The Making of the
National Labor Relations Board

The Making of the
National Labor Relations Board

A Study in Economics,
Politics, and the Law

Volume I (1933–1937)

James A. Gross
New York State School of Industrial and Labor Relations
Cornell University

State University of New York Press
Albany, New York, 1974

FIRST PUBLISHED IN 1974 BY
STATE UNIVERSITY OF NEW YORK PRESS,
99 WASHINGTON AVENUE, ALBANY, NEW YORK 12210
© 1974 STATE UNIVERSITY OF NEW YORK
ALL RIGHTS RESERVED
PRINTED IN THE UNITED STATES OF AMERICA

LIBRARY OF CONGRESS CATALOGING IN PUBLICATION DATA

Gross, James A   1933—
The making of the National Labor Relations Board.

Includes bibliographical references.
CONTENTS: 1. 1933–1937.
1. United States. National Labor Relations Board.
I. Title.

KF3372.G76   353.008'3   74–5284
ISBN 0–87395–270–7
ISBN 0–87395–271–5 (microfiche)

FOR LINDA,
JIM, JOHN, JUSTIN, AND CAITLIN

Contents

034018

Illustrations

Acknowledgments

Many very kind and very capable people made it possible for me to write this book. I am especially indebted to Frank McCulloch, former Chairman of the National Labor Relations Board now on the faculty of the University of Virginia Law School, who had confidence enough in the project to give me access to the board's records, and to my colleagues, Maurice Neufeld, Donald Cullen, Kurt Hanslowe, Robert Doherty, Emil Mesics, Gerd Korman, and David Lipsky whose scholarly advice vastly improved the manuscript and whose friendship and good humor kept me linked with humanity while laboring in archival tunnels and the records warehouse that once was my office.

I am also pleased to acknowledge my debt of gratitude to the staff of the National Archives and Records Service in Washington, D.C., particularly to Mr. Joseph Howerton of the Industrial and Social Branch, Civil Archives Division, and Mr. George Perros of the Legislative, Judicial and Diplomatic Records Division whose expertise and personal concern made my visits there most worthwhile. Congressman Howard Robison of New York also facilitated my work by successfully petitioning the Clerk of the House of Representatives to permit me to examine and reproduce several restricted record groups at the National Archives.

It is almost unfair merely to mention the names of others who helped me so much. People such as Bruce Friend, who worked so diligently and effectively as my Graduate Research Assistant and later as a Research Associate in Washington, D.C.; Judith Byne who conducted oral history interviews so expertly and graciously; Gould Colman of the Cornell Oral History Project, who provided interviewing skills, a little entrepreneurship, and much financial and personal encouragement; Ogden Fields, former Secretary of the NLRB; his successor, John Truesdale; and Meta Barghausen, personal secretary to all NLRB chairmen since J. Warren Madden, who guided me through the board's files; Dana Eischen, Ben Wolkinson, John Glenn, Joseph Shedd, David Middlebrooks, Stephen Poor, Frances Hardin, and Richard Miserendino, who worked with me as Graduate Research Assistants at various stages of the project, and Mrs. Nancy Voorheis who, without complaint, typed and xerographed so many drafts of this manuscript.

Earlier drafts of the manuscript were read in whole or in part by my colleagues Maurice Neufeld, Donald Cullen, Kurt Hanslowe, David Lipsky, Gerd Korman, Vernon Jensen, Emil Mesics, John Windmuller, and George Brooks; and by Philip Ross of the State University of New York at Buffalo; Russ Allen of Michigan State University; Charles Fahy, former General Counsel of the NLRB and Solicitor General of the United States now Senior Circuit Judge for the U.S. Court of Appeals, District of Columbia Circuit; Donald White of Boston College, and Tim Bornstein, former Special Assistant to the Chairman of the NLRB now on the faculty of the University of Massachusetts. Although I have not accepted all of their suggestions, I do thank them sincerely for taking valuable time away from their own work to improve my own. Charlotte Gold, Director of Publications for the School of Industrial and Labor Relations, free-lanced the editorial work on the manuscript, and her deft and intelligent touch is very much evident and appreciated.

I am deeply grateful to my good friend Tim Bornstein for his intercessions on my behalf which opened the way to many valuable sources of information at the NLRB and for his family's generous hospitality which made my brief but too frequent separations from my own family much easier to take.

I am also grateful to those who helped finance the project. A National Endowment for the Humanities Summer Fellowship and two grants from the American Philosophical Society aided my work appreciably. The Research Committee of the New York State School of Industrial and Labor Relations and the Cornell University Research Grants Committee also provided substantial support for the project as did the former Dean of the School of Industrial and Labor Relations, David Moore, and the current

Dean, Robert McKersie, who authorized indispensable summer support.

There are so many more to thank, particularly those men and women who helped to make the history of the NLRB and who shared their recollections with us in the oral history phase of the study. I trust that the extensive use which I make of their comments in this volume and in the volume to follow will be sufficient indication of how very valuable their cooperation was in the writing of this book.

Introduction

Administrative agencies, such as the National Labor Relations Board (NLRB), have become vital and pervasive forces in our society. Their rise has been one of the most important political and legal developments in the last century. The NLRB is worthy of a major study not only because the board is an important administrative agency which has had a widespread effect on administrative law and other administrative bodies, but also because of the large part it played in the growth of the strongest labor movement in the world. One administrative law expert rates the board's administration of the National Labor Relations Act (the Wagner Act) as "the outstanding instance during the present century of an aggressive program sustained over powerful opposition of regulated parties . . . "[1] and another considers "the first five years of the administration of the Wagner Act" as "the most high powered and effective law enforcement in our history."[2]

This study, the first of two volumes, analyzes the relationship between the NLRB and the development of a national labor policy and the growth of administrative processes and legal methods in United States labor relations. It begins with the creation of the National Labor Board (NLB) in 1933 and culminates in the Supreme Court's historic decisions in 1937 sustaining the constitutionality of Senator Robert Wagner's National Labor Relations Act (NLRA). The second volume continues this analysis of

1. Kenneth Culp Davis, *Administrative Law Text* (St. Paul, Minn.: West Publishing Co., 1959), p. 8.
2. Louis L. Jaffe, *Administrative Law* (New York: Prentice-Hall, 1953), pp. 79–80.

the board's history into the period immediately following the passage of the Taft-Hartley Act in 1947.

The present volume explains how three successive national labor boards, the National Labor Board from August 1933 to June 1934, the old National Labor Relations Board from June 1934 to July 1935, and the Wagner Act National Labor Relations Board beginning in July 1935, responded to the political and economic conflicts of the period. These boards, proceeding less by ideological premeditation than by the pressure of circumstances, hammered out the essentials of a labor policy on a case-by-case basis in a series of turbulent and dramatic conflicts with employers and unions, President Roosevelt, Congress, the National Recovery Administration (NRA), the Department of Labor, the National Association of Manufacturers, the Liberty League, the press, and the Department of Justice and the federal judiciary, including the Supreme Court of the United States.

In the course of these struggles, what began in 1933 as a tripartite National Labor Board created to settle strikes through mediation, nonlegalistic informal discussions, and voluntary cooperation eventually became, in 1935, a quasijudicial body of neutrals deciding cases by setting forth principles of law, conducting formal hearings, issuing rules and regulations, and requiring legalistic uniformity in procedure.

The NLB and the old NLRB, in particular, accelerated a transition, a fundamental and historically significant change, that would shift the control of decision-making authority from the employers and unions in dispute (where the NLB's original commission to seek a settlement acceptable to the parties placed the power) to a national labor board that would issue decisions on the merits of individual cases and would, in the process, develop a "case law" of labor-management relations. This gradual shift in the locus of decision-making power, from the parties to the national labor board, had other profound and lasting effects on the formulation and the administration of labor policy. The rejection of mediation, partisan representation, and voluntarism meant that American labor policy would henceforth be developed by law and litigation through legislative enactment, the growth of a body of NLRB case precedent, and the application of administrative law. The great and lasting significance of the work of the NLB and the old NLRB is found in their assertion of the first principles of a national labor policy and in their preparations for establishing administrative processes and legal methods in the emerging field of industrial relations.

Since they had no labor law or clear and unequivocal labor policy statement by the New Deal administration to guide them, the NLB and the old NLRB made labor policy with each substantive interpretation of the generalized and abbreviated terms of Section 7(a) of the National Industrial Recovery Act (NIRA). Moreover, they learned from their experiences about the defects of Section 7(a) in confronting specific cases, internal organization problems, hostile employers, and political pressures. These lessons were then translated into the provisions of, first, Senator Wagner's unsuccessful labor disputes bill in 1934 and, ultimately, the Wagner Act of 1935. Almost every provision of the Wagner Act, from the definition of the words "employee" and "representative" to each of the employer unfair labor practices, is rooted in the experiences of these two pre-Wagner Act boards. The personnel of the old NLRB, played an active role in writing the Wagner Act that has been unknown or vastly underestimated until now.

Although the new Wagner Act board worked to develop a body of case law interpreting the National Labor Relations Act, the employers' bitter opposition to the law made it impossible for the NLRB to function as Congress intended until the act was sustained by the Supreme Court. Constitutionality, therefore, became the overriding objective of the NLRB and influenced its every action. The act remained essentially inoperative from September 1935 to April 1937 while the board formulated a litigation strategy designed to withstand the Supreme Court test. Only those who were privy to the Supreme Court's deliberations know why the Court sustained the Wagner Act in 1937. Whatever the reason, the constitutional litigation conducted by the NLRB made a vital contribution not only to the ratification of the Wagner Act labor policy, but also to the creation of a radically changed role for the federal government in labor relations. In fact, the NLRB's contribution had historical significance well beyond labor relations, since the Court's Wagner Act decisions eliminated long-standing restraints on the exercise of national power by establishing precedents for submitting to federal regulation affairs that had never before been considered the business of the federal government.

Senator Robert Wagner's National Labor Relations Act of July

1935 was one of the most important laws enacted by Congress to that date in the twentieth century. The Wagner Act's general principles of worker self-organization and election of representatives without interference from management with subsequent recognition by and bargaining with management were not new ideas. They had appeared repeatedly over the years in the reports of industrial commissions, the rulings of the War Labor Board in World War I, court decisions, and railway labor legislation. Yet, the drive to create a permanent national labor board that would give practical effect to these principles in previously inviolate areas of private industry incited more sustained opposition than any other proposal made during the early years of the New Deal administration.

American employers realized that the balance of power between themselves and their employees was at issue. Their power would be seriously lessened if the proponents of New Deal labor legislation succeeded in getting the principle of the right to organize for collective bargaining written into substantive legislative provisions and into the decisions of a national labor relations board. It took the desperate crises of the Great Depression before Congress and the president were willing to accept these principles as the foundation for a national labor policy.

The experiences of Senator Wagner's National Labor Board, Lloyd Garrison's and Francis Biddle's old NLRB, and J. Warren Madden's Wagner Act NLRB provide the underlying explanations of how this labor policy and the powers and procedures of a national labor board came to be.

This study of the national labor relations boards during these years focuses on the boards themselves as the primary objects of investigation. In a reversal of the usual line of labor relations inquiry, legislative histories, the details of legal doctrines, and the problems of labor and management have been considered only to the extent that they contribute to a better understanding of the actions and reactions of the labor boards. Millis and Brown's classic study, *From the Wagner Act to Taft-Hartley* (1950), for example, traces the development of a national labor policy by concentrating on the doctrines evolved by the NLRB and the legislative amendments proposed by others and Irving Bernstein's *The New Deal Collective Bargaining Policy* (1950) is an analysis of the legislative history of the Wagner Act.

The unique study of the NLRB developed here, however, is based primarily on previously untapped NLRB records found in the files of the board and at the National Archives in Washington and on a series of approximately fifty in-depth oral history interviews with people prominent in the history of the board. The board files contained the detailed minutes of meetings dating from 1934, interoffice memoranda, work reports and memorandums on internal matters, correspondence (both general and related to policy matters), digests of issues arising in cases, criticisms of the handling of cases, press releases, and unpublished internal studies of the board. The National Archives held the records of the National Labor Board (such as certain records of the NLB's chairman, Senator Robert Wagner, and a substantial collection of William Leiserson's papers and correspondence) and the records of the old NLRB including many of the papers of Chairman Lloyd Garrison and board members Harry Millis and Edwin S. Smith— all of whom were historically important figures in the history of labor relations in the 1930s and 1940s.

Some of the most valuable documents in the Archives were those pertaining to the preparation of the board's case before the Special House Committee to Investigate the NLRB (the Smith Committee) and a complete collection of the Smith Committee's own records—including internal reports and recommendations from the committee's general counsel (Edmund Toland), analyses and reports from the committee's investigators and staff, internal committee correspondence, and all of the committee and NLRB exhibits which were introduced in evidence at the hearing but were not published.

The oral history portion of the study was invaluable. The recollections of those interviewed provided an otherwise unattainable sense of the climate of the times both inside and outside the NLRB. They also provided a depth of meaning and historical connections which frequently could not be obtained from documents alone as well as an excellent sense of the intensity and influence of the human dimension in the history of the board.

Although the literature of administrative law and labor history contains much about the legal powers of agencies such as the NLRB, their procedures, and the judicial review of their decisions, little is known about the part judicial, part political, and part ideological decision-making processes of these agencies and the role that individual expertise plays. Examining the history of the 1930s as seen and made by those who shaped the policies of the NLRB and its predecessors, the National Labor Board and the old NLRB, in those early years should increase our understanding of the exercise of this kind of governmental authority. This approach should make the work important to social historians, political scientists, and legal scholars as well as to specialists in the field of industrial and labor relations.

1 The National Labor Board: From Successful Mediation to *Budd Manufacturing* and *Weirton Steel*

The National Recovery Administration and the Conflict over Section 7(a)

When Franklin Delano Roosevelt was inaugurated as president of the United States in the spring of 1933, the nation was suffering through the fourth year of its most disastrous economic depression.[1] The tragic number of people unemployed had increased

1. Excellent works dealing with the New Deal period include Irving Bernstein, *The New Deal Collective Bargaining Policy* (Berkeley and Los Angeles: The University of California Press, 1950); Irving Bernstein, *Turbulent Years* (Boston: Houghton Mifflin Company, 1970); Arthur M. Schlesinger, Jr., *The Age of Roosevelt: The Crisis of the Old Order* (Boston: Houghton Mifflin Company, 1957); Arthur M. Schlesinger, Jr., *The Coming of the New Deal* (Boston: Houghton Mifflin Company, 1959); Arthur M. Schlesinger, Jr., *The Politics of Upheaval* (Boston: Houghton Mifflin Company, 1960); William E. Leuchtenburg, *Franklin D. Roosevelt and the New Deal, 1932–1940* (New York: Harper and Row, 1963); Sidney Fine, *The Automobile Under the Blue Eagle* (Ann Arbor: The University of Michigan Press, 1963); Richard C. Cortner, *The Wagner Act Cases* (Knoxville: University of Tennessee Press, 1964); Jerold S. Auerbach, *Labor and Liberty: The LaFollette Committee and the New Deal* (Indianapolis, Ind.: Bobbs-Merrill, 1966); Bernard Sternsher, *Rexford Tugwell and the New Deal* (New Brunswick, N.J.: Rutgers University Press, 1964); Frank Freidel, *F.D.R. and the South* (Baton Rouge: University of Louisiana Press, 1965); Raymond Moley, *The First New Deal* (New York: Harcourt, Brace and World, 1966); Frances Perkins, *The Roosevelt I Knew* (New York: The Viking Press, 1946); Broadus Mitchell, *Depression Decade, From New Era Through New Deal, 1929–1941* (New York: Holt, Rinehart and Winston, 1947); and

from 13,204,000 in November 1932 to 15,071,000 in March 1933 and panic and hopelessness had caused many to believe that the country's long history of economic growth had come to a permanent end.[2]

The people had lost faith in the virtues of rugged individualism and the allegedly self-generating forces of economic recovery and they were desperately receptive to almost any kind of remedial action, including unconventional experiments in economic policy by the federal government. Most legislators, moreover, agreed with Senator Robert Wagner's judgment that this "sad tide of affairs, bringing deprivation and disaster to the whole nation, justifies an experiment"[3] and with Congressman Samuel B. Hill who responded to a colleague's learned dissertation on the unconstitutionality of one of the New Deal's experiments by pointing out that it was "little satisfaction to the man who is starving for want of the opportunity to work to tell him that he is starving to death constitutionally."[4]

The time was right for what one historian of the period has called the "Roosevelt Revolution"—a turning point in American history—"a greater upheaval in American institutions than in any similar period in our history, save perhaps for the impact on the South of the Civil War."[5] The first one-hundred days of Roosevelt's New Deal administration produced "the most extraordinary series of reforms in the nation's history."

It had committed the country to an unprecedented program of government-industry cooperation; promised to distribute stupendous sums to millions of staple farmers; accepted responsibility for the welfare of millions of unemployed; agreed to engage in farreaching experimentation in regional planning; pledged billions of dollars to save homes and farms from foreclosure; undertaken huge public works spending; guar-

---

James MacGregor Burns, *Roosevelt: The Lion and the Fox* (New York: Harcourt, Brace and World, 1956). For a useful survey of New Deal literature, see Richard S. Kirkendall, "The New Deal as Watershed: The Recent Literature," *The Journal of American History*, vol. 54, March 1968, pp. 839–852.

2. Bernstein, *Turbulent Years, op. cit.*, p. 1.

3. 77 *Cong. Rec.* 5158 (1933).

4. 77 *Cong. Rec.* 4222 (1933).

5. Leuchtenburg, *op. cit.*, p. xii.

anteed the small bank deposits of the country; and had, for the first time, established federal regulation of Wall Street . . . . as the President sat at his desk in the White House signing several of the bills Congress had adopted, including the largest peacetime appropriation bill ever passed, he remarked, "More history is being made today than in [any] one day of our national life." Oklahoma's Senator Thomas Gore amended: "During all time."[6]

The politics of the New Deal, however, were flexibly pragmatic rather than ideologically rigid. The administration's goal was to create a friendly, cooperative partnership out of many diverse interests with the federal government acting as a "broker state," unifying, harmonizing, and mediating among the major interest groups.[7] The New Deal's pursuit of "a true concert of interests . . . meant in practice something for everyone."[8]

No piece of New Deal legislation better epitomized this pragmatism than the National Industrial Recovery Act—"an omnibus proposal that had a little for everyone."[9] That act was an amalgam of the recommendations for recovery advocated by diverse interest groups. The advocates of self-regulation for business obtained a government suspension of the antitrust laws to permit industry to form trade associations to set production quotas and fix prices through a system of codes of industrial self-government, those who advocated national planning attained their goal of government licensing of business, the advocates of labor organization and shorter hours of work received a guarantee of the right of employees to organize and to bargain collectively through representatives of their own choosing as well as a stipulation that the codes would set minimum wages and maximum hours, and, finally, the advocates of public works as a counter to the downswing of the business cycle received $3.3 billion for public works projects.[10]

Balancing multiple interest groups to obtain cooperation, however, also made the administration "the prisoner of its own interest groups" in that Roosevelt "often shied away from decisions

6. *Ibid.*, p. 61.
7. Burns, *op. cit.*, pp. 192–193.
8. Richard Hofstadter, *The American Political Tradition* (New York: Alfred A. Knopf, 1951), p. 330.
9. Leuchtenburg, *op. cit.*, p. 57.
10. *Ibid.*, pp. 57–58.

that might antagonize one or another of the elements in the coalition."[11] The crucial interest group in the industrial recovery program was, of course, business. In part because of industry's importance and in part because he wanted to avoid an early test of the doubtful constitutionality of his new power, Hugh Johnson, the head of the National Recovery Administration (NRA) that administered the NIRA, "decided that everything else had to be subordinated to winning the uncoerced assent of major industries to the codes."[12] The emphasis, therefore, was on cooperation not conflict.

The first months of the New Deal were to an astonishing degree an adventure in unanimity. Though the business community had in the main gone for Hoover in 1932, prominent businessmen had supported Roosevelt; and neither Roosevelt's platform nor his personality seemed to hold any special problems for business after the election. . . . And most of the measures of Roosevelt's first month—in particular, the reopening of the banks, the cutback in government spending, and the return of beer—strengthened his conservative support. Even New Deal planning was for a moment acceptable. After all, few businessmen cared what happened in agriculture; and NRA not only drew on ideas long urged by business leaders but depended on close business-government collaboration.[13]

The NRA became "the first bastion of government-business cooperation." In 1933 and 1934 "it offered businessmen their most important bridgehead in Washington."[14]

Although it is clear that the Recovery Act was built around a system of codes of industrial self-regulation, it is equally clear that Roosevelt "had little idea what he was letting himself in for"[15] when he agreed to the insertion of the following provisions (Section 7(a)) into the NIRA:

Every code of fair competition, agreement, and license approved, prescribed, or issued under this title shall contain

11. *Ibid.*, p. 87.
12. Schlesinger, *The Coming of the New Deal, op. cit.*, p. 108.
13. *Ibid.*, p. 423.
14. *Ibid.*, p. 425.
15. Leuchtenburg, *op. cit.*, p. 107.

the following conditions: (1) That employees shall have the right to organize and bargain collectively through representatives of their own choosing, and shall be free from the interference, restraint, or coercion of employers of labor, or their agents, in the designation of such representatives or in self-organization or in other concerted activities for the purpose of collective bargaining or other mutual aid or protection; (2) that no employee and no one seeking employment shall be required as a condition of employment to join any company union or to refrain from joining, organizing, or assisting a labor organization of his own choosing; and (3) that employers shall comply with the maximum hours of labor, minimum rates of pay, and other conditions of employment, approved or prescribed by the President.[16]

Section 7(a) was actually an administration concession to the political strength which the AFL had demonstrated in its support of the Black thirty-hour bill which the president had opposed as unconstitutional and a drag on recovery. The administration, moreover, was unclear about what 7(a) meant or precisely how it could be enforced.[17] Despite the fact that the New Deal did not consider labor policy essential to the recovery program, there was the potential for major labor union advances under Section 7(a), as well as the possibility of no significant union gains at all. The outcome hinged upon how these provisions would be interpreted and enforced in the preparation and implementation of the National Recovery Administration's codes of fair competition. Section 7(a), as industry was well aware, provided neither enforcement powers nor procedures to accomplish the selection of the employees' representative nor any indication of what specific employer actions would be prohibited. In addition, its wording was susceptible to interpretations that would sanction company unions, proportional rather than exclusive representation, and individual rather than collective bargaining. It would also permit an employer to avoid bargaining with a labor union which represented his employees.

16. For a discussion of industry's efforts to introduce amendments protecting the open shop and labor's opposition, see Bernstein, *The New Deal Collective Bargaining Policy, op. cit.*, pp. 35–37.
17. Leuchtenburg, *op. cit.*, p. 107.

Since there was also no provision in the NIRA for either national or industry labor boards to pass upon these questions, organized labor and organized employers relied on their political and economic power to pressure the New Deal administration to read into Section 7(a) the strongest endorsements of their own positions. Industry generally had the political power advantage as long as the New Deal recovery program remained an experiment in industrial self-government dependent upon employer cooperation rather than government control. On June 19, 1933, for example, three days after the enactment of the NIRA, General Hugh S. Johnson, head of the National Recovery Administration, announced, "Basic codes containing provisions respecting maximum hours of labor, minimum rates of pay, and other conditions of employment, which are in themselves satisfactory, will be subject to approval, *although such conditions may not have been arrived at by collective bargaining.*"[18] This directive effectively excluded organized labor from participation in the code-making process, since very few unions in 1933 possessed the bargaining power needed to guarantee a role in code drafting and implementation.[19]

Although General Johnson's decision had given employer groups control of even the labor provisions of the codes in most industries, the NRA administrator was sensitive to public protests by his Labor Advisory Board[20] and sought the safer high ground of "perfect neutrality," as well as a "square deal" for labor by declaring on July 7, 1933: "It is the duty of this Administration to require the inclusion in all codes of the mandatory provisions of Section 7. . . ."[21] Many employers, however, particularly those in the basic industries, were unwilling to duplicate the language

18. Lewis L. Lorwin and Arthur Wubnig, *Labor Relations Boards* (Washington: The Brookings Institution, 1935), p. 57 (emphasis added).
19. The exceptions were the unions in the coal industry, building trades, needle trades, and the printing industry. See Sumner Slichter, "Labor Under the National Recovery Act," *Harvard Business Review*, vol. 12, no. 2 (January 1934), p. 148.
20. Lorwin and Wubnig, *op. cit.*, p. 57. The Labor Advisory Board was appointed by the secretary of labor and the leaders of organized labor and the representatives of unorganized workers on the board advised the NRA on labor policy.
21. *Ibid.*, p. 60, quoting NRA Release Number 34.

of Section 7 in their codes and pressed the NRA to approve codes in which the employer draftsmen had substantially modified the statutory labor provisions.

At this point, any idealized version of a code "gave way to the realities of an out-and-out bargaining process in which selfish interests were played against one another."[22] The automobile industry, for example, after negotiations with the NRA and over the strenuous objections of the AFL, obtained approval of its code which added an "individual merit clause" to the terms of Section 7(a) so that "employers in this industry may exercise their right to select, retain, or advance employees on the basis of individual merit, without regard to their membership or non-membership in any organization."[23]

The words "efficiency" and "merit" had developed special anti-union connotations over the years of employer resistance to employee organization and, as a consequence, other employer associations were quick to demand that merit clauses be included in their codes.[24] When General Johnson, again under Labor Advisory Board pressure, had second thoughts about the wisdom of the merit clause in the automobile code and stated that the NRA would not approve any qualifications of Section 7(a) in future codes, all the members of the Industrial Advisory Board threatened to resign.[25]

As these controversies persisted throughout the summer of 1933, General Johnson and Donald R. Richberg, general counsel of the NRA, were caught in the pressures and counterpressures brought to bear on the NRA by organized labor and organized employers. On more specific 7(a) issues, the NRA agreed with industry that company unions were not prohibited if membership was voluntary and if such organizations were free of coercion, interference, or restraint by the employer. The NRA also contended that "employers . . . can make collective bargains with organized employees, or individual bargains with those who

22. Leverett S. Lyon *et al.*, *The National Recovery Administration: An Analysis and Appraisal* (Washington: The Brookings Institution, 1935), p. 85.
23. Lorwin and Wubnig, *op. cit.*, pp. 66–67.
24. *The New York Times*, September 14, 1933, p. 1, col. 7, and p. 6, col. 1.
25. Edwin Witte, "The Background of the Labor Provisions of the N.I.R.A.," *University of Chicago Law Review*, vol. 1, no. 3 (January 1934), p. 572.

13

choose to act individually."[26] Because of union strength in some industries, however, and the threat of major industrial strikes that would seriously impede the recovery program, not all of the NRA explanations of Section 7(a) were unfavorable to organized labor. The NRA, for example, did not approve the soft coal codes until employers in those industries removed their company-union and individual-bargaining interpretations of 7(a) from those documents.

It is clear, therefore, that the NRA had tried to reconcile the labor provisions of the NIRA with the basic purposes of the rest of the act in ways that would not delay industrial recovery—"the NRA [was] surrounded by the spears of opposed interests on none of which it [wished] to impale itself."[27] The result was a series of "vague, confusing, and somewhat meaningless" public statements which raised many of the issues inherent in Section 7(a) but settled none of them.[28] Even in those industries where organized labor was strong enough to repulse employer alterations of Section 7(a), the NRA had prohibited only the inclusion of these modifications in the formal language of the code provisions. The NRA had not prohibited the practice of these modifications by employers in the field. The end result was self-confessed confusion on the part of the NRA's Hugh Johnson who complained that

> Management has just carved out of that Section the interpretations that suit their point of view and published it all over their plants . . . and, on the other hand, the labor people have carved out of the President's speeches or simple statements I have made, or Richberg has made, whatever they like until the whole thing is in confusion.[29]

For workers, however, the meaning of Section 7(a) was plain: President Roosevelt wanted them to join unions. When they did and employers refused to recognize their unions or rushed to install company-sponsored employee representation plans to

26. Lorwin and Wubnig, *op. cit.*, p. 74, quoting NRA Release Number 463. See also Emmett B. McNatt, "Organized Labor and the Recovery Act," *Michigan Law Review*, vol. 32, no. 6 (April 1934), pp. 780–810.
27. Lyon *et al.*, *op. cit.*, p. 230.
28. Lorwin and Wubnig, *op. cit.*, p. 83.
29. Schlesinger, *The Coming of the New Deal*, *op. cit.*, p. 146.

forestall unionization, a strike wave followed. There were more strikes in 1933 than in any year since 1921, particularly in the second half of 1933 when "man days lost due to strikes which had not exceeded 603,000 in any month in the first half of 1933 spurted to 1,375,000 in July and to 2,378,000 in August."[30] This increase in strike action was so severe that President Roosevelt issued a plea for industrial peace and, on August 5, 1933, created the National Labor Board to "consider, adjust and settle differences and controversies that may arise through differing interpretations of the President's Re-Employment Agreement. . . ."[31] The New Deal was being forced to piece together a labor policy on a crisis-by-crisis basis.

The National Labor Board: The First Three Months

The president shaped the National Labor Board in the NRA mold of voluntary cooperation and self-government and made Senator Robert F. Wagner its chairman. Senator Wagner expressed the underlying philosophy of this approach most clearly in a letter which he wrote to the chairman of a newly established regional board shortly after the NLB began its operations:

30. Bernstein, *Turbulent Years, op. cit.*, pp. 172–173.
31. The complete text of the president's statement and the announcement by the National Recovery Administration on August 5, 1933 are found in U.S. Congress, Senate Committee on Education and Labor, *Hearings on S. 2926*, "A Bill To Equalize The Bargaining Power Of Employers And Employees, To Encourage The Amicable Settlement Of Disputes Between Employers And Employees, To Create A National Labor Board, And For Other Purposes," 73d Cong., 2d Sess., (Washington: GPO, 1934), part I, pp. 39–40 (hereinafter cited as *Senate Hearings on the Labor Disputes Act*). See also *The New York Times*, August 6, 1933, p. 1, col. 8. The president's Re-Employment Agreement was a blanket code which governed industry until particular codes were submitted and approved by the NRA. Those covered by the NRA were required to agree to observe the requirements of Section 7(a) of the NIRA.

The recent surge of strikes and similar industrial disturbances has been due almost entirely to misunderstandings and misconceptions of the new rights and obligations conferred and imposed upon industry and labor alike in the program to make America safe for industrial democracy. Out of confusion which must necessarily accompany the beginning of any new scheme of so vast a scope, have risen cross-currents of distrust and antagonism between labor and industry, which have no substantial basis in fact. The very brief experience of the National Labor Board has already demonstrated that practically all of the recent industrial conflicts can be amicably settled when the parties have been brought together to discuss their differences in an atmosphere of calmness and disinterestedness and with a clearer knowledge of their respective rights and duties. Cooperation based on mutual trust and understanding must be the keynote henceforward. [32]

The board's structure reflected these principles. It "brought together" three industry representatives selected by the NRA's Industrial Advisory Board, three labor representatives chosen by the NRA's Labor Advisory Board, and Senator Wagner, representing the public interest as their chairman. [33] (There was precedent for this tripartite setup: the National War Labor

32. Letter from Senator Robert F. Wagner to the Honorable Marion Smith, October 22, 1933. National Archives, Record Group 25, records of the National Labor Relations Board, National Labor Board, and National Labor Relations Board I (hereinafter cited as NA, RG25): office of the executive secretary, correspondence and reports relating to regional boards, 1933–1935, Region VI, Atlanta.
33. NA, RG25, undated and unsigned memorandum. Office of the chairman, board and personal correspondence of Senator Wagner. The letter of appointment sent by President Roosevelt to members of the National Labor Board read as follows: "Upon joint recommendation of the Labor Advisory Board and the Industrial Advisory Board of the National Recovery Administration I have created a National Labor Board to function under the National Industrial Recovery Act as an agency to investigate and pass upon the merits of controversies concerning or arising out of labor relations, which may operate to impede the efforts of the government to effectuate the policy of that Act.
"I have appointed you as a member of the National Labor Board

Board in World War I consisted of five representatives of employers, five union representatives, and two representatives of the public in the belief that "the success of the principles formulated . . . would be conditioned upon their acceptance by both capital and labor and that it was therefore essential that both parties should formulate them. . . .")[34]

The six partisan members who, along with Senator Wagner, served without pay were Walter C. Teagle, chairman of the Industrial Advisory Board and president of the Standard Oil Company of New Jersey; Gerard Swope, president of the General Electric Company; Louis E. Kirstein, general manager of William Filene Sons Company; Dr. Leo Wolman; chairman of the Labor Advisory Board and professor of economics at Columbia University; and William Green, president of the American Federation of Labor of America; and John L. Lewis, president of the United Mine Workers of America. Their job, according to Senator Wagner, was "to get rid of the whole idea of war to the limit and to substitute for it the idea of agreements through mediation. . . ."[35] Their legal powers, should the method of voluntary cooperation fail, were "shadowy and uncertain."[36] The NLB had received a very vague mandate from the president "to consider and settle" differences over the interpretation of the president's Re-Employment Agreement. Because the president had created the NLB on August 5, 1933 without issuing a formal executive order, its status in the administrative hierarchy of the New Deal, its jurisdiction, and even its duration were in doubt. As the *The New York Times* commented on August 6,

What final and permanent form this mediation plan will take is not predicted, and President Roosevelt himself has no

---

and will appreciate deeply your acceptance of the responsibility thus imposed upon you as a most important contribution to public service."
34. U.S. Department of Labor, Bureau of Labor Statistics, *National War Labor Board* (Washington: GPO, 1921), Bulletin No. 287, p. 10.
35. *The New York Times*, November 20, 1933, p. 3, col. 5. In this article Senator Wagner is quoted as saying, "The chief hope that I had when accepting the President's appointment to the Chairmanship of the National Labor Board was that its influence might work a change in our people's ideas about industrial disputes."
36. *Senate Hearings on the Labor Disputes Act, op. cit.*, p. 208.

definite design. The single board may be replaced in time, he told newspapermen, by individual boards set up for each industry group.[37]

Although the stability of the recovery program may have made it politically necessary for President Roosevelt to surround the NLB with vagueness and uncertainty, the president had made the NLB vulnerable to the power conflicts of the day and had, in effect, subjected the board's jurisdiction, functions, organization, powers, and doctrines to the pressure of events.

The First Steps: Inexperience and Flexibility

The NLB established simple procedures at the outset. A labor dispute became an NLB case whenever the board sent a mediator to the troubled locality or called the parties to the dispute to Washington.[38]

> Normally, however, it is only when the mediator has failed to bring the parties together, that they are called to Washington. The Board then attempts to bring them to an agreement, following a hearing at which both parties are represented. At this hearing issues are presented *anew* and the chairman and members of the Board endeavor to persuade the parties to make reasonable concessions to one another, in the interests of the Recovery Program, in order to settle the strike.[39]

The board, with a total of nine people[40] on its staff and with no field organization, worked under the stress of a heavy caseload

37. *The New York Times*, August 6, 1933, p. 1, col. 8.
38. NLRB files, "Summary of Activities of National Labor Board," memorandum from Paul M. Herzog to the National Labor Board, October 26, 1933, p. 1.
39. *Ibid.*, pp. 1–2.
40. William Leiserson was secretary, Benedict Wolf was executive officer, Milton Handler was general counsel, Jesse I. Miller and Heber Blankenhorn were assistants to the chairman, Paul M. Herzog was assistant secretary, John D. Moore was technical

from the very beginning. The work pace was bewildering. The board's staff often worked from eighteen to twenty hours a day including Saturdays and Sundays and some panel sessions were held at two and three o'clock in the morning. Milton Handler, the NLB's general counsel,

> found that the board was not very well organized and . . . was devoting all of its time to putting out fires and there was a new fire virtually every day . . . . we would have one, two or three hearings a day . . . . we were so heavily burdened with the emergencies of each day . . . that we went from one crisis to another.[41]

Because of the tremendous workload and a limited staff, it was not unusual for Senator Wagner, as chairman of the NLB, to be called into the field to settle a strike[42] even though the board did have the assistance of mediators from the Conciliation Service of the United States Department of Labor.[43] The NLB's staff was not only small in number but also short on labor relations experience. According to General Counsel Handler, "virtually no one on the board [had] very extensive or comprehensive knowledge of labor law or labor problems" and he, himself, "had just a general knowledge of labor law but . . . was in no sense an expert."[44]

Philip Levy, who came to the NLB when "the legal staff consisted of one and I was . . . that one,"[45] accepted Milton Handler's offer to join the NLB less than one year after graduation from the Columbia Law School. Paul Herzog, who became chairman of the NLRB in 1945, had not yet finished law school when he became assistant to the board's secretary, William Leiserson. The

advisor to the board, Estelle Frankfurter was in charge of research and statistics, and Beatrice Stern was assistant executive officer.

41. Oral history interview with Milton Handler, April 15, 1970, pp. 7–8, on file in the Labor Management Documentation Center, New York State School of Industrial and Labor Relations, Cornell University (hereinafter referred to as ILR, Cornell).
42. Oral history interview with Benedict Wolf, May 19, 1968, p. 8, on file in the Labor Management Documentation Center, ILR, Cornell.
43. Lorwin and Wubnig, op. cit., pp. 125–126.
44. Oral history interview with M. Handler, op. cit., p. 6.
45. Oral history interview with Philip Levy, March 15, 1969, on file in the Labor Management Documentation Center, ILR, Cornell.

NLB, moreover, lost mediation skills as well as administrative effectiveness when it assigned its first employee, Leiserson (in the beginning the only key staff member with extensive practical and academic experience in labor relations), to administrative rather than mediation work.

Although he remained with the board for several more months, Leiserson asked to be relieved of his duties as secretary in October 1933. He told Senator Wagner:

> I am fitted neither by experience nor by aptitude for administrative work, such as devolves on a secretary, and a trained secretary might have succeeded in getting the Board's work organized on an efficient basis long before this. . . . I shall be glad to come back to assist you in mediation and arbitration work . . . where I really can be helpful.[46]

The fundamental objective of the NLB members and staff was to get cases settled by preventing or settling strikes that interfered with the recovery effort. NLB hearings in Washington, consequently, were nonlegalistic, informal, and friendly discussions designed to facilitate agreement between the union and the employer.

> Witnesses were not under oath; there was no power in the Board to compel by subpoena the attendance of persons or the production of records. The introduction of testimony, statements, and affidavits was not limited by the rules of evidence which hold in the courts; and because the primary intent of the hearing was to compose a dispute, not to make findings as to guilt or innocence, the Board did not adhere to very strict canons of fact finding.[47]

The typical settlement made between the parties to a dispute and the NLB provided for the end of the strike and the reinstatement of the strikers without discrimination; an NLB-supervised secret-ballot election to determine who, if anyone, would represent the workers; an employer agreement to bargain collectively with the elected representatives, if any; and the submission of all differences unresolved by negotiations to an arbitration board or

46. NLRB files, letter from W. Leiserson to Senator Robert F. Wagner, October 19, 1933, pp. 3–4.
47. Lorwin and Wubnig, *op. cit.*, p. 126.

to the NLB "for final decision."[48] The NLB resorted to a decision only after all its mediation efforts had failed to achieve a voluntary settlement and the parties refused to submit their dispute to arbitration.

Mediation Succeeds:
A Review and Reevaluation

Since the NLB went into battle armed only with what Senator Wagner called "public sentiment" and the prestige of its members ("the benefit of having them [the parties] in Washington was that you would get them before a panel of important industrialists and labor leaders who could then exercise some influence"),[49] the success of the NLB's operation depended ultimately upon the voluntary cooperation of employers and unions.

Despite the lack of enforcement powers and an inexperienced staff, the board, during its first three months, was able to settle approximately 88 percent of its cases (58) through mediation either in the field or in Washington[50] and had to resort to decisions in just 8 cases, only one of which involved a basic interpretation of Section 7(a).[51] Some of the board's success can be explained as a patriotic response to the president's recovery

---

48. *Senate Hearings on the Labor Disputes Act, op. cit.*, p. 30. This typical settlement was first announced on August 11, 1933 in the resolution of the Reading hosiery strike in Berks County, Pennsylvania and became known as the "Reading Formula." See Lorwin and Wubnig, *op. cit.*, pp. 95–99.

49. Oral history interview with B. Wolf, *op. cit.*, p. 10.

50. NLRB files, memorandum from Paul M. Herzog to the National Labor Board, *op. cit.* By October 26, 1933 the NLB had handled a total of 110 cases—44 of those cases were still pending or had been referred elsewhere. Of the remaining 66 cases, 58 were settled in Washington or in the field and only 8 were settled by a decision of the NLB. See also *The New York Times*, October 30, 1933, p. 5, col. 3.

51. *Decisions of the National Labor Board* (Washington: GPO, 1934), "*Berkeley Woolen Mills and United Textile Workers*," vol. I, pp. 5–6 (hereinafter referred to as *Decisions of the NLB*). This case is described later in the text.

program and the codes of fair competition which were being set up throughout the summer and fall of 1933. The settlements themselves, moreover, reinforced the success of the NLB. Settlements permitted the board to avoid the risk of alienating either labor or management by making it unnecessary for the board to take public positions concerning the meaning of 7(a).

A more substantial explanation for the NLB's excellent record, however, is that in its first three months of work the board had not encountered its formidable open-shop foes in the basic industries such as automobiles and steel. Although the NLB kept only crude aggregate case statistics,[52] the board's successor, the old National Labor Relations Board, did a detailed internal study of NLB-conducted elections[53] which supports this conclusion. These NLB election statistics give an unusually detailed picture of the board's work, particularly since the representation election was a standard component of all NLB settlements. This study found that in 73 percent of the 406 cases for which the size of the unit was known, elections were held in small establishments with from one to 250 employees eligible to vote.[54] Only two NLB elections in those first three months covered units where more than 1,000 workers were eligible to vote: the 45 Reading, Pennsylvania, hosiery mills in August 1933 and the P. R. Mallory Company of Indianapolis, Indiana, in October.[55]

These election statistics and the decisions issued by the NLB

52. Lorwin and Wubnig, *op. cit.*, p. 217: "The official figures were not of a high statistical order. They were gathered hastily and offhand in the rush of more urgent work. There was a considerable amount of double counting, in the sense that the same cases were sometimes included in the separate totals of the regional and the national boards.... There was reason also to suspect that the published figures were presented for propagandistic rather than informative purposes."

53. NLRB files, "Elections Conducted by the National Labor Board and Regional Labor Boards, August 5, 1933–July 9, 1934," memorandum from Emily Clark Brown to the National Labor Relations Board, August 16, 1934. Portions of this study appear in Emily Clark Brown, "Selection of Employees' Representatives," *Monthly Labor Review*, vol. 40, no. 1 (January 1935), pp. 1–18.

54. There were a total of 546 plants or other units covered by this study so that 406 cases represent approximately 74 percent of the total.

55. NLRB files, memorandum from Emily Clark Brown to the National Labor Relations Board, *op. cit.*, Part III, Table VIII.

from August through October 1933 show clearly that the NLB's initial work was concentrated in coal yards; laundry and cleaning establishments; the hosiery, jewelry, and shoe industries; dress and clothing shops; and street railways. Employers in these industries had sufficient incentive to cooperate with the NLB since their firms were the least likely to survive a union strike—being small firms in highly competitive industries with low-profit margins and little labor relations expertise.

Big Industry Responds to Section 7(a): The Employee Representation Plan

The NLB's showdown with the powerful employers in the mass production industries was, of course, inevitable. Under the inspiration of the NIRA, the AFL, long beset by low morale, weak organizing efforts, corruption, exclusionary racial practices, and jurisdictional disputes, had freed itself from its craft restrictions long enough to spread unionism among the unskilled and semi-skilled workers in automobile, rubber, steel, meat packing, and other industries.[56] Employers in these industries had counter-attacked by encouraging their employees to form employee representation plans within their own companies. A National Industrial Conference Board (NICB) survey of such plans in November 1933 revealed that 45 percent of the employees in the manufacturing and mining companies studied were covered by employee representation plans—a 169 percent increase in the number of employees covered by representation plans just one year earlier.[57] (Of these plans for employee representation, 61.3

56. For an analysis of jurisdiction problems in organizing the mass production industries, see Fine, *Blue Eagle, op. cit.*, pp. 142–181.
57. National Industrial Conference Board, *Individual and Collective Bargaining Under the N.I.R.A.* (New York: November 1933), p. 17. Inquiries were addressed to 10,335 companies, "a fairly representative cross-section of industry." Replies were received from 3,314 companies with an aggregate employment of 2,585 wage earners representing approximately 27 percent of the estimated total number of workers employed in manufacturing and mining. *Ibid.*, pp. 12–13. (The earlier NICB study referred to was National Industrial Conference Board, *Collective Bargaining Through Employee*

percent had been installed after the NIRA was passed in June 1933.)

The NICB study also found that "the proportion of companies in which employee representation [was] in force [increased] as the size of the establishment [increased]": 44 percent of the plants which used these plans employed more than 500 workers.[58] The company union drive was so intense and so successful that the NICB concluded that "as regards both number of companies and number of employees covered, employee representation has made greater progress since the Recovery Act than union agreements. . . ."[59] A leading labor economist, Sumner Slichter, also verified the proliferation of employee representation plans:

> . . . The increase in wage earners covered by new employee-representation schemes since June 1933, probably exceeds the gains in trade union membership. . . . Large companies, such as the United States Steel Corporation, which have never tolerated employee committees have hastily organized them, and 85% of the workers in the steel industry are now said to be covered by employee representation plans. In the automobile industry, where employee committees have traditionally been frowned upon, plans have been established in the plants of General Motors, Chrysler, Packard, Hudson, and others. Chemical producers, radio manufacturers, shipbuilders, and a vast variety of other enterprises have set up plans.[60]

A major struggle between the NLB and big industry was shaping up over the determination of the employees' representatives and, although there was much disagreement over the benefits and failings of employee representation plans,[61] there was no

---

Representation (New York: June 1933). That study surveyed the years from 1919 to 1932.)

58. *Ibid.*, pp. 21 and 23–24.
59. *Ibid.*, p. 24.
60. Slichter, *op. cit.*, p. 149.
61. *Senate Hearings on the Labor Disputes Act, op. cit.*: John L. Lewis, p. 143; William Green, p. 71; Senator Wagner's article on company unions from the *The New York Times*, reproduced on pp. 176–180; John Carmody, pp. 307–312; series of testimonials from employees of Youngstown Steel, American Rolling Mills, Wheeling Steel, and other companies, pp. 780–882; and Nathan Miller, p. 885.

doubt that the fate of Section 7(a) would be determined by the outcome of that struggle.

NLB Weaknesses Hidden by Case Statistics

The NLB, moreover, despite the impressive case statistics of the first three months, had come to understand its own weakness and vulnerability. One weakness was inherent in the part-time, voluntary-service nature of the board membership. Since the partisan members of the NLB remained responsible for the operation of powerful corporations and important unions, it was "very rare" that the full board was present for a mediation hearing in Washington.[62] Employer members in particular were frequently absent.

It should be noted that the failure of the employer members of the Board to continue to participate in its work was in no way deliberate but resulted from the change in personnel of the Industrial Advisory Board of the NRA. While the employer members were constantly in Washington as a result of their work with the NRA, they were also available for National Labor Board work. When they ceased to be members of the Industrial Advisory Board their presence in Washington was infrequent, and attention to their duties as members of the National Labor Board diminished almost to the point of complete disappearance.[63]

Although President Roosevelt responded to Senator Wagner's request and expanded the Board from seven to eleven members in October 1933,[64] the attendance problem remained

62. Oral history interview with M. Handler, *op. cit.*, p. 7.
63. Benedict Wolf papers, unpublished manuscript (10 chapters, 312 pages), pp. 12–13, from this author's files.
64. *The New York Times*, October 7, 1933, p. 24, col. 3. The employer members added were Austin Finch, president, Thomasville Chair Company, and Edward Nash Hurley, chairman of the board, Hurley Machine Company. Shortly after the death of Hurley in early

unresolved[65] and continued to aggravate the workload difficulties of an already understaffed agency. Senator Wagner, who as the only public member of the board usually presided over the hearings in Washington,[66] remained a U.S. Senator with full senatorial duties so that, although he was a strong chairman,[67] he was not at the board full time. In Senator Wagner's absence "very often the only person sitting on the Board" was Father Francis Haas,[68] a labor member of the NLB, who as a partisan representative on the NLB assumed the responsibility for conducting the mediation sessions and for reporting to the full board when it met in conference to issue decisions whenever mediation failed.[69] This arrangement helped to undermine employer confidence in the impartiality of the NLB.

William Leiserson was convinced, however, that even with all of the NLB members present, the board could not function effectively as a mediating body as long as it was "constituted as it is with representatives of industry and labor."[70]

The reason for this is that when mediation is attempted by the Board as a whole, the representatives of industry and labor on the board show their divergent opinions to the par-

---

November, Pierre S. duPont was appointed to the board. The labor members added were Major George L. Berry, president of the International Pressmen's and Assistants' Union, and Father Francis J. Haas, director of the National Catholic School of Social Service.

65. As late as February 25, 1934, the NLB was still "hoping for a reorganization to ensure attendance at all times of both industrial and labor members and to expedite solution of the type of cases in which members feel delay makes equitable adjustment hopeless." *The New York Times*, February 25, 1934, p. 15, col. 1.

66. Oral history interview with M. Handler, *op. cit.*, p. 7.

67. Oral history interview with Leon Keyserling, March 19, 1969, pp. 4–5, on file in the Labor Management Documentation Center, ILR, Cornell.

68. Oral history interview with Estelle Frankfurter, January 21, 1970, p. 42, on file in the Labor Management Documentation Center, ILR, Cornell.

69. Most of the decisions of the board were made by the entire board meeting in conference. Oral history interview with M. Handler, *op. cit.*, p. 7.

70. NLRB files, letter from W. Leiserson to Senator Wagner, *op. cit.*, p. 1.

ties involved in the disputes, and this impresses the parties that they have support for their respective positions, thus making a settlement almost impossible. Successful mediation can be accomplished only when the parties have a single mediator to deal with, who is impartial and who suggests concessions to be made by both parties.[71]

Mr. Leiserson told Senator Wagner that it was a "fatal error" for mediators to represent either employers or employees. He recommended a change in the structure of the NLB whereby all mediation work would be turned over to the Senator as the neutral member of the board with "a staff of mediators to assist you, all of whom are neutrals representing the government only...."[72] The board, in Leiserson's plan, would sit "only as a judicial tribunal and an agency for deciding questions of policy for the guidance of its mediators."[73] Senator Wagner's basic operating principle of "bringing the parties together" was too deeply rooted, however, to change the board's structure before its effectiveness had been conclusively disproved by experience. Partisan representation was never completely eliminated until the Wagner Act (National Labor Relations Act) was passed in 1935.

The NLB's mediation staff was also "woefully undermanned"[74] for the enormous task it had been assigned. The board's impressive case statistics did not show the many labor disputes that the NLB was unable to reach. Leiserson felt, therefore, that the board was unfair to labor when it told workers that strikes were unnecessary:

> We tell working people not to strike, that there is machinery established for mediating and arbitrating disputes. As a matter of fact, however, we have made the barest beginning toward establishing such machinery.... At present, I do not think we are justified in making any such statement. For every dispute we deal with, there are many others we never touch because of lack of facilities.[75]

71. *Ibid.*
72. *Ibid.*
73. *Ibid.*, p. 2.
74. *Ibid.*
75. *Ibid.*, pp. 2–3.

The NLB responded by establishing regional labor boards in twelve major cities by the end of October 1933.[76] As Senator Wagner described them to the public, these local boards were duplicates of the NLB in Washington:

The Boards vary in number of members but each is composed on the same principle, namely, equal representation of industry and labor with an impartial chairman like the National Labor Board's composition. We took nominations from Chambers of Commerce and employers' associations, and nominations from Labor organizations in making our selections. We consulted public organizations for suggestions of men who could serve as impartial chairmen. . . .[77] The fact that these public spirited men are willing to take time from their many duties to act, without remuneration, in the establishment of industrial peace throughout the country attests to their patriotism and keen social consciousness. Under an impartial chairman, labor and industry will sit around a common conference board and adjust the differences that come before them.[78]

The regional boards were local "mediation tribunals"[79] set up "to adjust disputes and compose differences, and [their methods were] all directed to the attainment of that single objective."[80]

76. The twelve cities were New York, Chicago, Philadelphia, Boston, San Francisco, Cleveland, St. Louis, Seattle, New Orleans, Detroit, Minneapolis, and Atlanta. *The New York Times*, October 28, 1933, p. 5, col. 1. Regional boards were later established in Buffalo, Indianapolis, Kansas City, Los Angeles, Newark, Pittsburg, San Antonio, and Toledo, for a total of twenty regional boards.

77. NA, RG25, NRA Release No. 1280, October 19, 1933, p. 1. Office of the executive secretary, Region VI, Atlanta, correspondence and reports relating to regional boards, 1933–1935.

78. NA, RG25, NRA Release No. 1296, October 20, 1933, p. 1. Office of the executive secretary, Region VI, Atlanta, correspondence and reports relating to regional boards, 1933–1935.

79. NA, RG25, letter from M. Handler to Campbell MacCulloch, December 7, 1933, p. 1. Regional board records, Los Angeles Regional Labor Board, 1933–1934.

80. *Ibid*. Some of the new regional boards "muddled along" when faced with defining their powers, jurisdictional boundaries, and organizational setup. One executive secretary concluded, for example,

034018

In an unintended description of the state of this early board's development, William Leiserson told the regional board members,

A dignified office should be secured. A telephone should be installed. A light and well ventilated place is needed where the atmosphere is cheerful. Furniture should be rented. Get a suitable room for nothing if possible; if not, the government will go as high as $30.00 or $40.00 per month rent.[81]

The NLB instructed its local boards to "make settlements even though you are told it violates all the laws of the land, if it meets the dictates of sound judgment and common sense. . . ."[82] The NLB emphasized the importance of flexibility and informality in successful mediation and told the regional boards that "from the very nature of [their] duties and functions . . . it [was] neither feasible nor desirable that any inflexible rules of procedure be prescribed. . . ."[83] William Leiserson urged, "Don't consult lawyers; keep them out."[84]

---

that the NLB was within the NRA because he "received a supply of stationery from the National Labor Board which is all National Recovery Administration stationery." Letter from Campbell Mac-Culloch to George Creel, November 18, 1933. The same executive secretary commented on another occasion; "We're all out here on the end of a limb and much of the time I suspect someone has sawed that limb off close to the Washington trunk." Letter from C. Mac-Culloch to G. Creel, January 2, 1934. The chairman of the San Francisco Regional Board wrote, "When I am in Washington I mean to find out just what area is covered by each regional board. Quite frankly, I do not know as yet what my territory is." Letter from G. Creel to C. MacCulloch, November 16, 1933. All of these letters are from NA, RG25. Regional board records, Los Angeles Regional Labor Board, 1933–1934.

81. NA, RG25, regional board records, minutes of the Indianapolis Board, Region X, Chicago, November 1933–September 1934.

82. NA, RG25, "Excerpts from Advice Given to One of the Regional Boards by Dr. Leiserson," January 20, 1934, p. 3. Regional board records, Region I, Boston, correspondence from and reports to headquarters, instructions from Washington, 1933–1935.

83. NA, RG25, NLB, "General Instructions for Regional Labor Boards," October 1933, p. 3. Regional board records, Region I, Boston, correspondence from and reports to headquarters, instructions from Washington, 1933–1935.

84. NA, RG25, minutes of the meeting of the Indianapolis Regional

The board's call for informality in procedure and flexibility in substantive determinations, however, ignored the inevitable growth of internal controls in any expanding organization and was inconsistent with the need to define the rights guaranteed by Section 7(a). The need for some uniformity in procedures and records, for example, forced the NLB to write rules and regulations to govern the regional boards in handling complaints. Despite William Leiserson's anxiety about lawyers in labor relations, moreover, the board had to make those regulations more formal by incorporating legal principles such as the adequacy of notice and the opportunity to be heard.[85]

The NLB, in addition, was just beginning to recognize the potential incompatibility of its two goals: strike settlements based on formulas mutually acceptable to employers and unions and the interpretation of Section 7(a) "setting forth the applicable principles of law."[86] The board, consequently, in a further reduc-

---

Labor Board, December 8, 1933, p. 3. Regional board records, Region X, Chicago, minutes of the Indianapolis Board, November 1933–September 1934.

85. NA, RG25, "Excerpts From Advice . . .," *op. cit.*, pp. 1–3. Complaints to the regional labor board had to be specific and in writing. A copy of the complaint was sent to the person or organization complained against with a request for the other side of the story. "It is most important that the employer receive this notice of complaint because (a) he must answer it; and (b) he is thereby prepared for a visit from a representative of the Board, or for any further means of proceeding that the Board may decide upon." The secretary then tried to settle the dispute by telephone, by going out into the field, or by calling the parties to his office. If the secretary was unable to settle the case, "he must lay it before the Board." If the board could not obtain a settlement, then the case was scheduled for hearing: "Notify the parties for hearing, calling the case by such and such a name, and giving the place and date of hearing. . . . Tell them they are requested to be present with such witnesses as they deem necessary. Do not limit the number of witnesses they desire to bring. Let them bring as many as they wish and let each person be heard. They may bring their lawyers if they desire."

86. NA, RG25, "Statement of Jurisdiction and Powers of the National Labor Board and Regional Labor Boards," May 15, 1934, p. 1. Regional board records, Region I, Boston, correspondence from and reports to headquarters, instructions from Washington, 1933–1935.

tion in flexibility, made the regional boards dependent upon Washington for policy decisions "to insure uniformity of interpretation."[87] The NLB reserved the right to review all regional board conclusions concerning violations of the president's Re-Employment Agreement and the NRA's codes of fair competition and required the regional offices to submit "all questions of law"[88] to the NLB, limiting themselves "to a statement of facts and recommendations" which did not "discuss questions of law or state conclusions of law regarding alleged violations of the statute."[89]

The NLB itself, however, did not "state conclusions of law"[90] during its first three months of work chiefly because Senator Wagner believed that the success of the board depended upon the unanimity of its labor and management members:

> Senator Wagner sought . . . to avoid any public expressions of differences in viewpoint. His idea was that the Board's influence depended largely on public opinion. To command public opinion, it would be well to make a display of unanimity. Such a display would exhibit the cooperation of management and labor in the interests of the recovery program.[91]

As a consequence, after three months of avoiding unequivocal interpretations of Section 7(a), NLB mediators continued to function without policy guidance from the board and to work with employers and unions that were still ignorant of their rights under the NIRA. Leiserson told Wagner in October 1933 that this was one of the most serious problems facing the board.

> I feel that many of our cases have been unduly delayed and mishandled because when they come to the Board from the

87. NA, RG25, "NLB, General Instructions for Regional Labor Boards," October 1933, p. 4. Regional board records, Region I, Boston, correspondence from and reports to headquarters, instructions from Washington, 1933–1935.
88. *Ibid.*
89. NA, RG25, letter from M. Handler to C. MacCulloch, *op. cit.*, p. 2. Regional board records, Los Angeles Regional Labor Board, 1933–1934.
90. The only exception to this statement was the NLB's decision in the *Berkeley Woolen Mills* case, *Decisions of the NLB, op. cit.*, vol. I, pp. 5–6.
91. Lorwin and Wubnig, *op. cit.*, p. 119.

mediators, the Board has attempted to mediate them all over again, instead of . . . deciding them on the basis of the provisions of the Recovery Act. . . . Instead the Board attempted to mediate with the result that the whole matter of collective bargaining vs. individual bargaining involved in these cases was left as something to be fought out in industrial conflicts and settled on the basis of relative economic power, as it was before Congress enacted section 7-a. . . .

There are a number of matters of policy that need to be decided by the Board. . . . I refer particularly to such questions as recognition of the union, minority representation, written agreements with unions, and form of ballot, whether the name of a union may appear as a candidate for representative, etc. . . . . In most of the cases that have come to the Board these questions were involved, but the Board has not decided them because it has undertaken to mediate the cases, thus avoiding a decision on the basic question of policy. Had the Board sat as an arbitration or judicial tribunal, the policy questions would have been settled long ago on the basis of decisions in the cases submitted to it, and the questions people are asking about the rights of employers and workers under the N.R.A. would not have to go unanswered . . . . many questions of policy would have been cleared up, and most of the difficulties of the Board's staff and mediators would be out of the way.[92]

Yet, the defects inherent in an NLB structure which combined not only employer and union representatives but also mediation and judicial functions became most obvious the one time in the first few months that the board did take a definite public stand on a controversial 7(a) issue. The board, by deciding unanimously in the *Berkeley Woolen Mills and United Textile Workers* case that "employees have the right to choose anyone they may wish as their representative and are not limited in their choice to fellow employees"[93] established itself as prolabor in the opinion of employers and, consequently, undermined its own mediation effectiveness.

92. NLRB files, letter from W. Leiserson to Senator Wagner, *op. cit.*, pp. 1 and 3.
93. *Decisions of the NLB, op. cit.*, vol. I, p. 6.

A Fight for Control of Section 7(a):
The Challenge of the NRA

The NLB, therefore, chose to decide policy questions only as a last resort and then only on a case-by-case basis in dealing with actual controversies.[94] The board directed its regional offices to follow this same approach, "refusing to discuss theoretical questions of law with representatives of the employers or to render decisions upon abstract questions of law which are not involved in a concrete case presented to the Board for decision."[95] The NLB's cautious approach to policy making, however, left it vulnerable to the maneuverings of the NRA which, in its administration of the recovery program, was "highly sensitive to outside forces" in a "continuous effort . . . to adjust itself to the balance of power in capital-labor relations. . . ."[96] General Hugh Johnson, NRA head, and Donald R. Richberg, NRA general counsel, seized the policy-making initiative from the NLB in the early months of the NRA and issued a series of public statements reading Section 7(a) to mean that company unions were not prohibited, that exclusive representation was not required, and that minority or porportional representation was permitted ("Messrs. Johnson and Richberg thus introduced the concept of plurality in labor representation for collective bargaining within one and the same labor unit").[97] It was also understood that workers were free to bargain individually, that the closed shop was contrary to public policy, and that employers were not obliged to assent to a contract of any kind.[98] The NRA interpretations, moreover, were advanced as governmental policy and "whatever their legal soundness . . . [they] had the practical effect of placing the NRA on the side of anti-union employers. . . ."[99]

In September 1933, before the NLB had established regional

---

94. NLRB files, letter from W. Leiserson to Senator Wagner, *op. cit.*, p. 3.
95. NA, RG25, letter from M. Handler to C. MacCulloch, *op. cit.*, p. 1. Regional board records, Los Angeles Labor Board, 1933–1934.
96. Lyon *et al.*, *op. cit.*, p. 443.
97. *Ibid.*, p. 463.
98. *Ibid.* For a review of NRA interpretations of Section 7(a), see pp. 461–466.
99. *Ibid.*, p. 465.

offices, General Johnson also moved to establish NRA jurisdiction over local labor disputes by directing local NRA compliance boards to mediate local labor controversies.[100] Although the local compliance boards were designed to provide balanced representation for employers, employees, and consumers,[101] these NRA boards were generally dominated by employers "unfriendly to organized labor"[102] and "hundreds of letters and telegrams . . . poured into the offices of the National Labor Board and into the Department of Labor from labor unions protesting against the appointment of open-shop advocates on local compliance boards, who immediately began to take part in mediating labor disputes."[103]

Senator Wagner, confronted with the first critical struggle for control of Section 7(a), was reported to have threatened to resign as chairman of the NLB,[104] an action that would have severely weakened labor's confidence in the NRA. After the NRA's Labor Advisory Board "called on General Johnson," the NRA administrator announced on September 19, 1933 "that he would see to it that a letter was sent out to the local compliance boards canceling their efforts to mediate labor disputes."[105] The NLB's desire to secure its jurisdiction over Section 7(a) guaranteed the early

100. *The New York Times*, September 20, 1933, p. 5, col. 1. NRA compliance boards had been established in many cities to adjust disputes arising under NRA codes prior to the creation of the NLB.
101. Charles L. Dearing *et al.*, *The ABC of the NRA* (Washington: The Brookings Institution, 1934), pp. 68–73.
102. Lorwin and Wubnig, *op. cit.*, p. 264. See also J. Henry Richardson, "The New Deal in the United States," *The Economic Journal*, vol. 44, December 1934, pp. 608–610.
103. *The New York Times*, September 20, 1933, p. 5, col. 1.
104. *Ibid.* See also *The New York Times*, September 23, 1933, p. 7, col. 5.
105. *The New York Times*, September 20, 1933, p. 5, col. 1. General Johnson said, "It is contemplated that in the near future the National Labor Board will set up regional agencies for mediation in the case of labor disputes. Until that time, when there is an active or threatened lockout or strike in a community which is brought to the attention of the local NRA compliance board, this board should report that fact immediately to the National Recovery Administration for reference to the National Labor Board. . . ." *The New York Times*, September 23, 1933, p. 7, col. 5.

creation of a system of regional labor boards after the withdrawal of the NRA.[106]

The Steel and Automobile Industries Confront a Powerless NLB

The NLB, however, never did have control over the enforcement of its own decisions. Unfortunately for the board, that power was controlled by the Compliance Division of the NRA and the U.S. Department of Justice. Its use depended ultimately not upon the findings and recommendations of the NLB, but upon the willingness of the Compliance Division to deprive an employer of his Blue Eagle and of the attorney general to initiate legal proceedings. The board, after some "internal friction," remained divided on the relative merits of legal force and moral suasion,[107] but chose initially to extend its mediation efforts to include problems of noncompliance with its decisions, "ostensibly [ignoring] the assumption that settlements might be impossible because some employers were firmly opposed to recognizing the authority or accepting the principles of the Board."[108]

In a dispute involving taxi cab drivers employed by the Philadelphia Rapid Transit Company,[109] for example, the board sent William Leiserson to Philadelphia to continue mediation efforts

106. One NRA official was concerned about the void created by the NLB action: "Not the least of my bitterness was that the National Labor Board took away all power from the NRA for the adjustment of industrial disputes, although neither at the time, nor since, have they had any machinery at all to exercise this authority thus assumed. . . ." NA, RG25, letter from G. Creel (then chairman of a NRA district recovery board) to C. MacCulloch, October 12, 1933. Regional board records, Region XVI, San Francisco, general correspondence, 1933–1935, Los Angeles Regional Board, 1933–1934.
107. *The New York Times*, February 25, 1934, p. 15, col. 1; *The New York Times*, February 26, 1934, p. 38, col. 2.
108. Lorwin and Wubnig, *op. cit.*, p. 134.
109. *Decisions of the NLB, op. cit.*, vol. I, pp. 66–67.

after the PRT Co. refused to comply with the NLB's decision of December 18, 1933.[110] The NLB persisted in its efforts to mediate the company's noncompliance, even though the strike was causing great public inconvenience and disorder with taxi cab drivers being beaten and their cabs stoned and burned in the center of the city[111] and despite heavy pressure from city officials who demanded that the case be turned over to the Department of Justice for "immediate action" to end the PRT's "brazen defiance of the National Government."[112]

Mediation continued for three weeks until January 9, 1934, when Senator Wagner answered critics of this extended mediation approach in his announcement of the ratification by the parties of an agreement, "largely that recommended by the Philadelphia Regional Labor Board on December 6 and by the National Labor Board on December 18":[113]

> This outcome is worth pondering by those who have hastily assailed the National Labor Board system whenever a recommendation or ruling was not accepted instantly. Friendly critics have shouted for us to be belligerent and hostile critics have dared us to be. That was not the policy of the Board. Why? Because the Board knows that voluntary agreements are always preferable and that lasting agreements generally grow out of second thoughts rather than controversial first thoughts. In the Philadelphia taxi case . . . when acceptance

110. NA, RG25, records of the National Labor Relations Board. Documents from the unfair labor practices and representation case files. Informal files (hereinafter referred to as NA, RG25, informal files), NRA Release Number 2422, December 21, 1933, *Philadelphia Rapid Transit Company* case.: ". . . the National Labor Board was in touch by telephone with its Secretary, Dr. William Leiserson, who is in Philadelphia attempting to avert the strike. Dr. Leiserson reported to the Board late today that he would have another meeting with the strike committee this evening."

111. NA, RG25, informal files, *Philadelphia Ledger*, December 4, 1933, p. 1, *Philadelphia Rapid Transit Company* case.

112. NA, RG25, informal files, letter from S. Davis Wilson to Senator Robert F. Wagner, December 30, 1933, *Philadelphia Rapid Transit Company* case.

113. NA, RG25, informal files, NRA Release Number 2648, January 9, 1934, *Philadelphia Rapid Transit Company* case.

was not immediate, we remained patient but persistent. This persistence had its reward. . . .[114]

The *Edward G. Budd Manufacturing* and *Weirton Steel* Cases

The NLB needed more than patience and persistence to meet the challenges of the powerful steel and automobile industries whose cases (the *Edward G. Budd Manufacturing Co.* and the *Weirton Steel Co.*) confronted the NLB in December 1933. The Budd Manufacturing Company[115] employed 5,000 workers in peak seasons in the production of automobile bodies and frames. The company notified its employees on September 1, 1933 (two days after 1,000 Budd employees attended a mass meeting called by the Metal Trades Council of Philadelphia) that an employee representation plan was being prepared by the management. That plan was submitted to the employees on September 5, 1933, nominations for the various offices were made on the same day, and, on September 7, 1933, 92 percent of the employees voted for their representatives who, in turn, accepted a constitution and bylaws prepared by the Budd Company. When management told the United Automobile Federal Union, which claimed 1,000 Budd employees as members, that the company "could not recognize the American Federation of Labor inasmuch as Budd had employee representation that was operating satisfactorily,"[116] approximately 1,500 Budd employees went on strike on November 14, 1933—a strike which the company told Secretary of Labor Perkins "has been brought about apparently by professional union organizers who already have attempted unsuccessfully to force their purposes on Ford and others."[117] The company refused to appear

114. *Ibid.*
115. *Decisions of the NLB, op. cit.*, vol. I, pp. 58–61. Other material for the background of this case was found in NA, RG25, informal files, *E. G. Budd Company* case.
116. *Decisions of the NLB, op. cit.*, p. 59.
117. NA, RG25, informal files, letter from Samuel Barker to Frances Perkins, November 20, 1933, *E. G. Budd Company* case.

before the NLB or to agree to a new representation election as ordered by the NLB on December 14, 1933. Finally, Senator Wagner gave the case to the national compliance director on January 11, 1933.

> Mr. Budd cannot have been under any illusion that the National Labor Board would merely drop this case.... Mr. Budd will not take the judgment of his peers—the outstanding industrial leaders composing half the memberships of the Philadelphia and National Boards—that an impartially supervised election is necessary.... In view of this attitude ... the National Labor Board has no choice but to transmit the case to the National Compliance Director.[118]

The NLB expected that the Compliance Board would "withdraw the Blue Eagle from Budd and order the cancellation of all his Government contracts."[119] Neither happened.

Ernest Weir, chairman of both the Weirton Steel Company, which employed 13,000 workers, and National Steel, the country's fourth biggest steel company, repudiated an October 1933 strike-ending agreement with Senator Wagner in which the NLB was to specify the "procedures and method"[120] for a representation election to be held in December 1933 and, over vigorous NLB objections, conducted his own election under the rules of the Weirton employee association. As *Business Week* reported in its December 23 issue:

> In Pittsburgh, ancient citadel of steel, the battle is of the greatest importance.... Traditionally the steel industry is open shop. Recently the Amalgamated has been boring in on steel employees. [The] Presence of William Green, head of the A.F. of L. on the Labor Board, and ... Administration aid to the organization [have] been endured with suppressed fury by many a hard-boiled steel operator who couldn't think of anything to do about it.... Weir is a big independent. He has

118. NA, RG25, informal files, NRA Release Number 2678, January 11, 1934, p. 1, *E. G. Budd Company* case.
119. NA, RG25, informal files, letter from M. Handler to William H. Davis, January 5, 1934, *E. G. Budd Company* case.
120. "Weirton Fights," *Business Week*, December 23, 1933, p. 6. See also *The New York Times*, October 17, 1933, p. 1, col. 5.

more freedom of movement than would be possible for companies with far-flung interests and numerous points of vulnerability. From congratulatory wires and letters you might assume that Mr. Weir was the most popular man in the industry. . . .[121]

After fruitless mediation efforts by William Leiserson and Milton Handler,[122] the Justice Department, at the request of the NLB, sent agents of the Federal Bureau of Investigation to observe Mr. Weir's election (a sweeping victory for the company union), to "see what was going on," to interview workers, and to put together affidavits in preparation for legal proceedings.[123] These legal proceedings were still unresolved 18 months later when the Supreme Court ruled the NIRA unconstitutional.

William Green, president of the AFL, wanted to "pillory Mr. Weir as a public enemy" and lamented the tragedy of the destruction of "the faith that . . . workers have in the Government and in the National Labor Board" when the Weirton and Budd companies continued to display the Blue Eagle and to enjoy government contracts and the benefits and protection of the code while "eight hundred men walk the streets because they tried to take advantage of their legal rights."[124] The *Philadelphia Record* stated that it was the duty of the NLB "to hold such an election whether Budd likes it or not."[125]

121. "Weirton Fights," *op. cit.*, pp. 6–7.
122. Oral history interview with M. Handler, *op. cit.*, p. 32.
123. *Ibid.*, pp. 32–33.
124. *Senate Hearings on the Labor Disputes Act, op. cit.*, pp. 104, 105, and 106. The specific reference to 800 men concerns the E. G. Budd Company.
125. NA, RG25, informal files, *Philadelphia Record*, November 19, 1933, *E. G. Budd Company* case.

2 The NLB and the Labor Disputes Bill

Executive Order Number 6511 and the Intensification of Industry's Challenge to the Authority of the NLB

The *Weirton* and *Budd* crises had conclusively demonstrated the weakness inherent in the board's total dependence upon the voluntary cooperation of employers and unions, the force of public sentiment, and the influence and prestige of its members. The NLB, therefore, moved to strengthen its own position by obtaining an executive order which would detail the board's administrative authority and would finally clear up the confusion and uncertainty over the NLB's legal status which had persisted since the creation of the board by press release on August 5, 1933.

General Counsel Milton Handler remembers:

> I drafted the executive order. . . . After I cleared the executive order with Senator Wagner, I asked him whether I should then clear it with the State Department. . . . He [said] "I don't need any State Department to clear this order. . . . I'll call the president, make an appointment with him, give him the executive order, and have it signed. . . ." When he came back, I asked him for the order. He was very sheepish. He said that after chatting with the president and listening to the president talk about a variety of things, he stuck his hand in his pocket to pull out the executive order to present to the president for signature. To his dismay he found that he had lost the order. . . . After a period of some weeks, Senator Wagner

again made an appointment with the president and this time he returned with the bacon.[1]

President Roosevelt, on December 16, 1933, "approved and ratified" in Executive Order Number 6511 "all actions heretofore taken by this Board in the discharge of its functions. . . ."[2] The executive order formally validated powers which the board had already assumed—to establish local or regional boards, to review the determinations of the regional boards, and to make rules and regulations governing board procedure. It also confirmed the board's expansion of its own jurisdiction beyond disputes arising under the president's Re-Employment Agreement to those arising under "any duly approved industrial code of fair competition," such as the Automobile Code under which the Budd Company operated. Another provision which anticipated the establishment of individual labor boards for each industry gave the NLB the discretion "to decline to take cognizance of controversies" in fields where other settlement agencies existed.

Although the executive order ratified the mediation functions of the NLB, it conferred no new powers on the board, made no reference to the board's decision-making authority, and gave no authorization for the conduct of representation elections. Senator Wagner for the first time indicated publicly that he would ask Congress "for legislation to give the Board further power."[3]

The National Association of Manufacturers (NAM), however, responded with a vigorous public attack on the NLB, charging that the executive order had given the board so much power that it was now the "Supreme Court of Labor."[4] The NAM reviewed the decisions of the NLB and found that "its lines of thinking and the direction in which it is moving" one-sided:[5] the board had ordered that strikers be given preference in poststrike reinstate-

1. Oral history interview with M. Handler, *op. cit.*, pp. 10–11. See also *The New York Times*, December 20, 1933, pp. 1, col. 5, and 6, col. 5.
2. NA, RG 25, "Statement of Jurisdiction and Powers . . .," *op. cit.*, p. 4. For the complete text of Executive Order Number 6511, see *Senate Hearings on the Labor Disputes Act, op. cit.*, pp. 48–49.
3. *The New York Times*, December 20, 1933, pp. 1, col. 5, and 6, col. 5.
4. *Commercial and Financial Chronicle*, vol. 137, no. 3574, (December 23, 1933), p. 4397.
5. *Ibid.*

ments,[6] that strikers be permitted to vote in the election of representatives,[7] and that employee representatives did not have to be chosen from among the employees.[8] The association was most disturbed that the NLB "had been active in promoting and supervising the election of worker representatives."[9] The NAM's distress over representation elections was understandable. Employers promoting employee representation plans "had little to gain and much to lose"[10] from an NLB representation election, whereas trade unions had everything to gain and little to lose: "In fact, a major reason why trade unions were willing to abide by Board recommendations urging them to call off strikes was their belief that in a free election they were quite likely to win against the company unions."[11]

Trade unions had won 75 percent of the 31 representation elections held by the board from August through December 1933— a union success rate that remained constant throughout the life of the NLB.[12] The NLB's advocacy of the representation election under these circumstances convinced industry that the board's (including the employer members') "underlying purpose always is to carry out the demands of labor, and especially organized labor."[13]

> . . . the theory upon which all governing boards are nominally constituted . . . is . . . that the opposing sides shall have individual and equal representation in order that they may

6. *Decisions of the NLB, op. cit., "Art Metals Construction Company and Its Employees,"* vol. I, pp. 24–25 and *"Shoe Manufacturers of New York and Brooklyn and Shoe and Leather Workers Industrial Union,"* vol. I, pp. 35–36.
7. *Ibid.*
8. *Ibid., "Berkeley Woolen Mills and United Textile Workers,"* vol. I, pp. 5–6.
9. *Commercial and Financial Chronicle, op. cit.,* p. 4398.
10. Lorwin and Wubnig, *op. cit.,* pp. 218–219.
11. *Ibid.,* p. 219.
12. Slichter, *op. cit.,* p. 151. Among the 546 plants "or other units" in which the board conducted elections "in 408 cases or 74.7 percent, a trade union won the election. Of 103,714 votes counted, 71,931 or 69.4 percent were cast for trade union representation." Emily Clark Brown, "Selection of Employees' Representatives," *op. cit.,* p. 1.
13. *Commercial and Financial Chronicle, op. cit.,* p. 4398.

have fair and impartial treatment. But let no one be deceived by this suggestion of fair and judicial treatment. The representatives chosen are almost invariably heads of large labor organizations who can be depended upon to present an unyielding front in advocating the demands of so-called labor, *while even the representatives of the manufacturers are usually chosen from among those who are known from their expression of views to have a strong leaning towards labor.* [14]

Milton Handler, who attended all the board hearings and who "in the main wrote all the opinions for the board with the assistance of [his] staff,"[15] had a different view of the workings of the board:

I think our hardest problem was a matter of personality, getting all of the people together . . . Senator Wagner had no executive talent, he was a great procrastinator. You could never get a decision out of him on administrative matters. When it came to issues before the board, he liked to listen. Leo Wolman . . . could brilliantly analyze the issues . . . . he would give you the pros and cons and it would be fascinating to listen to him . . . . [but] you could practically never get a decision out of him. The labor people to a very large extent engaged in bloc voting, they voted as a class. The employers were very extraordinary, they were very fair. . . . Pierre duPont tended towards bloc voting, but Teagle and Swope were very, very fair-minded men and they called the shots as they saw them.[16]

NLB staff member Benedict Wolf recalled:

My experience with Pierre duPont [was] that when he spent a little time in Washington subject to discussions with us, he would be well educated to the purpose of the act and interested in carrying out its functions. . . . and then he'd go back to Wilmington for two weeks . . . (listening . . . to the people in his own organization who must have told him what a horrible thing the whole [7a] idea was) . . . and by the time

14. *Ibid.*, p. 4397 (emphasis added).
15. Oral history interview with M. Handler, *op. cit.*, p. 16.
16. *Ibid.*, p. 40.

he came back, we'd have to go through the whole process all over again. [17]

Executive Order Number 6511, in fact, did nothing to discourage employer challenges to the authority of the NLB. Senator Wagner told President Roosevelt in a report summarizing the work of the NLB and its regional boards from August 5, 1933 to February 1, 1934 that "the statistics bear out what the Boards in many regions have been reporting for some time; namely, that the willingness to use the Boards, displayed by the majority, is encountering the impediment of a small minority whose desire for industrial peace is not uppermost. *This impediment is increasing.*"[18] Senator Wagner found it "disquieting" that only 69 percent of the cases before the labor boards had been settled, that "some settlements had been unsatisfactory," and that there had been a sharp increase in the number of settlements by board decisions "for it is another indication of resistance to agreement. . . ."[19] Even including the 88 percent voluntary settlement rate for the first three months of the board's work, the combined statistics of the NLB and its regional boards showed that by February 1, 1934 just one-half of the settlements had been the result of voluntary agreement of employers and unions.[20] Moreover, the NLB, which from August through October 1933 had successfully mediated approximately 7 voluntary settlements for every one of its decisions, could obtain only 2 voluntary settlements for each of its decisions from November 1, 1933 to February 1, 1934.[21]

17. Oral history interview with B. Wolf, *op. cit.*, pp. 14–15.
18. NA, RG25, NRA Release Number 3414, "National Labor Board Reports to the President," February 21, 1934, p. 2 (emphasis added). Office of the executive secretary, Region VI, Atlanta. Correspondence and reports relating to regional boards, 1933–1935.
19. *Ibid.*, pp. 2–3.
20. *Ibid.*, p. 1.
21. Figures based on NLRB files, memorandum from Paul M. Herzog to the National Labor Board, *op. cit.*, and "Work of National Labor Board and Regional Boards," *Monthly Labor Review*, vol. 38, no. 3 (March 1934), pp. 527–528. The *Monthly Labor Review* lists 103 cases settled by agreement. When the 58 voluntary agreements obtained from August through October are subtracted from that total, it

The NLB as a Judicial Body

The board, under the pressure of these circumstances, moved reluctantly and cautiously into its role as a quasijudicial body formulating principles rather than fashioning compromises. No authority had been given to the board to make decisions as a quasijudicial agency, it had no body of precedent on which to rely, and it received no help from the NRA compliance agencies. (Only four employers had been deprived of their Blue Eagles by the middle of June 1934 when the board was terminated and, in fact, even the removal of the Blue Eagle had no effect on most employers in most industries.)[22] The board, furthermore, was so convinced that the NLB needed the trust, support, and cooperation of the parties, particularly employers, to secure voluntary agreements (which alone promised "durable peace"[23]) that the mediation criterion of acceptability to the parties was also used to guide the making of Board decisions.[24] The board's crucial decisions concerning the choice of representatives, company unions, recognition, and collective bargaining were, therefore, susceptible to compromise according to the circumstances and pressures of each case.

A Last Attempt to Obtain Voluntary Settlements

The NLB never found that company unions violated Section 7(a) as long as "the plan had been established and was maintained

---

leaves 45 cases settled by agreement from October 1933 through January 1934. Subtracting the 8 decisions issued by the NLB in the first three months from the 29 decisions listed in the *Monthly Labor Review* table leaves 21 cases settled by decision from October to January 1934.

22. Lorwin and Wubnig, *op. cit.*, p. 221.
23. NA, RG25, NRA Release Number 3414, *op. cit.*, pp. 2–3.
24. Lorwin and Wubnig, *op. cit.*, p. 222: "Its [the NLB's] primary intention, however, was not so much to act like a court of law as it was to evolve a set of principles and devices—a theory of labor relations

through the free expression of the worker' will,"[25] particularly
if the employees were given the opportunity to choose between
"inside and outside unions" as they were in the *Federal Knitting
Mills* case.[26] The board, however, would find a violation of Section
7(a) whenever the employees had been denied their freedom to
choose their own representatives and wherever "the new union
[was] the creature of the company and not of its employees."[27]
Even these rulings, however, were subject to compromise. On
January 21, 1934, for example, the board did find such a violation
of Section 7(a) in the *Dresner* case[28] and ordered its Chicago
Regional Board to conduct a representation election restricting
voter eligibility to those employees on the company's payroll of
September 5, 1933 (the day before the employees of Dresner went
on strike) "who are in the company's employ or who manifest a
desire to be reinstated."[29] The company refused to cooperate with
the board and another hearing was held so that the company
could show cause why the NLB should not send the case "to
the enforcement authorities of Government" following which
"numerous attempts were made to adjust the dispute."[30] When

---

    —which would appeal to employers and workers alike because of
relationality and justice."
25. Lorwin and Wubnig, *op. cit.*, p. 154.
26. *Decisions of the NLB, op. cit.*, "*The Federal Knitting Mills, Friedman, Blau, Farber Co., Interstate Knitting Mills, Stone Knitting
Mills and United Textile Workers' Union*," vol. I, p. 70. In this case
"(1) in each shop votes were taken for an inside as against an outside
union; (2) thereafter there was an election of representatives and
no coercion was evidenced before or during such election; (3) subsequent to such election collective bargaining was freely entered
into between the employers and employees representatives; (4)
controls on membership are to run from three to six months and are
then renewable. . .; (5) the constitutions of these associations were
drafted by the employees themselves." See NA, RG25, informal files,
memorandum from Estelle S. Frankfurter to the National Labor
Board, January 25, 1934, p. 2, *Cleveland Knitting Mills* case.
27. *Decisions of the NLB, op. cit.*, "*S. Dresner and Son and United
Leather Workers International Union*," vol. I, p. 27.
28. *Ibid.*
29. *Ibid.*
30. NA, RG25, informal files, letter from M. Handler to Wilber Katz,
June 22, 1934, *S. Dresner & Son* case.

the NLB finally decided to conduct an election without the consent of the company four months after the board's decision, the Dresner Company obtained an injunction prohibiting the board's representation election.

The board, inadequately staffed to handle litigation ("we did not have on our staff . . . any lawyer with court experience who could have been sent to Chicago to conduct the litigation"),[31] advised by the Department of Justice that the state courts would rule against the government ("this view was based upon the known hostility of the courts in that section of the country to the NRA"),[32] and convinced that litigation would delay the election "for an indefinite period of time,"[33] approved an agreement negotiated by the Department of Justice and the company to resolve the issue.[34] Under the terms of that agreement, the NLB, in return for the dismissal of the injunction, abandoned all attempts to prosecute the Dresner Company or to remove the company's Blue Eagle,[35] agreed to drop its charges that the company had violated Section 7(a),[36] and consented to an election "to be held under the supervision of an impartial third person not connected with the National or the Local Board."[37]

Moreover, the board, also contrary to its January decision, agreed that the poll would be conducted in two parts:

31. NA, RG25, informal files, letter from M. Handler to the National Labor Relations Board, November 26, 1934, pp. 1–2. *S. Dresner & Son* case.
32. *Ibid.*, p. 2.
33. NA, RG25, informal files, letter from B. Wolf to Herbert L. Petty, August 16, 1934, p. 1, *S. Dresner & Son* case.
34. NA, RG25, informal files, letter from M. Handler to the National Labor Relations Board, *op. cit.*, p. 2. Handler opposed this settlement: "My own inclination was to reject the proposed settlement. I was confident that there was no merit in the injunction suit and that the government would prevail in higher courts." *Ibid.*
35. NA, RG25, informal files, memorandum from B. Wolf re *S. Dresner & Son*, October 20, 1934, *S. Dresner & Son* case.
36. NA, RG25, informal files, letter from William Rice to Wilber Katz, August 18, 1934, and letter from Lloyd Garrison to United Leather Workers International Union, August 2, 1934, *S. Dresner & Son* case.
37. NA, RG25, informal files, letter from Harold M. Stephens to Francis Biddle, February 9, 1935, *S. Dresner & Son* case.

The first poll would be of those working at the time in the Dresner factories. These ballots were to be segregated and the results were not to be announced. A second poll was then to be held outside the factory, of those on the preferential list. It was [planned] to combine the results of the two polls and to certify the victorious union as the bargaining agency. [38]

A University of Chicago professor, Wilber Katz, conducted a secret ballot election on Dresner Company premises in June 1934, [39] but when the United Leather Workers Union, which had no part in the settlement agreement, learned of the first election and its outcome (three to one against the union), [40] "it refused to participate in the second" [41] unless "it [was] held in accordance with the previous ruling of the National Labor Board." [42] The union persisted in its efforts to obtain enforcement of the board's January 31, 1933 order until February 18, 1935 when the NLB's successor, the first NLRB, told the union that ". . . it would not be in the public interest to conduct an election now on the basis of employees who were on the payroll a year ago. Too much water has passed over the dam." [43]

The NLB also frequently resorted to compromise to evade the issue of union recognition. William Green, president of the AFL,

---

38. NA, RG25, informal files, letter from M. Handler to the National Labor Relations Board, *op. cit.*, p. 3.

39. *Ibid.*, p. 2.

40. NA, RG25, informal files, memorandum from B. Wolf re *S. Dresner & Son*, *op. cit.*

41. NA, RG25, informal files, letter from M. Handler to the National Labor Relations Board, *op. cit.*, p. 3.

42. NA, RG25, informal files, letter from B. Wolf to Charlton Ogburn, October 3, 1934, *S. Dresner & Son* case. "The Union protested the June 26th election, particularly with reference to the fact that the poll was conducted on company property and with the cooperation of the company as well as in the absence of prior advice to the union representatives." The union also charged the company with intimidating the employees who voted. See NA, RG25, informal files, letter from B. Wolf to Herbert L. Petty, August 16, 1934, p. 2, *S. Dresner & Son* case.

43. NA, RG25, informal files, letter from Francis Biddle to Charlton Ogburn, February 18, 1935, p. 1, *S. Dresner & Son* case. The union had also been told by the NLRB that the board had no power to

charged, for example, that "the Board has been consistently forced to straddle the real issue in many of the cases, and the real issue is that of union recognition for collective bargaining."[44] Union recognition was the issue when the H. C. Frick Company and the United Mine Workers of America failed to negotiate a collective bargaining agreement in the captive mines of western Pennsylvania in January 1934.[45] The Mine Workers demanded union recognition in the form of an agreement between the Frick Company and the UMWA as an organization whereas the H. C. Frick Company refused to recognize the union and insisted that any agreement be made between the company and John L. Lewis and others as individuals who represent "the majority voting."[46] The board compromised and, in a decision which was called "at best an expedient designed to prevent defiance,"[47] ruled that the contracts be made between the mine operators and John L. Lewis *et al.* in their individual capacities as international or district officers of the union.[48] The NLB sidestepped the basic issue by holding that "whether a contract made and executed in this form does or does not, as a matter of law, amount to recognition of the Union is a question not before us and one which we need not here decide."[49]

upset "an agreement with the company entered into by the Department of Justice and the NLB." See NA, RG25, informal files, memorandum from B. Wolf re *S. Dresner & Son, op. cit.*, and letter from W. Rice to W. Katz, *op. cit.*

44. *Senate Hearings on the Labor Disputes Act, op. cit.*, p. 70.

45. *Decisions of the NLB, op. cit.*, "*H. C. Frick Coke Company, National Mining Company, and Sharon Limestone Company and the United Mine Workers of America*," vol. I, p. 44. This dispute arose under the terms of the presidential agreement which had settled the bitter strikes in the captive mines of western Pennsylvania in October 1933. *Ibid.*, pp. 44–45.

46. NA, RG25, informal files, "Summary of the Captive Mine Contracts Hearing," Jesse I, Miller, n.d., p. 2, *H. C. Frick Coke Company* case.

47. *The New York Times*, February 4, 1934, sec. 8, p. 3., col. 1. "Clearly the decision accommodated itself to the balance of forces in what had been a major industrial disturbance and was designed as far as possible to 'save face' for both of two powerful antagonists." Lorwin and Wubnig, *op. cit.*, p. 189.

48. Lorwin and Wubnig, *op. cit.*, p. 175.

49. *Decisions of the NLB, op. cit., H. C. Frick Coke Company . . .*," p. 48.

The NLB's general counsel summarized the board's position on union recognition in a letter to the Chicago Regional Board one week after the Frick decision:

Regarding the question of union recognition, I find no affirmative requirement in the statute that the employer must recognize a union. He must meet and bargain collectively with the representatives of the workers. The union, or the union officials, may constitute such representatives and the agreement may be made with the employees acting through their representatives, or it may be made with the representatives directly. No compulsion, however, can be exercised by the National Labor Board controlling the form and nature of the agreement that is made. *Many of our proposed settlements have been wrecked on the rocks of this question of union recognition, and we have made use of various compromises. The decision in the Captive Mines controversy indicates one of the compromises which is most frequently involved.*[50]

Employer recalcitrance also influenced the NLB's definition of the essential requirements of collective bargaining. The board, without finding that a refusal to reduce a collective bargaining agreement to writing violated the NIRA, held in the *Pierson Manufacturing Company* (December 28, 1933) and *Harriman Hosiery* (January 4, 1934) cases that any agreement reached "*shall be reduced to writing*"[51] since "only a written agreement can give both parties the sense of certainty and security which is essential to lasting industrial peace."[52] Yet, when confronted with noncompliance in these two cases, Senator Wagner wrote the Pierson Manufacturing Company on January 18, 1934 that "the Board

50. NA, RG25, letter from M. Handler to the Chicago Regional Board, January 26, 1934, p. 1 (emphasis added). Office of the executive secretary, Region X, Chicago, correspondence and reports relating to regional boards, 1933–1935.

51. This precise language is used in the board rulings in both cases. See *Decisions of the NLB, op. cit.,* "*Pierson Manufacturing Co. and United Garment Workers of America Local No. 247,*" vol. I, p. 53, and "*Harriman Hosiery Mills and United Textile Workers of America,*" vol. I, p. 68 (emphasis added).

52. *Decisions of the NLB, op. cit.,* "*Pierson Manufacturing Company . . .,*" p. 53.

ruled that the agreement which had been reached by the management and the employees *should* be reduced to writing"[53] and the NLB's general counsel explained that the *Harriman* case ruling

[was] merely a statement of the Board's views regarding the proper method of adjusting a dispute and bringing the efforts at collective bargaining to the successful conclusion. The ruling does not have the force and effect of law, however . . . . the form that the agreement takes is a subject for collective bargaining and is thus exclusively within the control of the parties.[54]

Despite these compromises in pursuit of employer and union cooperation, the board had begun to develop a common law of labor relations from mid-December 1933 to February 1, 1934[55] by ruling that an employee discharged for union activity be reinstated with back pay from the date of his discharge,[56] that the employees' right to bargain collectively imposed a corresponding duty on the employer,[57] that the parties approach negotiations with open minds and exert every reasonable effort to reach an agreement,[58] that self-organization and representation elections concerned employees exclusively and employers must keep "hands

53. NA, RG25, informal files, letter from Senator Wagner to the Pierson Manufacturing Company, January 18, 1934, p. 1 (emphasis added), *Pierson Manufacturing Company* case.

54. NA, RG25, letter from M. Handler to the Chicago Regional Board, *op. cit.*, pp. 1–2. Handler added that "all the statute requires is that both parties manifest an earnest and sincere desire to reach an agreement and the failure to sign a written agreement may impugn the good faith of the parties. While not in itself a violation of the statute, such failure or refusal may be evidentiary of a refusal to bargain collectively."

55. This summary of NLB rulings is based on NLRB files, "National Labor Board Principles With Applicable Cases: August 5, 1933 to July 9, 1934," August 21, 1934.

56. *Decisions of the NLB, op. cit.,* "*United Airlines, Inc. and David L. Behncke et al.,*" vol. I, p. 81.

57. *Ibid.,* " *S. Dresner & Son and United Leather Workers International Union,*" vol. I, p. 26.

58. *Ibid.,* "*The Harriman Hosiery Mills and United Textile Workers of America,*" vol. I, p. 68.

off,"[59] that strikers be given reinstatement priority over employees hired after the strike began,[60] that all strikers be reinstated at the end of a strike when the board believed the strike was justified or when the strike was caused by an employer's violation of the law,[61] and that, in many cases involving representation elections and reinstatement, strikers were to be treated as employees.[62]

Executive Order Number 6580 and NLB Acceptance of Its Judicial Function

Noncompliance was spreading, however, and the NLB was seriously threatened:

> Despite the executive order of December 16, the Labor Board came close to collapse during the month of January 1934. The machinery of the Board began to creak; members failed to attend hearings; the handling of cases became chaotic, protracted, and indecisive. Rumor spread that Senator Wagner would resign. In the meantime, the Weirton and Budd companies continued their "defiance"; and the

59. *Ibid.*, "*S. Dresner & Son and United Leather Workers International Union,*" vol. I, p. 26, and "*Edward G. Budd Manufacturing Company and United Automobile Workers Federal Labor Union No. 18763,*" vol. I, p. 58.

60. *Ibid.*, "*S. Dresner & Son and United Leather Workers International Union,*" vol. I, p. 26.

61. *Ibid.*, "*S. Dresner & Son and United Leather Workers International Union,*" vol. I, p. 26; "*Edward G. Budd Manufacturing Company and United Automobile Workers Federal Labor Union No. 18763,* vol. I, p. 58; and "*The Motor Truck Association of Western Massachusetts and International Brotherhood of Teamsters, Chauffeurs, Stablemen and Helpers, Local Union No. 404,*" vol. I, p. 62.

62. Although the board "made no explicit ruling stating that strikers are employees," see *ibid.*, "*Edward G. Budd Manufacturing Company . . .,*" vol. I, p. 58; "*The Motor Truck Association of Western Massachusetts . . .,*" vol. I, p. 62; and "*The Philadelphia Rapid Transit Company,*" vol. I, p. 66.

example once given was infectious. Not only the National Board, but even more so the regional boards, ran head-on into an attitude of stubborn resistance on the part of many employers. . . . Moreover, the strike situation was becoming ominous once more. . . .[63]

A beleaguered NLB again sought the support of President Roosevelt as it had in December 1933. The president responded on February 1, 1934 with Executive Order Number 6580,[64] which was intended to strengthen the board's authority to conduct elections in *Weirton* and *Budd* situations by empowering the NLB to "make the arrangements for and supervise the conduct of an election, under the exclusive control of the Board and under such rules and regulations as the Board shall prescribe."[65] Executive Order Number 6580 as amended on February 23, 1934[66] also took "a definite step in the direction of establishing the Board as an independent agency"[67] by depriving the NRA's Compliance Division of its power to review the findings of the NLB—a power which had been used to frustrate and to delay the removal of Blue Eagles. In the *Budd* case, for example, the Compliance Division had conducted its own hearing *de novo* including "an investiga-

63. *Lorwin and Wubnig, op. cit.*, p. 107.
64. The full text of Executive Order Number 6580 is reproduced in *Decisions of the NLB, op. cit.*, p. vii.
65. *Ibid.*, p. vii.
66. The full text of Executive Order Number 6612-A is reproduced in *ibid.*, p. viii.
67. E. G. Latham, "Legislative Purpose and Administrative Policy Under the National Labor Relations Act," *The George Washington Law Review*, Vol. 4, no. 4 (May 1936), p. 437. See also Louis Stark, Stark, "Labor Board Made Independent; New Powers Added," *The New York Times*, March 4, 1934, p. 1, col. 3. Stark wrote, "In so modifying his Executive Order of February 1, President Roosevelt ended a long conflict between the National Labor Board and the NRA. . . . It is understood that the matter was discussed at a recent cabinet meeting after Secretary Perkins had conferred at length with General Johnson. The Secretary maintained that the Labor Board's findings should not be subject to review by the Compliance Board, and that the function of the latter in cases when invoked by the Labor Board, was to enforce the recommendations of the Labor Board. The General, it is said, held that the Compliance Board

tion at the plant of the Company in Philadelphia . . ."[68] after which it devised its own plan to resolve the controversy[69] eventually resulting in a settlement with the Budd Company which the board found "at complete variance with the basis of settlement which the Compliance Division assured us would be adopted."[70]

Making the board's findings nonreviewable by the Compliance Division, however, moved the NLB, as did the establishment of regional boards, further from the flexible, industrial relations problem-solving approach to industrial disputes and closer to the more legalistic, judicial method. The NLB instructed its regional boards that "evidence on facts bearing on the controversy should be taken in order to make possible a later transcription of the testimony"[71] and set forth the "matters . . . [which] . . . should be set out in detail in the transcript . . . " emphasizing the need for "a certain uniformity in the collection of evidence. . . ."[72] This was one of the earliest signals of the changing nature of the board that earlier had berated "legal emissaries,"[73] but whose general counsel, Milton Handler, would later tell a Senate committee:

> Now, the bipartisan aspect of the Board . . . is chiefly valuable in the peaceful settlement of disputes, in the exercise of the mediation functions of the Board. When it comes to the purely judicial work of the Board, where you are inquiring into questions of law violation, obviously the value of the layman is somewhat diminished. They contribute greatly to an understanding of the problem, but you must have a corps of disinterested public representatives who are competent

might hold hearings of its own and, as in the Budd and Ford cases, make its own findings of fact, whether they coincided with those of the Labor Board or not."

68. NA, RG25, informal files, memorandum from the National Compliance Board to the administrator for Industrial Recovery, February 17, 1934, p. 1, *E. G. Budd Company* case.

69. *Ibid.*, pp. 4–5.

70. NA, RG25, informal files, memorandum from M. Handler to Jesse I. Miller, April 6, 1934, *E. G. Budd Company* case.

71. NA, RG25, memorandum from Jesse I. Miller to the regional boards, April 16, 1934, p. 2. Regional board records, Region IV, Philadelphia.

72. *Ibid.*, pp. 2–3.

73. *Decisions of the NLB, op. cit., "S. Dresner & Son and United Leather Workers International Union,"* vol. I, p. 26.

by training and experience to handle questions of law and judicial problems that arise in such cases.[74]

The president had, in addition, armed the NLB with its First statement on a question of policy by specifying in Executive Order Number 6580 that the doctrine of majority rule was controlling in representation elections.[75]

The president's endorsement of the board's already functioning election procedure (the NLB had conducted about 40 representation elections prior to the February 1 executive order),[76] his promulgation of the majority rule principle, and his loosening of the NLB's ties to the NRA[77] understandably led the board to believe that "the Administration would support firm, vigorous and unrelenting enforcement of its doctrines of collective bargaining."[78] The NLB, therefore, was ready to make more decisive interpretations of Section 7(a) even at the risk of exposing dissent within the board to public view and to confront the challenge of General Hugh Johnson and Donald Richberg of the NRA who placated aroused employers two days after the publication of Executive Order Number 6580 by telling them that the president's order did "not restrict . . . the right of minority groups or of individual employees to deal with their employer separately."[79] The board, in addition, "fortified by the executive order of February 23 . . . decided to stake its prestige on a firm prosecution of the Weirton case . . . [and] . . . turned the case over to the Department of Justice with a recommendation for immediate action."[80] Senator Wagner also chose the end of February 1934 as the most favorable time to submit his labor disputes bill to the Senate.

74. *Senate Hearings on the Labor Disputes Act, op. cit.*, p. 31.
75. Latham, *op. cit.*, p. 436 and *The New York Times*, February 2, 1934, p. 8, col. 4.
76. NA, RG25, "Statement of Jurisdiction and Powers . . .," *op. cit.*, p. 1.
77. Under the terms of Executive Order Number 6612-A, which amended the February 1, 1934 order, although the board's findings were not reviewable, the Compliance Division retained the power "to take appropriate action."
78. Lorwin and Wubnig, *op. cit.*, p. 230.
79. NRA Release Number 3125, February 4, 1934, summarized in Lorwin and Wubnig, *op. cit.*, p. 270.
80. *Ibid.*, p. 111.

The board's decisions did become more decisive after the February executive order. On March 1, 1934 the board in the *Denver Tramway* case established the cornerstone principles of majority rule and exclusive representation by deciding that the bargaining agent elected by a majority of the employees voting in a representation election was empowered to represent all of the employees eligible to vote in that election.[81] The board took this position (and reaffirmed it on March 8, 1934 in the *Houde Engineering Company* decision)[82] over the vigorous and (for the first time) public dissent of board member duPont who maintained in the unpublished portion of his written dissent that General Johnson's interpretations of Section 7(a) and Executive Order Number 6580 were correct and that "any attempt to read into [Section 7(a)] an intent to impose election of representatives by majority vote would lead to disastrous results."[83] The board in the *Hall Baking Company* case once again, as in the captive mine cases confronted an employer that refused to make a collective bargaining agreement "with the union as such, or with the officials as representatives of the employees, if the union titles are appended to their

81. *Decisions of the NLB, op. cit., "The Denver Tramway Corporation and the Amalgamated Association of Street and Electric Railway Employees of America, Division 1001,"* vol. I, p. 64.
82. *Ibid.,* "*Houde Engineering Company and United Automobile Workers Federal Labor Union No. 18839,*" vol. I, p. 87. The *Houde* case is discussed at length in the next chapter.
83. Mr. duPont's dissenting opinion appears in *Decisions of the NLB, op. cit., "The Denver Tramway Corporation . . .,"* vol. I, p. 65. The informal file in the *Denver Tramway* case contains a 6-page typewritten analysis by duPont of Section 7(a) and Executive Order Number 6580, a portion of which was printed in vol. I, p. 65. In the unpublished portions of his dissent, duPont noted that the word "majority was not used in Section 7(a)," that majority rule was not mentioned on the official ballot prepared by the NLB and that the voter was invited to "indicate the one you favor as your agency for collective bargaining." He also noted that neither organization received a majority of the votes (basing his figures on the total number of employees eligible to vote rather than on the total number voting) and stated: "Under a law confirming to employees the 'right to organize and bargain collectively through representatives of their own choosing' how can we deny that right to over half of the employees of the Denver Tramway Corporation."

names."[84] The company, in addition, reminded the NLB of an *H. C. Frick Company* type compromise on union recognition which the board had made earlier in the *Philadelphia Bakery Companies* case and contended that entering into a written agreement with the union "would be illegal and in contravention of [that] decision. . . ."[85] The board on March 8, 1934, again with member duPont dissenting, refused to compromise on the issue of union recognition and decided that "as the statute [conferred] complete freedom upon the employees in their choice of representatives," there was "no valid reason" why an employer should decline to enter into a contract with the union chosen by the employees to be their representative.[86]

The NLB, in other important decisions subsequent to Executive Order Number 6580, ruled that an election was simply an "administrative device" used by the board to determine the "identity and authority of the employees' representatives,"[87] that the principle of majority rule and the election by secret ballot made it unnecessary for a union to disclose to an employer either the names "of those voting for the representatives so elected" or the union's membership lists,[88] and that strikers remained employees while on strike and were entitled to displace their replacements whenever the board found that the strike had been caused by the employer's violation of Section 7(a).[89]

84. *Decisions of the NLB, op. cit., "Hall Baking Company and Bakery Drivers Union Local No. 264,"* vol. I, p. 83.

85. NA, RG25, informal files, letter from Daniel B. Shortal to the National Labor Board, December 7, 1933, *Hall Baking Company* case.

86. *Decisions of the NLB, op. cit., "Hall Baking Company and Bakery Drivers Union Local No. 264,"* vol. I, pp. 83–84.

87. *Ibid., "The B/J Aircraft Corporation and the General Aviation Manufacturing Corporation and Aeronautical Workers Federal Labor Union No. 18541,"* vol. I, pp. 55–57.

88. *Ibid., "Houde Engineering Company and United Automobile Workers Federal Labor Union No. 18839,"* vol. I, p. 87. See also NA, RG25, informal files, letter from B. Wolf to the Buffalo Regional Board, January 3,1934, and memorandum from P. Herzog to the board members, July 23, 1934, *Houde Engineering* case.

89. *Decisions of the NLB, op. cit., "A. Roth and Company and International Ladies Garment Workers' Union,"* vol. I, p. 75, and *"Joseph*

The NLB assumed that it spoke from a position of strength when it issued these decisions and when, in the *National Lock Company* case,[90] it made its most definitive statement concerning the obligations of collective bargaining and the rights of employee organization under Section 7(a):

> The collective bargaining envisaged by the statute involves a duality of obligation—an obligation on the part of employees to present grievances and demands to the employer before striking, and an obligation on the part of the employer to discuss differences with the representatives of the employees and to exert every reasonable effort to reach an agreement on all matters in dispute. . . . Section 7(a) cannot be altered by omission or qualification by those unsympathetic with its major objectives. . . . Its mandates are unequivocal. Representation is not restricted under the statute to fellow employees. There is no limitation on the form of organization which may be established by the workers. . . . Organization and representation are matters which concern employees exclusively. The employer has no right to initiate a plan of organization, or to participate in any way, in the absence of any request from the employees, in their designation of representatives and their self-organization. In fact such actions are expressly forbidden by the statute.[91]

The President Abandons the NLB

Some members of the NLB, however, felt that the board's decision making was a futile exercise with little practical effect. Prior to the release of the board's decision in the *Hall Baking Company*

F. Corcoran Shoe Company and Brotherhood of Shoe and Allied Craftsmen," vol. I, p. 78.

90. *Ibid.*, "*National Lock Company and Federal Labor Union No. 18830*," vol. I, p. 15.
91. *Ibid.*, p. 19.

case, board member Leo Wolman told General Counsel Milton Handler:

> I have read the Hall Baking Company decision, and I doubt that it will do any good. The crowd in this case are the same group with whom we had such prolonged dealings in both the Philadelphia and Pittsburg baking cases. They have taken a definite and deliberate position on the matter of whom they will make contracts with, and have expressed their views to the Board in no uncertain way on many occasions. The decision, as it stands, therefore, will only be summarily rejected by them, and I doubt the wisdom of issuing it.[92]

Although Wolman's reaction was to some extent influenced by his dedication to the settlement of labor disputes by compromise and voluntary agreement rather than by decision, it was true that employers, including the Denver Tramway Corporation, A. Roth and Company, the Hall Baking Company, Houde Engineering Company, and the National Lock Company, had blocked the board's efforts to put its doctrines into effect—and "it was not merely a question of individual employers, acting singly, but of an organized campaign of non-compliance in which entire industries acted in concert, supported by their trade associations and by the leading employer organizations."[93]

The NLB had reached an impasse with employers and the NRA by the middle of March 1934. If the NLB was to continue, that deadlock had to be broken by a firm commitment by the New Deal administration to the labor policy emerging from the decisions of the board. The administration was unwilling to make that commitment.

> Basic to the inability of both the NLB and the NLRB to enforce their rulings on Section 7(a) was the reluctance of the Administration to face the fundamental issue raised by the statute, namely the part to be played by trade unions in American industry. To encourage vigorous enforcement of Section 7(a) as interpreted by the two Labor Boards would have precipitated an industrial battle to the finish between

92. NA, RG25, informal files, memorandum from L. Wolman to M. Handler, March 3, 1934, *Hall Baking Company* case.
93. Lyon *et al.*, *op. cit.*, p. 483.

trade unions and anti-union employers. These consequences the Administration was not ready to face, partly because of the possible effects on re-employment and recovery, partly because of the long-range implications of collective bargaining through trade unions upon the economic structure.[94]

The Automobile Settlement

The NLB's moment of truth arrived in March 1934 when the automobile manufacturers, fearing the consequences of the NLB's majority rule for the industry's company union plans, refused to recognize the United Automobile Workers (a grouping of AFL federal unions) or to permit the board to conduct a representation election.[95] President Roosevelt intervened and, along with General Hugh Johnson, who acted as chief negotiator for the government, devised a settlement which averted a general strike but which "reduced much of the Labor Board's statements of principles to scraps of paper."[96] The settlement denied the board the authority to hold a representation election in the industry, rejected the principle of majority rule, and accepted Messrs. Johnson and Richberg's "doctrine of pluralism in collective bargaining"[97] through proportional representation.[98] Since it seemed to commit the president to a NRA labor policy that was irreconcilable with the doctrines set forth by the NLB, the automobile settlement "was a staggering blow to the prestige and authority of the Board."[99]

94. *Ibid.*, pp. 486–487.
95. Lorwin and Wubnig, *op. cit.*, pp. 112–113. See also Fine, *op. cit.*
96. Herman Feldman, "Increase In Nation's Strikes Spurs Debate on Labor Issues," *The New York Times*, March 27, 1934, sec. 9, p. 3, col. 6.
97. Lorwin and Wubnig, *op. cit.*, p. 356.
98. *The New York Times*, March 26, 1934, p. 1, col. 6. The White House statement included the vague arrangement whereby "no such disclosure in a particular case shall be made without specific direction of the President."
99. Lorwin and Wubnig, *op. cit.*, p. 113. The settlement also created an Automobile Labor Board with jurisdiction over "questions of

Although the NLB had never been immune from union as well as employer disenchantment with its decisions,[100] the government's action severely weakened labor's already wavering confidence in the board. There was a major outbreak of violent strikes across the nation in the spring of 1934 in part because unions, convinced that it was unlikely that they would achieve their objectives by submitting their disputes to the NLB, came to prefer "direct action" and expressed a strong "resentment at the Board's interference."[101] Labor erupted in 1934 with "1856 work stoppages involving 1,470,000 workers by far the highest count in both categories in many years" including the "social upheavals . . . of auto parts workers . . . in Toledo, of truck drivers in Minneapolis, of longshoreman and then virtually the whole labor movement on the shores of San Francisco Bay, and of cotton-textile workers in New England and the South."[102] Without government support many attempts at unionization failed.

---

representation, discharge and discrimination" arising under the automotive parts and equipment code. *Ibid.*, p. 358.

100. In the *Brocton Shoe Manufacturers' Association* case, for example (*Decisions of the NLB, op. cit.*, vol. I, p. 21), the NLB ordered an election to allow the employees to chose between a "rump" union, the Brotherhood of Shoe and Allied Craftsmen, and the AFL's Boot and Shoe Workers' Union, which had a contract in effect with the company at the time of the board's decision. The AFL union telegrammed Senator Wagner that the board "apparently lacked the courage to make decisions based on [the] legal validity of contracts," that William Leiserson "apparently unable to openly destroy the American Federation of Labor organizations seeks to breed outlaw unions," and that the board's decision was "influenced either by cowardice . . . or a willful effort to nullify all contracts held by the American Federation of Labor." NA, RG25, informal files, telegrams from Frank W. Gifford and James O'Connel to Senator Wagner, November 3, 1933, *Brocton Shoe Manufacturers'* case.

101. *Decisions of the NLB, op. cit.*, "*The Haverhill Shoe Manufacturers and United Shoe and Leather Workers' Union*," vol. II, p. 1. Certainly, the increase in economic activity in the spring of 1934 stimulated an increase in strike activity. Yet, 75 percent of the strikes during this period were over the issue of union recognition which was within the jurisdiction of the NLB.

102. Bernstein, *Turbulent Years, op. cit.*, p. 217.

The result might have been decidedly different if there had been any feeling that the government would promptly and vigorously act to suppress any attempt at intimidation on the part of the employers. More than any other single happening the Denver Tramway case tended to discourage the leaders of organized labor in this community as it was found that, even after an election had been held and won by a regular labor organization, the Government failed to back them up in their demand for the right of collective bargaining.[103]

By the middle of June 1934, enforcement of board decisions was so unlikely that the Justice Department advised Senator Wagner to stop giving "advance publicity" to cases sent by the board to the Compliance Division for removal of the Blue Eagle since "it would better serve the purposes of the National Recovery Administration . . . to make no mention of the reference of cases to this Department than to advise the public and the offender of such reference and then find that no action is justified."[104]

Although it issued several decisions of doctrinal importance concerning collective bargaining,[105] plant shutdowns and the

---

103. NA, RG25, informal files, letter from T. S. Hogan to the National Labor Board, June 7, 1934, *Denver Tramway* case.

104. NA, RG25, informal files, letter from Harold Stephens to Senator Wagner, June 14, 1934, pp. 1–2, *A. Roth and Company* case.

105. See, for example, *Decisions of the NLB, op. cit., "National Aniline & Chemical Company and Analine Chemical Workers' Local No. 18705,"* vol. II, p. 38. In this case the board ruled that "The objective sought by the law is the making of collective agreements. To be sure, the substance of these agreements is wholly a matter of negotiation. . . . But an attitude of unwillingness to enter into any obligation with respect to future relations thwarts the statute. . . . If this is not a denial by the company of its employees' right to bargain collectively, the promise of Section 7(a) is tinsel. Congress did not write vain words, and we must not empty 'the right to bargain collectively' of serious meaning" (see pp. 39–40). In *ibid., "Connecticut Coke Company and United Coke and Gas Workers' Union No. 18829,"* vol. II, p. 88, the board held that "true collective bargaining involves more than the holding of conferences and the exchange of pleasantries. It is not limited to the settlement of specific grievances. Wages, hours, and conditions of employment

---

transfer of work to avoid unionism,[106] and the reinstatement status of strikers proven guilty of violence,[107] the NLB was simply lingering on after the automobile settlement handling "mostly petty cases involving alleged discriminatory discharges of union workers."[108]

The Defeat of the Labor Disputes Bill and the End of the NLB

Prior to the automobile settlement, Senator Wagner had sought legislative support for the NLB by introducing his labor disputes

---

may properly be the subject of negotiation and collective bargaining. While the law does not compel the parties to reach agreement, it does contemplate that both parties will approach the negotiations with an open mind and will make a reasonable effort to reach a common ground of agreement. The definite announcement by the company that it will not make an oral or a written agreement deprives collective bargaining of any content or objective" (see p. 89).

106. *Ibid.*, "*Maujer Parlor Frame Company et al. and Furniture Workers Industrial Union*," vol. II, p. 78. In this case the board decided that "the obligations of the statute cannot be evaded by a change in the physical location of the plant" and "that a condition in harmony with the law can best be brought about through the reinstatement [of the displaced employees]" (see p. 80). See also *ibid.*, "*Bear Brand Hosiery Company (Beaver Dam Plant) and Branch No. 66, American Federation of Hosiery Workers*," vol. II, p. 67; *ibid.*, "*George Royle and Company and Upholstery Weavers and Workers Local Union 25 and Jacquard Loom Fixers Local No. 1270*," vol. II, p. 90.

107. The NLB consistently ruled that the employer was under no obligation to reinstate strikers found guilty of violence during a strike. *Decisions of the NLB, op. cit.*, "*Bee Line Bus Company and Amalgamated Association of Street and Electric Railway Employees*," vol. II, p. 24; *ibid.*, "*Eagle Rubber Company and United Rubber Workers Federal Labor Union No. 18683*," vol. II, p. 31; *ibid.*, "*SKF Industries, Inc. and Anti-Friction Bearing Workers Union, Local No. 1*," vol. II, p. 46; and *ibid.*, "*Bornot Cleaning and Dyeing, Inc. and Cleaners, Dyers, Spotters, and Pressers Local No. 18233 and Teamsters, Chauffeurs, Stablemen & Helpers Local No. 501*," vol. II, p. 15.

108. Lorwin and Wubnig, *op. cit.*, p. 113.

bill into the Senate on March 1, 1934: "A Bill To Equalize The Bargaining Power Of Employers And Employees, To Encourage The Amicable Settlement Of Disputes Between Employers And Employees, To Create A National Labor Board, And For Other Purposes."[109] Wagner's bill, which applied to "the small as well as the larger employer; the financial, commercial, agricultural, and household employer as well as the industrial employer,"[110] rejected the individualistic tradition of labor relations as outmoded and as a prime cause of industrial strife. Its provisions, instead, encouraged collective action and linked the right to organize for collective bargaining to six employer unfair labor practices and to a national labor board empowered to conduct representation elections and to prevent these employer unfair labor practices by issuing cease and desist orders. These board-enforced unfair labor practices, called the "guts of the act" by Henry I. Harriman, the president of the United States Chamber of Commerce,[111] would have profoundly affected the employer-employee relationship by requiring employers to recognize and to "deal with" the representatives of their employees and "to exert every reasonable effort to make and maintain agreements with such representatives concerning wages, hours and other conditions of employment" and by prohibiting employers from dominating or supporting any labor organization and from interfering by any means with the right of their employees to organize for collective bargaining.[112]

In 1933 Senator Wagner had placed his confidence in partisan representation on this expert board which sought to mediate industrial disputes. Despite the sharp increase in mediation failures which had forced the NLB more and more to resort to "decisions," Wagner retained partisan membership on the board in the labor disputes bill and took the position that, although many judicial functions had been written into the bill, mediation would remain the board's "chief function."[113] The one point on which both the

109. S. 2926, 73d Cong. 2d Sess. introduced into the Senate on February 28 (calendar day, March 1), 1934.
110. Lorwin and Wubnig, *op. cit.*, p. 235.
111. *Senate Hearings on the Labor Disputes Act., op. cit.*, p. 499.
112. The provisions of the Labor Disputes Act are reproduced in *ibid.*, pp. 1–7.
113. *Ibid.*, p. 10.

opponents and supporters of the labor disputes bill agreed, however, was that the experiences of the NLB had proved that its partisan representation and mediation approach had failed to bring about union recognition and collective bargaining and that what was needed was an independent, neutral, quasijudicial agency free from the necessity of compromise.[114] Secretary of Labor Frances Perkins testified at the Senate Labor Committee hearing on the bill: "we have come to the time when the establishment of a judicial tribunal to determine certain things in the relationship between employers and employees is definitely indicated,"[115] and added that she felt it "desirable to separate the duty of conciliation from the duty of a judicial board."[116] Milton Handler, the general counsel of the National Labor Board, told the Senate Committee that "if a board exercising judicial functions is to command the highest respect, it ought to be put on an entirely independent basis"[117] and the general counsel of the United States Steel Company concluded:

> Now this [the Labor Disputes Act] proposes to set up this board with its extraordinary powers—judicial, executive, powers of mediation and conciliation. I say, gentlemen, that no board, for such purposes, constituted as this board is proposed to be, will ever properly function. You might have representatives of particular interests on a board merely for mediation or conciliation, but when you clothe the board with any such powers as these the individuals composing it

114. NLRB files, "An Analysis of S.2926, The (Wagner) Labor Disputes Act," memorandum from G. S. Wheeler, December 8, 1934, p. 7. See also *Senate Hearings on the Labor Disputes Act, op. cit.*: Frances Perkins, pp. 21 and 27; Milton Handler, p. 33; Otto Beyer, pp. 228–229; William Leiserson, p. 236; Franklin Edmonds, p. 405; Guy Harrington, p. 463; Henry Harriman, p. 500; Roy F. Hall, p. 560; Charles S. Craigmile, p. 570; Walter Carroll, pp. 612–613; and Nathan Miller, p. 889.

115. *Senate Hearings on the Labor Disputes Act, op. cit.*, p. 18.

116. *Ibid.*, p. 21. Frances Perkins, however, was opposed to an independent board and wanted any labor board "located in the Department of Labor." *Ibid.*, p. 24.

117. *Ibid.*, p. 33.

should be selected to represent one interest and one alone, and that is the public interest.[118]

Senator Wagner publicly acknowledged the substance and sources of these criticisms when, in reply to the comment of the general counsel of the Philadelphia Chamber of Commerce that "it would be much better to have a permanent commission composed of a group who represent the public . . . in order that they may gradually build up a tradition of rights . . .,"[119] he said, "I might remind the chairman that the proponents of the bill, who appear in favor of the legislation, generally also favor that proposition."[120]

Senator Wagner's Labor Disputes Act "reflected in [its] details the agony of the Labor Board."[121] "Every one of its provisions [was] addressed to specific evils that [had] become abundantly manifest during the 10 months experience of the National Labor Board."[122] Consequently, President Roosevelt's automobile settlement dealt a "terrific jolt" to the NLB and to the labor disputes bill which was being considered by the Senate Labor Committee at the time.[123] The President had ignored the limitations which the labor disputes bill had sought to place on the participation of company unions in collective bargaining and had stated publicly that he hoped the automobile formula would develop into a new system of industrial relations for all of industry and labor.[124] *Business Week* expressed the opinion that given "the trend and tone of the President's statement . . . the National Labor Board must revise

118. *Ibid.*, p. 889.
119. *Ibid.*, p. 405.
120. *Ibid.*
121. Oral history interview with Philip Levy, *op. cit.*
122. 78 *Cong. Rec.* 12018 (1934). William Leiserson, Milton Handler, William Rice, and Benedict Wolf of the NLB staff participated in the preparation of the Labor Disputes Act (see Bernstein, *The New Deal Collective Bargaining Policy, op. cit.*, p. 63.
123. Thomas Emerson papers, "Analysis of the Labor Disputes Act— S. 2926," n.d. (processed), p. 1 (in T. Emerson's possession). The Senate Labor Committee held hearings on the Labor Disputes Act from March 14 to April 9, 1934.
124. *The New York Times*, March 26, 1934, p. 1, col. 6., and "Labor Charter," *Business Week*, March 31, 1934, p. 5.

its postulates and perhaps curtail its ambitions. . . ."[125] The National Association of Manufacturers, in addition, argued vigorously against the act, fully aware that from the very beginning "in the highest quarters, there [was] unwillingness to support legislation of this character."[126]

On March 26, 1934, the day after the president's settlement was announced, Senator Wagner felt constrained to soften his bill by eliminating three very important provisions: (a) the ban on employer initiation (as distinguished from domination) of company unions,[127] (b) the retroactive ban on "any term of a contract or agreement of any kind which conflicts with the provisions of [the] act"[128] and (c) the provision which specified that board findings of fact, if supported by evidence, were conclusive on the reviewing court.[129] The president's settlement also persuaded Senator Wagner to add a provision which banned intimidation or coercion *from any source*, including labor unions.[130]

Even with these major concessions, however, the Labor Disputes Act remained far too inconsistent with the principles of the automobile settlement to have any chance of passage and only "an ominous strike situation at a time when the government had no adequate disputes machinery"[131] kept the issue of labor legislation before Congress. Control of the legislation passed from Senator Wagner and the NLB to Senate Labor Committee chair-

125. "Labor Charter," *op. cit.*, pp. 5–6.
126. Letter from James Emery, general counsel, National Association of Manufacturers, quoted in Bernstein, *The New Deal Collective Bargaining Policy, op. cit.*, p. 62, fn. 39.
127. "Freedom of the employer to initiate the company union plan and the freedom of the employee from domination by the plan go ill together and may well lead to emasculation of the guarantees of the Labor Disputes Act." Thomas Emerson papers, "Analysis of the Labor Disputes Act . . .," *op. cit.*, pp. 2 and 6–7. For a discussion of the company union provision, see *Senate Hearings on the Labor Disputes Act, op. cit.*, pp. 346–348.
128. *Senate Hearings on the Labor Disputes Act, op. cit.*, pp. 360–361.
129. *Ibid.*, p. 368.
130. *Ibid.*, pp. 347–348.
131. Bernstein, *the New Deal Collective Bargaining Policy, op. cit.*, p. 76. See also *The New York Times*, May 26, 1934, p. 1, col. 7; May 27, 1934, sec. 9, p. 3, col. 6; and June 3, 1934, sec. 8, p. 2, col. 1.

man, David I. Walsh, and the Department of Labor. Their drastic revisions[132] transformed the Labor Disputes Act into the National Industrial Adjustment Act, [133] which was reported out of the Labor Committee on May 26, 1934. The Walsh bill was still too strong for industry to accept and the added objections of organized labor and the press pointed to a "prolonged and acrimonious debate" which the president and Congress wanted to avoid.[134] An imminent general strike in the steel industry, however (aggravated by a lower court's refusal on May 29, 1934 to grant a preliminary injunction which would have compelled the Weirton Steel Company to allow an NLB representation election),[135] kept the pressure on the administration. What the president needed was a "noncontroversial bill that would move through both houses quickly, preferably with Republican support."[136] After instructing Charles Wyzanski of the Labor Department and Donald Richberg of the NRA to draft such a bill, President Roosevelt "called a White House Conference of the majority leaders, Senator Joe Robinson and Representative Joseph W. Byrns, Walsh, Wagner, Miss Perkins, Wyzanski and Richberg" at which time the president dictated Public Resolution Number 44 "essentially in the form" in which it was sent to Congress on

132. Bernstein, *The New Deal Collective Bargaining Policy, op. cit.*, p. 72. "Their alterations included eliminating the economic analysis in the declaration of policy, restricting coverage, paring the scope of the unfair labor practices, removing the duty to bargain, placing the board in the [Labor] department, protecting the Conciliation Service, and restricting jurisdiction to disputes that burdened commerce." Section 10 of the Walsh bill authorized the board to use either majority rule or proportional representation in elections. *Ibid.*, p. 74.

133. For a copy of the Labor Disputes Act (S. 2926) as amended by the National Industrial Adjustment Act and the accompanying *Senate Report*, see National Labor Relations Board, *Legislative History of the National Labor Relations Act* (Washington: GPO, 1949), vol. I, pp. 1070–1112.

134. Bernstein, *The New Deal Collective Bargaining Policy, op. cit.*, p. 76.

135. Lorwin and Wubnig, *op. cit.*, pp. 114 and 333.

136. Bernstein, *The New Deal Collective Bargaining Policy, op. cit.*, p. 77.

June 13, 1934,[137] three days before the strike deadline in the steel industry. The House and the Senate passed the measure on June 16, 1934, one day after it was formally received.[138]

Public Resolution Number 44 authorized the president to establish "a board or boards" to investigate labor disputes arising under Section 7(a) which obstructed or threatened to obstruct commerce. Such boards had the power to conduct secret ballot representation elections and to subpoena the documents and witnesses needed to carry out their election powers. This was all that was left of the Labor Disputes Act as the resolution provided no authority except to investigate, left the critical powers of enforcement under the control of the NRA and the Department of Justice, and made no mention of unfair labor practices ("the guts" of the Labor Disputes Act),[139] not even to forbid an employer to discharge a man for joining a union: "Public Resolution Number 44 was at bottom a compromise which avoided the basic issues raised by the NLB's efforts to interpret and apply Section 7(a)."[140]

During the Senate debates, when Senator Robert LaFollette had persisted in advocating the Labor Disputes Act, a disappointed and resigned Senator Wagner asked him to withdraw his support:

> . . . this is really one of the most embarrassing moments of my whole political life. Every Senator knows and I think the public knows that I have devoted myself to the task of preventing strikes and composing differences after strikes occur since early in August, when the President of the United States asked me to leave behind a very pleasant vacation and assume the duties of the chairmanship of the National Labor Board. From then until now I have devoted all my time not spent in the Senate to the work of that Board. From last August until

137. *Ibid.*, pp. 77–78.
138. 78 *Cong. Rec.* 12120–12122, 12045 (1934). In the Senate, Resolution Number 44 became S. J. Resolution Number 143 and in the House, H. J. Resolution Number 375. See *The Legislative History of the National Labor Relations Act, op. cit.*, vol. I, pp. 1160–1161 and 1224–1225.
139. See Henry I. Harriman's characterization of the unfair labor practices section of the Labor Disputes Act in this chapter, p. 65.
140. Lorwin and Wubnig, *op. cit.*, p. 261.

the session began I rarely left Washington except to go where a strike was in progress or was threatened. I might add, although I do not need to, I know that for this I received no compensation of any kind. Many a night, on one occasion for three nights in succession, I remained up until 4 o'clock in the morning with a group of workers and industrialists for the purpose of preventing a strike which I knew would have been a serious impediment to our recovery program. I make these preliminary remarks so that nobody will doubt my devotion to this cause, a devotion which has resulted in some sacrifice of my health. . . .

But . . . the President feels that at this time that this temporary measure ought to be passed to relieve an emergency situation. . . . Therefore, I will ask the Senator to withdraw his amendment at this time. *We will fight for it next year, when the country will have become sufficiently educated as to the need for it.*[141]

The vice president of industrial relations for the United States Steel Corporation expressed a contrary view in a private communication:

I view the passage of the joint resolution with equanimity. It means that temporary measures which cannot last more than a year will be substituted for the permanent legislation proposed the original Wagner bill. I do not believe there will ever be given as good a chance for the passage of the Wagner Act as exists now, and the trade is a mighty good compromise. I have read carefully the joint resolution, and my personal opinion is that it is not going to bother us very much.[142]

It was not yet politically advantageous for the New Deal administration to commit itself to a policy of collective bargaining. The NLB had been pioneering in labor relations for ten months of intense testing and experimentation, setting forth the first principles of a labor policy, developing the legal method in

141. 78 *Cong. Rec.* 12041, 12044 (1934) (emphasis added).
142. Bernstein, *The New Deal Collective Bargaining Policy, op. cit.*, p. 81. A more complete version of the letter is found in the *Legislative History of the National Labor Relations Act, op. cit.*, vol. II, p. 2912.

industrial relations, and devising effective administrative procedures. The drive for a national labor policy of collective bargaining was just beginning, not ending when the NLB was abolished by Executive Order Number 6763[143] issued on June 29, 1934, with its personnel, pending cases, unexpected funds and records, papers, and property transferred to a newly created National Labor Relations Board.

143. Executive Order Number 6763, which abolished the NLB effective July 9, 1934, is reproduced in *Decisions of the National Labor Relations Board* (Washington: GPO, 1935), vol. I, pp. vii–ix: and vol. II, pp. vii–x (hereinafter referred to as *Decisions of the NLRB-I*).

3 The Old National Labor Relations Board: Challenges to a Judicial Approach

The National Labor Relations Board had inherited the NLB's problems as well as its staff, unexpended funds, and property. The NLRB was as weak after the president's executive order on June 29, 1934 as the NLB had been before it. Although Executive Order Number 6763 authorized the NLRB to make investigations, hold hearings, and make findings of fact, it conferred no decision-making authority on the board. It gave the board the powers needed to order and conduct representation elections, yet omitted the majority rule principle contained in Executive Order Number 6580[1] (February 1, 1934) and permitted an employer to have the board's election order reviewed in the circuit courts of appeals.

It made the board more independent than its predecessor by instructing other persons and agencies in the executive branch of the government that the NLRB's jurisdiction in 7(a) and Public Resolution Number 44 cases was exclusive once asserted and that the Board's findings of fact were nonreviewable. At the same time, however, it created the NLRB "in connection with"[2] the Department of Labor and made provision for the establishment "of special labor boards for particular industries vested with powers that the President is authorized to confer by Public Resolution 44." The president had, in fact, deprived the NLRB of jurisdiction in the automobile and steel industries by allowing the Automobile

1. See Chapter II, pp. 53–56.
2. The NLRB's relationship with the Department of Labor was a critical issue during the life of the pre-Wagner Act NLRB and throughout the preparation of and debates over the Wagner Act. The NLRB's efforts to become independent of the Department of Labor are discussed later in this chapter.

Labor Board to continue to function and by creating the National
Steel Labor Relations Board the day before he issued Executive
Order Number 6763.[3]

The most critical defect in the president's executive order was
that it left the board unable to enforce its own decisions. This
same fatal powerlessness which had afflicted the NLB was the
fundamental reason for the eventual failure of this new board to
enforce Section 7(a).

The president, however, ignoring the contradictions and ambi-
guities of Public Resolution Number 44 and Executive Order
Number 6763, announced on June 30, 1934 that he had ". . . established upon a firm statutory basis the additional machinery by
which the United States Government will deal with labor relations, and particularly with difficulties arising in connection with
collective bargaining, labor elections, and labor representation."[4]
Although the statutory basis remained inadequate, the "additional machinery" had changed drastically. Those who planned
the organization of the new labor board, "hoping to profit by the
mistakes as well as the successes of the old board,"[5] convinced the
president to appoint an impartial board of three full-time, paid
neutrals to replace the voluntary, part-time, partisan representatives who had served on the National Labor Board: Lloyd K.
Garrison, dean of the University of Wisconsin Law School (who
had "no experience at all in the labor field" at the time Secretary
of Labor Frances Perkins informed him that the president wanted

3. The National Steel Labor Relations Board was established by
   Executive Order Number 6751 on June 28, 1934. For the contents of
   this executive order, see Lorwin and Wubnig, *op. cit.*, pp. 336–338.
4. NLRB files, "Statement Issued by the President Upon the Signing of
   an Executive Order Creating The National Labor Relations Board,"
   June 30, 1934, p. 1. See also *The New York Times*, July 1, 1934, p. 20,
   col. 2.
5. Louis Stark, "New Labor Board May Be Neutral," *The New York
   Times*, June 22, 1934, p. 2, col. 6. The president stated on June 30,
   1934, "For many weeks, but particularly during the last ten days,
   officials of the Department of Labor, the National Recovery Administration and the National Labor Board have been in conference
   with me and with each other on this subject." NLRB files, "Statement Issued by the President . . .," *op. cit.*, p. 1. See also *The New
   York Times*, July 1, 1934, p. 20, col. 2.

him to serve as chairman of the NLRB),[6] Edwin S. Smith, former commissioner of labor and industries in Massachusetts ("I know quite definitely [it was] at the instance of Miss Perkins [that] I was recommended"),[7] and Harry A. Millis, former vice-chairman of the NLB's Chicago Regional Board and nationally known arbitrator and chairman of the Department of Economics at the University of Chicago.[8]

6. Oral history interview with Lloyd K. Garrison, December 22, 1969, p. 5, on file in the Labor Management Documentation Center, ILR, Cornell. Garrison graduated from the Harvard Law School in 1922 and had been counsel for the New York City Bar Association for five years during which time he was active in investigations of ambulance chasing by lawyers and bankruptcy abuses. He then served as a special assistant to the solicitor general of the U.S. heading a two-year investigation of bankruptcy subsequent to which he became dean of the University of Wisconsin Law School. *Ibid.*, pp. 5-6. See also *The New York Times*, July 1, 1934, p. 20, col. 1.

7. Oral history interview with Edwin S. Smith, December 26, 1968, p. 5, on file in the Labor Management Documentation Center, ILR, Cornell. Smith remembered that "Miss Perkins called me . . . from Washington and wanted to know if I would be agreeable to being appointed as a member of the . . . board . . . . and Frances, I think, was . . . in fact I know, was quite anxious to play an important role in the organization and work of the board. . . . I think that she was quite eager, in fact, to have the board closely attached by whatever devices were appropriate to the Labor Department." *Ibid.*, pp. 14-15. Smith, after graduating from Harvard, worked for several years as a reporter on Springfield, Massachusetts and Hartford, Connecticut newspapers. He then spent three years with the Russell-Sage Foundation in the Division of Industrial Studies, then under the direction of Mary VanKleeck. As a result of his work while studying the Filene Department Store for the foundation, he became personnel director of Filene's and then secretary to Lincoln Filene. As Filene's secretary, he became active in the successful campaign of the democratic candidate for governor of Massachusetts, Governor Ely, who subsequently appointed Smith commissioner of labor and industries in the state of Massachusetts. While commissioner, Smith "became acquainted with Frances Perkins who then held the same position in New York State." *Ibid.*, p. 5. See also *The New York Times*, July 1, 1934, p. 20, col. 1.

8. Millis, who was a graduate of the University of Indiana, had been a professor at the University of Chicago since 1916. He had been the

A Judicial Approach and a Formal Organization: Decision and Reaction

Mr. Garrison met his new colleagues immediately after his arrival in Washington during the first week in July 1934. Garrison recalled that the board members "in turn met with Miss Perkins":[9]

> ... she arranged to have us go over and see the president. We had about a half an hour with the president. Rather to my surprise, he didn't make any comments at all on the nature of the task before us or what his concept of our job was or anything to do with labor for that matter. He spent the time gossiping about some experiences he'd had on a recent trip across the country during which he was entertained by Governor Olsen of Minnesota. He told us some funny stories connected with that, and it was all very affable and very pleasant, but it wasn't particularly educational.[10]

Garrison explained that he and the new members of the NLRB, without specific instructions from the president, "had first of all to decide what sort of body we should be" and "the history of the National Labor Board made it clear which way we should go."[11] The board members deliberated with Paul Herzog, who "had all the workings of that Board [the NLB] at his fingertips,"[12] Milton Handler, who "spent a period of time giving the new members of the Board, in a very concentrated dosage, the total experience that [the NLB] had had,"[13] and with Benedict Wolf, who briefed the members of the NLRB on the seventy-seven cases left unfin-

director of investigations in the Pacific States for the United States Immigration Commission in 1908 to 1910 and the chairman of the board of arbitration in the men's clothing industry in Chicago from 1919 to 1923. He was also a nationally known economist and was president of the American Economic Association at the time of his appointment to the NLRB. See *The New York Times*, July 1, 1934, p. 20, col. 1.

9. Oral history interview with L. K. Garrison, *op. cit.*, p. 8.
10. *Ibid.*, pp. 8–9.
11. Lloyd K. Garrison, "The National Labor Boards," *The Annals*, vol. 184, March 1936, p. 138.
12. Oral history interview with L. K. Garrison, *op. cit.*, p. 9.
13. Oral history interview with M. Handler, *op. cit.*, p. 23.

ished by the National Labor Board.[14] The new board then decided that, unlike the NLB, it could not act as both mediator and judge.

We must be one or the other. If we were to be mediators only, most of the cases before us would remain undisposed of, for they could not be settled by agreement. We were unwilling to pass these cases by, because Section 7(a) was the law and we had been set up to bring about compliance with it. Therefore we determined to sit as judges and not to engage in mediation.[15]

While working to dispose of the cases that had been pending before the National Labor Board, the board members continued throughout its first month of operation to devote "as much time as possible to the consideration of the many questions of policy confronting us."[16] The board, after the initial discussions with NLB personnel, conferred with its regional board chairmen and executive secretaries; members of the National Labor Board and the Steel and Automobile Labor Boards; and representatives of the Department of Justice, the National Recovery Administration, and the Department of Labor. It then developed a general outline of policy which the board proposed to pursue[17] and communicated its intentions to President Roosevelt in August 1934.

The members of the board told the president that there was no shortcut to the interpretation and application of Section 7(a) and that "if Section 7(a) is to be enforced, *as it must be enforced*, some agency of the Government must pass authoritatively upon each unsettled case as it arises, *and that we take to be the duty of this*

14. Oral history interview with B. Wolf, *op. cit.*, pp. 6–7. See also the NLRB files, press release, July 19, 1934.
15. Garrison, *op. cit.*, p. 140. The new chairman of the NLRB had observed that the NLB had been "hampered by differences which arose between its industry and labor members" over the interpretation of Section 7(a), that "the members were too busy with their own affairs to be able to sit upon the increasing number of cases," and that "cases were frequently heard by only one member of the Board and sometimes only by a member of the staff." *Ibid.*, p. 139.
16. NLRB files, "Report to the President By the National Labor Relations Board for the Period July 9, 1934 to August 9, 1934, Inclusive," August 1934, p. 1.
17. *Ibid.*, p. 4.

Board."[18] Although the NLRB decided to reject strike prevention as its primary objective, the board did tell the president that "every effort [would] be made to promote harmonious settlements of controversies and to reduce to a minimum the cases requiring decision and enforcement."[19] It planned to avoid the mixing of the judicial and mediation functions which had prevented the NLB from acting "unitedly, promptly, and decisively"[20] by confining employer and union representation and mediation to the regional labor boards which were "in the field at the seat of the controversy."[21]

The NLRB also required each local board to "make such adequate records of the proceedings that if compliance with its recommendations does not follow, the cases may be immediately heard and disposed of by [the NLRB] without the necessity of taking further testimony."[22] The national board instructed its regional boards, moreover, that "settlements will not be urged unless they can be achieved without delay and without violating the principles of Section 7(a)."[23] (The difficulty of the local boards' assignment to apply a dual judicial-mediation approach to such fundamental issues as union recognition became clear when, in its formal instructions to the regional boards concerning mediation, the NLRB found that "no absolute rule [could] be laid down" and settled instead for a foggy guideline: "Principle ought not to be sacrificed to expediency, but on the other hand legalistic interpretations of 7(a) ought not to be insisted upon where genuinely harmonious relationships can be be brought about by agreement.")[24]

It was clear, however, despite the national board's decision to

18. NLRB files, "Report to the President . . .," *op. cit.*, p. 2 (emphasis added).
19. *Ibid.*, p. 3.
20. Garrison, *op. cit.*, p. 139.
21. NLRB files, "Report to the President . . .," *op. cit.*, p. 3.
22. *Ibid.*
23. *Ibid.*
24. NA, RG25, "Functions of the National Labor Relations Board and the Regional Labor Boards and Their Relations to Other Boards and Agencies of Government" (hereinafter cited as "Functions of the NLRB"), October 12, 1934, p. 14; Region XVI, miscellaneous correspondence, NLRB, 1933–1935.

continue mediation at the regional board level, that the NLRB had chosen to pursue mainly the judicial approach to labor dispute settlement—the approach which the NLB had used most reluctantly as a last resort. Chairman Garrison, a lawyer, undertook the vital job of reorganizing the board, particularly the regional offices, whereas nonlawyers, Millis and Smith, assumed responsibility for the organization of a research staff and the study of other existing labor boards such as the Automobile Labor Board.[25] Under Garrison's direction, the NLRB established a Legal Division whose seven members (all of whom were attorneys) digested and prepared cases for hearing, drafted decisions for the board members, worked with the Department of Justice on compliance questions, and acted as advisors to the board "on legal problems and matters of policy."[26]

Garrison and the other board members agreed that the key to

25. NLRB files, minutes of the meeting of the board, July 14, 1934, p. 6. These minutes summarized a conference which the national board held with representatives of the regional boards on July 14, 1934. Millis worked on the organization of a research staff and Smith conducted the study of other industrial boards. It was also decided "to devote immediate attention to the building of a field personnel, an increase in the legal staff, an arrangement with the NRA regarding the precise relations between the NRA and the National Labor Relations Board insofar as the removal and restoration of the Blue Eagle was concerned, and the formulation of general policies of the Board and the scope of the work of the Board." *Ibid.*

26. NLRB files, "Report to the President . . .," *op. cit.*, Exh. B, p. 1. The members of the Legal Division were William G. Rice, Jr., general counsel; Thomas I. Emerson, Nathan Witt, Laurence A. Knapp, Philip Levy, and Charles A. Wood, attorneys; and Paul M. Herzog, former assistant secretary of the NLB, who was now an assistant to the general counsel. The other divisions of the new board were (a) the executive office with Benedict Wolf, executive secretary, and Beatrice M. Stern, assistant executive secretary, who were responsible for supervising and directing the "administrative activities of the Board and of the Regional Boards, . . . the activities of the field staff . . . [and] . . . the development of cases for action by the Board," *ibid.*, p. 2; (b) the examiners—Patrick A. Donoghue, Rev. Francis J. Haas, John D. Moore, Frank H. Bowen, John A. Chumbley, Nathaniel S. Clark, John L. Connor, Robert H. Cowdrill, Victor E. Lowe, William Meyer, and Nathan Shefferman—who conducted

NLRB success was to be found in the perfection of the organization and machinery of the regional boards[27]—particularly in the improvement of the quality of the records in cases involving the violation of Section 7(a) since adequate statements of fact in the transcripts had been the exception in cases coming to the NLRB from the regional boards.[28] Gerhard Van Arkel, who was a board attorney in 1934 and became NLRB general counsel in 1946, characterized the quality of the pre-Wagner Act regional board personnel as:

> ... spotty, terribly spotty. ... I would almost have to list them one by one. Elinore Herrick in New York, for example, was a very driving personality and she was all over the lot. If a guy wouldn't deal with a union, she'd send the building inspectors around and so forth and get after him in all kinds of ways to sort of make him deal with the union. A lot of this, I think, was totally extracurricular activity from the point of view of the administration of the statutes. A large number of them were not lawyers and most of them did not have lawyers on their staffs so that the records which were made in the field were full of holes and this was always terribly embarrassing.[29]

field investigations of alleged violations of Section 7(a) and aided the regional boards in their work, *ibid.*, pp. 2–3; (c) the research staff— Estelle S. Frankfurter, research director and Heber Blankenhorn, member—which studied and analyzed regional board reports and the "economic phases of cases which came before the Board," *ibid.*, p. 3; and (d) the Division of Information—Wellington J. Voss, director of information—which provided the press with information on the board's activities, *ibid.*, p. 3.

27. NA, RG25, "Statement to the Regional Labor Boards," memorandum from B. Wolf to Alice M. Rosseter, August 17, 1934, p. 1. Regional board records, Region XVI, San Francisco, A. M. Rosseter, general records, 1933–1935.

28. NA, RG25, letter from H. A. Millis to Indianapolis Regional Labor Board, September 20, 1934, p. 2. Board members, records of Harry A. Millis concerning the organization and personnel of the NLRB, 1934–1935.

29. Oral history interview with Gerhard Van Arkel, September 4, 1970, p. 16, on file in the Labor Management Documentation Center, ILR, Cornell. The NLRB instructed the regional boards that "no em-

The board wanted to be able to decide cases involving violations of Section 7(a) without returning them to the regional boards to fill in gaps in the testimony and without calling witnesses to Washington where the NLRB would have to rehear the case from the beginning as the NLB had done. Yet, according to Chairman Garison, "it was fortunate" that in the early cases board members were forced to see and to hear union leaders, management officials, employees, foremen, and supervisors "because the experience gave us an insight into the human problems involved" and some experience in the treatment of various kinds of testimony.[30]

I remember vividly one of our earliest cases . . . very early in the game when we were still feeling our way as to procedure. . . . At the hearing the room was filled with employees of the company, there must have been a hundred of them there, and some officials of the company and their lawyers. The union was represented by Jacob Potofsky, the head of the Amalgamated Clothing Workers, who, although not a lawyer, conducted the proceedings for the union. . . . I remember the highly informal atmosphere that prevailed; many of the people in the audience . . . were very eager to express themselves and when a witness was on the stand and we would ask him some question that he couldn't answer, a dozen voices would spring up to answer it and pretty soon it became almost like a round table in which the three members of the board, sitting up on a little dais, would try to conduct a sort of round-robin questioning. . . . We were able somehow to keep order and it seemed to me a very educational process as far as we were concerned. I think we learned more by hearing from different people in the room in that informal fashion than by formally putting them on the stand and swearing them in and all that. But this case I mention only because it was so early and because very rapidly we developed rules of procedure that were published and we became more

---

ployee, temporary or permanent, [was] to be engaged without prior authorization and direction from this Board." NA, RG25, minutes of the meeting of the Philadelphia Regional Board, July 27, 1934, p. 1. Regional board records, Region IV, Philadelphia, minutes of the board, October 1933–July 1935.

30. Garrison, *op. cit.*, p. 141.

formal in our conduct of the cases as we went along. We were really feeling our way. It was a new experience for all of us and we sort of developed our own procedure from day to day.[31]

The members of the board agreed, however, that hearings "would have become a shambles" if they had tried to institutionalize the informal approach in the NLRB rules of procedure.[32] The national board, therefore, worked throughout the summer of 1934 to implement its decision to deemphasize the informal, nonlegalistic mediation approach in its reorganization of the regional boards, in the development of uniform rules of procedure, and in the delineation of the authority relationship between the NLRB and its regional boards.

The NLRB converted the NLB's twenty regional boards into a

31. Oral history interview with L. K. Garrison, *op. cit.*, pp. 15–18. Garrison also remembered that "The company did not bring any witnesses. They brought a pile of affidavits signed by different people, chiefly, as I recall, by company supervisors charging the union with intimidation, along with some affidavits from employees saying that they didn't want to join the union. . . . We [accepted the affidavits] with very great reluctance because we wanted to set a precedent for arriving at our decisions through the give and take of oral testimony. But we were finally persuaded to do it, partly because of the pressure of the cases that were piling up around us and the delays that would have . . . been very prejudicial to the complainants if we had had to put the case off and wait for witnesses to be brought up by the company." Garrison thought that the informal approach "happened to work out very well in that particular case by virtue of the fact that the audience consisted almost entirely of workers who had come here with an appearance of great sincerity and earnestness about trying to form a union. And Mr. Potofsky was very intelligent and a very orderly kind of person who knew his group and knew his people and they trusted him. . . ." *Ibid.*, pp. 15–19. The case referred to by Garrison is reported in *Decisions of the NLRB, op. cit., "Ames Baldwin Wyoming Company and Federal Labor Union No. 18658,"* vol. I, pp. 68–71.
32. Oral history interview with L. K. Garrison, *op. cit.*, pp. 19–20: "As a lawyer and as one who had had a little court experience, it was perfectly clear that cross-examination is the most powerful agency ever devised for getting at the truth. This is sort of in a lawyer's blood. They [the other members of the board] were not lawyers but they fully agreed." *Ibid.*, p. 19.

system of seventeen geographic districts with one regional labor board in each district and with a full-time, paid director (appointed by the NLRB) in charge of each regional board. The directors assumed the administrative responsibilities that had been shared by the executive secretaries and the unpaid neutral chairman of the NLB's regional boards[33] and they were expected to engage in mediation "to compose as many disputes as possible in the field and in the office."[34] It was the regional director, however, who had the "special responsibility"[35] in Section 7(a) cases "to see to it that a full and complete record [was] built up."[36]

The director, consequently, was to be present at all hearings (an unpaid,[37] three-member panel comprised of one public representative, one labor representative, and one representative of industry conducted the local board hearing and sat as a trial court and

---

33. According to board member Harry Millis, "unpaid chairmen, giving as much time as they could spare from their pressing duties, desired relief and very frequently resigned to rid themselves of the burden imposed upon them." NA, RG25, letter from H. A. Millis to Indianapolis Regional Labor Board, September 20, 1934, p. 2. Board members, records of Harry A. Millis concerning the organization and personnel of the NLRB, 1934–1935.

34. NA, RG25, letter from H. A. Millis to Towne Nylander, September 29, 1934, p. 1. Regional board records, Region XV, Los Angeles, general correspondence files, 1933–1935.

35. NA, RG25, letter from H. A. Millis to Frank X. Martel, August 29, 1934. Records of NLRB II, office of the secretary, Region VIII, Cleveland, correspondence relating to regional offices, 1934–1937.

36. NA, RG25, "Functions of the NLRB," op. cit., October 12, 1934, p. 21.

37. The board was convinced that panel members should not be paid. "Nearly always, Labor representatives are union officials or business agents and are paid for their full time by their organizations. Moreover, these men should have a very direct interest in the successful operation of the Regional Boards. Industry representatives are paid management men . . . who are comparatively well off, and, like Labor, they should have an interest in the maintenance and furtherance of industrial peace. Public representatives are outstanding people who are in a position to give some of their time without compensation and are not worth the while unless they have a substantial interest in and enthusiasm for the work. Added to this, if remuneration was offered, all sorts of undesirables would seek places on the panels and petty politicians would try to get in on their

handed down the decision).[38] The director assisted in preparing a case, keeping "a record of what had been developed and what must still be developed before a proper and complete record is made" and permitting "no hearing to come to a close until all pertinent testimony [had] been given, even though this [might] involve calling to the stand witnesses who [had] already testified, and questioning them himself."[39]

The national board, moreover, instructed its regional boards not to attempt mediation at all whenever a "substantial" Section 7(a) question was involved and a prompt settlement seemed unlikely "since nothing [was] more fatal to the enforcement of 7(a) than delay."[40] Prompt action on cases was not to be prevented by the "disinclination to arrive at something other than a unanimous decision"[41] characteristic of the NLB. The national board also decreased the diversity and flexibility in regional board procedures by issuing "standardized" rules and regulations "with sufficient uniformity to avoid confusion."[42] The rules required that unions file written complaints specifying the acts complained of, that the regional board give a notice of hearing sufficient "to

---

work." NA, RG25, letter from H. A. Millis to Roy C. Jacobson, October 19, 1934, p. 1. Records of NLRB II, office of the secretary, Region XIV, Colorado, correspondence relating to regional offices, 1934–1937.

38. The NLRB believed that "on the whole, the policy which should be followed by all of the Regional Boards is to select for each particular hearing one representative of labor, one representative of industry, and an impartial chairman, all three to be drawn from the appropriate panel by the regional director" since "the atmosphere is more informal, and the case proceeds more expeditiously than if a large number of people are sitting and asking questions, and the likelihood of obtaining not merely a unanimous opinion, but a settlement of the case, seems to be enhanced." NA, RG25, "Functions of the NLRB," *op. cit.*, October 12, 1934, p. 9.

39. NA, RG25, "Functions of the NLRB," *op. cit.*, October 12, 1934, p. 22 B.

40. *Ibid.*, p. 14.

41. NA, RG25, letter from H. A. Millis and Edwin S. Smith to R. Gordon Wagenet, November 19, 1934. Regional board records, Region XVI, San Francisco, instructions—general, 1933–1935.

42. NA, RG25, memorandum from B. Wolf to A. M. Rosseter, *op. cit.*, pp. 3–4.

give the employer a fair opportunity to prepare his defense,"[43] and that "in every 7(a) hearing all of the testimony . . . be taken down verbatim by an expert stenographer."[44]

The NLRB's instructions included lists of questions to guide the regional boards in their development of the evidence in discrimination cases, company union cases, and good faith bargaining cases. The national board's instructions also prescribed a form to be followed by the local boards in writing their opinions and recommendations[45] and set forth a detailed procedure for the conduct of a representation election dealing with the date and time of the election, the location of the polling places, eligibility to vote, the form of election notices and ballots, the supervision of elections, and the method of voting.[46] The national board also severely limited the regional board's use of mediation to obtain an employer's consent to representation election "because the initiation of mediation efforts has in the past resulted in long delays in adjusting the issues, and such delays have been extremely prejudicial to the rights of the petitioning employees."[47] The NLRB's decision not to delegate to the regional boards the authority to order a representation election[48] and its desire "to avoid the

43. NA, RG25, "Functions of the NLRB," *op. cit.*, October 12, 1934, p. 19.
44. *Ibid.*, p. 22.
45. *Ibid.*, pp. 23–25.
46. *Ibid.*, pp. 30–37.
47. NA, RG25, memorandum from the chairman of the NLRB to the regional labor boards, March 6, 1935, p. 2. Regional board records, Region XVI, San Francisco, miscellaneous correspondence, NLRB, 1933–1935. Whenever a request was made for a representation election, the regional director was required to communicate certain facts to the NLRB "immediately" and to propose an election hearing to take place not more than ten days after the director's transmission of this information to the NLRB. The board, in turn, "immediately [decided] whether to schedule the case for hearing before the Director of the Regional Board as its agent." The regional director was free to "initiate the usual mediation procedure in an attempt to secure the employer's consent to the election" while awaiting the NLRB's decision. *Ibid.*, pp. 1–2.
48. NLRB files, minutes of the meeting of the board, July 14, 1934, p. 5. the board did not want to have representation elections subject to the diverse policies and procedures of the various regional boards "since the election order can be reviewed in the Circuit Court [and]

necessity for holding a hearing in Washington on each request for an election" required the national board to issue to the local boards (as it had in the nonrepresentation 7(a) cases) a set of important guideline questions "that all hearings held on the question of granting requests for elections should develop. . . ."[49]

There were protests from the regions that local board members were experiencing a "feeling of lack of interest or of futility"[50] because "the limitations placed on [them] by the National Board [had] seriously handicapped their efforts."[51] Employer and union representatives on these boards had

> . . . a growing belief that the Regional Boards [were] merely inquistorial [sic] bodies investigating alleged violations of 7(a) and doing nothing else. The strong appeal to most of the men serving [on these boards had] grown out of the idea that they were a mediation and arbitration body engaged in keeping industrial peace. There is no objection whatsoever to dealing with 7(a) cases, but if the function of the board is really limited to 7(a) cases, this will cause a quick disintegration of [these boards]. They would feel they were acting only as something like committing magistrates.[52]

The members of one regional board complained

> . . . that only a small proportion of 7(a) cases are significant, and that most of these cases that come before its panels in-

---

great care must be taken in all the procedural steps leading to such an election order." The regional boards could order an election consented to by the parties. NA, RG25, "Functions of the NLRB," *op. cit.*, October 12, 1934, p. 37 A.

49. NA, RG25, memorandum on elections to all regional boards, July 31, 1934, pp. 1–2. Regional board records, Region I, Boston, election reports to Washington, 1933–1935.

50. NA, RG25, letter from Stanley W. Root to L. K. Garrison, September 22, 1934, p. 1. Records of NLRB II; office of the secretary, Region IV, Philadelphia, correspondence relating to regional offices, 1934–1937.

51. NA, RG25, minutes of the meeting of the Philadelphia Regional Board, September 21, 1934, p. 1. Regional board records, Region IV, Philadelphia, minutes of the board, October 1933–July 1935.

52. NA, RG25, letter from Marion Smith to Francis Biddle, February 22, 1935, p. 2. Records of NLRB II; office of the secretary, Region VI, Atlanta, correspondence relating to regional offices, 1934–1937.

volve but one disgruntled individual and are not important in any general sense . . . that under the new set-up they act much less vigorously and authoritatively in . . . mediation cases . . . . that in elections the actual effect of the change in policies has been to make it difficult for this Board to arrange elections [and] that since it cannot issue decisions in mediation efforts or election procedures, but must render merely recommendations, it cannot act effectively in such matters.[53]

Not all of the problems of the regional boards were related to the new instructions, however. Many regional officers reported to the NLRB that cooperation between the partisan labor and management representatives on the regional boards had become almost impossible because of the introduction of "labor politics" into local board hearings and the "buffeting" of employer representatives "by the Manufacturers Association and its attorneys for having acquiesced in [certain] agreements" proposed by the regional director.[54] In one hearing, for example, "a prominent labor member voted for the company and at the State convention of the American Federation of Labor the vote cast at this hearing was used to defeat him for the presidency of the State Federation."[55] Labor and management members of the local boards were charged with selling out if they voted with the other side:[56]

With rare exceptions the industrial and labor members of the panel do not cooperate in the manner we hoped for. The reason is that each of the members of these two groups belong [sic] to one of two associations; in other words, labor organizations or the merchants and manufacturers association

53. NA, RG25, letter from George W. Taylor to L. K. Garrison, September 15, 1934, p. 2. Records of NLRB II; office of the secretary, Region IV, Philadelphia, correspondence relating to regional offices, 1934–1937.

54. NA, RG25, letter from H. L. McCarthy to H. A. Millis, November 4, 1934, p. 2. Records of H. A. Millis, the organization and personnel of the NLRB, 1934–1935.

55. NA, RG25, letter from Roger M. Busfield to L. K. Garrison, July 26, 1934, p. 1. Records of L. K. Garrison, the organization and personnel of regional boards, June–November 1934 and January–March 1935.

56. NA, RG25, letter from Towne Nylander to the NLRB, September 25, 1934, p. 1. Regional board records, Region XV, Los Angeles, NLRB correspondence, 1933–1935.

and/or the Chamber of Commerce. The antagonism between these two groups . . . is still sufficient to cause the Board members to feel that they are representing interests which detract from the general efficiency of the Board, and they also feel a sense of responsibility in that their fellow association members are constantly checking up on their actions and do not hesitate to criticise them for apparently "going over to the opposition." Such criticism prevents the board members . . . from acting as they would if they were entirely free agents.[57]

The industrial members of several regional boards, moreover, vigorously objected whenever a regional director would prepare a complaint for an inexperienced union or whenever a regional director or the labor members of a local board would "build up" a union's case "by questioning"—although they admitted that "unions without the services of good lawyers, which they usually could not afford, were unable to present their cases properly"[58] and that "the unions needed the services of the labor members of the board, since these were probably the most intelligent labor leaders in the city."[59]

It would be the case decisions of the NLRB, however, and not the board's procedural and organizational changes that would thrust it into major conflict with industry and the New Deal administration. The board, in the process of carrying out its intention to "build up a body of labor law from [the] particular cases before [it],"[60] emphatically reaffirmed the precedents established in the opinions of the NLB and "made Section 7(a) mean as much as some employers feared at the time of its enactment."[61]

57. NA, RG25, memorandum re panel system, unsigned and undated, p. 1. Regional board records, Region XV, Los Angeles, general correspondence files, 1933–1935.

58. NA, RG25, memorandum from B. Wolf to the NLRB, n.d., p. 1. Records of NLRB II; office of the secretary, Region XIII, Texas, correspondence relating to regional offices, 1934–1937.

59. NA, RG25, memorandum from B. Wolf to the NLRB, December 19, 1934, p. 1. Records of NLRB II; office of the secretary, Region XII, St. Louis, correspondence relating to regional offices, 1934–1937.

60. NLRB files, "Report to the President by the National Labor Relations Board for the Period From July 9, 1934, to August 27, 1935, Inclusive," August 1935, p. 9.

61. Thomas Searing Jackson, "The National Labor Relations Board—

The *Houde Engineering Company* Case

Of all the NLRB's opinions, none was more controversial or more opposed by employers than the board's August 30, 1934 judgment concerning good faith bargaining and majority rule in the *Houde Engineering Company* case. When Paul Herzog briefed the newly arrived members of the NLRB on July 23, 1934, he told them that the issues raised in the *Houde* case had been "under consideration by the National Labor Board and the Buffalo Regional Labor Board since December, 1933"[62] and, according to Chairman Lloyd Garrison, the NLRB "devoted to no other case so much thought and discussion as to this one."[63]

Although the Houde Company, a manufacturer of shock absorbers and other automobile parts, had denied NLB jurisdiction and had refused to attend the board's hearings, it had taken the position in correspondence with the NLB that it was under no obligation to deal with a union of its employees until the names of those employees who had voted for that union were disclosed to the company. Since, just one week before its decision in the *Houde* case, the NLB had ruled that a company was obligated to bargain with the representative "*selected by a majority of those voting*" and that "any agreement reached . . . must apply alike to all employees of the Company,"[64] the board decided on March 8, 1934 that there "was no need for the disclosure of the names of those voting for the representatives so selected" and that a secret ballot election was the "best method" of resolving the Houde Company's challenge to the right of a union to represent its employees.[65]

A Landmark in Federal Settlement of Industrial Disputes," *George Washington Law Review*, vol. 3, November 1934, p. 62.

62. NA, RG25, informal files, memorandum from P. M. Herzog to NLRB members, July 23, 1934, p. 1. Documents from the unfair labor practices and representation case files, *Houde Engineering Company* case.

63. Garrison, *op. cit.*, p. 143.

64. *Decisions of the NLB, op. cit.*, "*The Denver Tramway Corporation and Amalgamated Association of Street and Electric Railway Employees of America, Division 1001*," vol. I, p. 64.

65. *Decisions of the NLRB*, "*Houde Engineering Company and United Automobile Workers Federal Labor Union No. 18839*," vol. I, p. 87.

The company refused "to commit itself to abide by the election results" although it did facilitate the election by providing the NLB with a payroll list of employees[66]—possibly because the board had extended the franchise to the large number of employees hired by the Houde Company since the union had first approached the company in the autumn of 1933. The representation election, conducted by the Buffalo Regional Board on March 23, 1934, established the United Automobile Workers Federal Union No. 18839 "beyond question as the representative of the majority, not merely of those voting, but of all the employees."[67] The company insisted, however, on its "right to deal with minority groups"[68] of its employees, particularly with the Houde Welfare and Athletic Association, which had obtained 30 percent of the vote in the representation election. During mediation efforts by the NLB, an employer member of the board "persuaded the Company to withdraw its demand that the Union disclose the names of its members on the understanding that the bargaining would be carried on with the representatives of both groups of employ-

66. NA, RG25, informal files, memorandum from P. M. Herzog to NLRB members, July 23, 1934, p. 1. *Houde Engineering Company* case.
67. *Decisions of the NLRB, op. cit., "Houde Engineering Corporation and United Automobile Workers Federal Labor Union No. 18839,"* vol. I, p. 38. The union received 1,105 of the 1,752 votes cast and the association 647. Since the board found that "about 400" employees did not vote, the union's 1,105 votes also represented a majority of the total number of employees eligible to vote—approximately 51 percent.
68. NA, RG25, informal files, memorandum from P. M. Herzog to NLRB members, July 23, 1934, p. 2. *Houde Engineering Company* case. The board noted that "For several years prior to the advent of the Union last fall athletic events among the men had been promoted by a loose-knit association, if it can be called such, which consisted simply of a treasurer and a chairman in charge of athletics. The association seems to have no formal name, no meetings of any sort and no listed members . . . [until] the employees began to join [the union] . . . . [Then] the name of the association became Houde Welfare and Athletic Association, and it was given a definite structure and form with members, officers and a grievance committee for the purposes of negotiating with the company." *Decisions of the NLRB, op. cit., "Houde Engineering Corporation and United Automobile Workers Federal Labor Union No. 18839,"* vol. I, p. 37.

ees."[69] The union, however, refused any compromise that would make it something less than the exclusive bargaining agent for the Houde employees.[70] The issue was still pending when the NLRB replaced the NLB.

The NLRB found that subsequent to the representation election, the company had met separately with the UAW committee and the association committee "every week or two on Saturday mornings" to discuss matters of "secondary" importance: "toilet facilities, safety measures, lighting and ventilation, coat-racks, slippery stairs, and so on."[71] The one issue of "general importance" that had been raised in the company's meetings with the two committees, a group insurance plan covering all of the Houde employees, was agreed to by the company and the association without consulting the union.[72]

On August 30, 1934 the NLRB, in its decision in the *Houde* case, found that "the phrases [of Section 7(a)] were full of meaning"[73] and proceeded to weave those meanings into a labor policy that would become the core of the Wagner Act approximately eleven months later. The basic elements of the board's decision were that "the fundamental purpose of Section 7(a) was to encourage collective bargaining," that under Section 7(a) "employees were to 'have the right to organize and *bargain collectively*', and to be free from interference in self organization 'for the purpose of collective bargaining,'" that "the right of employees to bargain collectively implies a duty on the part of the employer to bargain with their representatives," that "without this duty to bargain the right to bargain would be sterile," and that "the only interpretation of Section 7(a) which can give effect to its purposes is that the representative of the majority should constitute the exclusive agency for collective bargaining with the employer."[74]

Just as William Green, the president of the American Federation of Labor, was quick to characterize the NLRB's ruling as the

69. NA, RG25, informal files, memorandum from P. M. Herzog to National Labor Relations Board members, July 23, 1934, p. 2, *Houde Engineering Company* case.
70. *Ibid.*
71. *Decisions of the NLRB, op. cit.*, vol. I, p. 38.
72. *Ibid.*, pp. 38–39.
73. *Ibid.*, p. 35.
74. *Ibid.*, pp. 35 and 40.

"only safe guide which can be followed in the development of human relations in industry" and to congratulate the NLRB for a decision that "was economically sound, fair and just,"[75] the National Association of Manufacturers, within two weeks of the announcement of the board's *Houde* opinion, encouraged the nation's employers to ignore the board's decision "until competent judicial authority has passed on the ruling" and advised them to observe the contrary rulings "made by the President in settling the automobile strike, and also the continuing interpretations by Administrator Johnson and General Counsel Richberg ..."[76] which supported the rights of minority groups and individuals to bargain with their employers.[77] The NAM also urged employers to exercise "the utmost caution" in "submitting to the jurisdiction" of the NLRB.[78]

Several industry members of regional boards resigned or threatened to resign shortly after the publication of the NAM position. In Los Angeles, for example, where the industry members of the local board belonged to a manufacturer's association affiliated with the NAM, the NAM's stand "on the majority rule . . . left the industrial members with nothing else to do but resign since they can not very well belong to one organization which was openly defiant of another organization of which they were an important part."[79] The industry members of the Philadelphia Regional Board wanted to resign their positions because the reaction of organized employers to the *Houde* decision led them to believe

75. NA, RG25, informal files, telegram from William Green to L. K. Garrison, September 3, 1934, *Houde Engineering Company* case.
76. *The New York Times*, September 13, 1934, p. 1, col. 4.
77. Early in October, Richberg is reported by *The New York Times* as having said that he "saw no distinction between the National Labor Board's decision in the Houde case and the interpretation which he and General Johnson had previously announced." *The New York Times*, October 5, 1934, p. 1, col. 8. For William Green's challenge to Richberg's interpretation, see *The New York Times*, October 5, 1934, p. 6, col. 1.
78. *The New York Times*, September 13, 1934, p. 1, col. 4 and September 15, 1934, p. 15, col. 4.
79. NA, RG25, letter from Towne Nylander to the NLRB, September 25, 1934, p. 1. Regional board records, Region XV, Los Angeles, NLRB correspondence, 1933–1935.

that manufacturers would not come to the board for mediation except in "minor and inconsequential" cases."[80] Although discouraged by industry's reaction to the *Houde* decision, Chairman Garrison tried to reassure the regional boards:

> . . . I cannot believe that manufacturers generally will boycott the Regional Labor Boards. A suit to test the Houde ruling will be brought in the Department of Justice very shortly, and this should clear the air. I really think it would be calamitous to the public interest if manufacturers generally should refuse to permit mediation efforts to go forward, and if the industrial members of the Regional Boards should cease to help in attempting to bring about settlements.[81]

Even though there is no evidence of a mass boycotting of the NLRB by employers, the *Houde* decision did lead "to an almost complete strangulation of the labor boards in their efforts to obtain elections. . . ."[82] Large employers in particular[83]—such as the Firestone Tire and Rubber Company with 10,000 employees, the B. F. Goodrich Tire Company with 15,000 employees, and the Bendix Products Corporation with 4,000 employees—thwarted the board by taking advantage of the provisions of Public Resolution Number 44 and Executive Order Number 6763 which made it possible for employers to create "an insurmountable barrier of delay"[84] by having the board's election orders reviewed in the circuit courts of appeals.[85] (Of all the representation elections

80. NA, RG25, letter from George W. Taylor to L. K. Garrison, September 15, 1934, pp. 1–2. Records of NLRB II, office of the secretary, Region IV, Philadelphia, correspondence relating to regional offices, 1934–1937.
81. NA, RG25, letter from L. K. Garrison to G. W. Taylor, September 18, 1934, p. 1. Records of NLRB II, office of the secretary, Region IV, Philadelphia, correspondence relating to regional offices, 1934–1937.
82. Louis Stark, "Labor Unions Break with the New Deal," *The New York Times*, February 3, 1935, sec. 4, p. 6E, col. 1.
83. Garrison, *op. cit.*, p. 145.
84. NLRB files, "Report to the President by the National Labor Relations Board for the Period January 10, 1935 to February 9, 1935, Inclusive," February 1935, p. 2.
85. On this point Section 2 of Public Resolution Number 44, 73d Congress, reads, "Any order issued by such a board under the authority

conducted by the NLRB and its regional boards from July 10, 1934 to June 16, 1935, approximately 88 percent of the units contained fewer than 250 employees, whereas only 2 percent of the units involved over 1,000 employees.)[86] Thomas Emerson, an NLRB attorney, reported to the board chairman in March 1935 that "in every case where the employer has not consented to the holding of an election and the board has been compelled to use its power to order an election, the employer has succeeded in tying up the enforcement of the order almost indefinitely in the courts."[87]

of this section may, upon the application of such board or upon the petition of the person or persons to whom such an order is directed, be enforced or reviewed, as the case may be, in the same manner, so far as applicable, as is provided in the case of an order of the Federal Trade Commission under the Federal Trade Commission Act." Executive Order Number 6763 reads: "The Board is hereby authorized . . . to order and conduct elections and on its own initiative to take steps to enforce its orders in the manner provided in section 2 of Public Resolution 44, Seventy-Third Congress. . . ." Public Resolution Number 44 and Executive Order Number 6763 are reproduced in *Decisions of the NLRB-I, op. cit.,* vol. I, pp. v–ix and vol. II, pp. v–x.

86. George Shaw Wheeler, "Employee Elections Conducted by National Labor Relations Board, up to June 16, 1935," *Monthly Labor Review,* vol. 41, no. 4 (October 1935), pp. 956–959. The above percentages are based on the statistics presented in Table 3. *Ibid.,* p. 957. Although there was a grand total of 154 elections conducted by the NLRB (3) and the regional boards (151), 579 units were involved: "Usually an election involved only one unit, but an election might involve several units when a single election was to determine employee representation for several companies, or when different classifications of workers in one company voted for different sets of representatives. The results of elections are given by units since in one election the results for separate units might be different." (The regional boards reported no multiple unit elections from January 10 to June 16, 1935.) See NLRB files, "Elections to Determine Employee Representation Conducted by the National Labor Relations Board and the Regional Labor Relations Boards, July 10, 1934 to June 16, 1935," undated and unsigned, p. 1.

87. NLRB files, "Testimony before Senate Committee," memorandum from Thomas I. Emerson to Francis Biddle, March 8, 1935, p. 8. The author has been unable to locate any statistics that would indicate

Employer resistance was understandably intense since the board in the majority rule decision, had not only provided organized labor with a potent weapon against the company union, but had also established itself as the champion of the duty to bargain[88] by ruling that an employer was "obligated by the statute to negotiate in good faith with his employees' representatives; to match their proposals, if unacceptable, with counter-proposals;

---

the actual number of NLRB election orders that were taken to the courts. In a final report on litigation involving Section 7(a), the NLRB lists 12 cases from November 20, 1934 to May 4, 1935 in which employers had petitioned the courts to review NLRB election orders. See NLRB files, "Final Report on Litigation Involving Section 7(a)—Status as of Date of Schechter Decision," unsigned and undated, pp. 1–2.

88. The NLRB's six-month report to the president summarized the board's decisions on the duty to bargain: "The right of employees to bargain collectively carries with it a correlative duty on the part of the employer to bargain with their representatives. Without this duty to bargain the right to bargain would be sterile; and we do not believe that Congress intended the right to be sterile. The employer is obligated by the statute to negotiate in good faith with his employees' freely chosen representatives, to match their proposals, if unacceptable, with counter proposals, and to make every reasonable effort to reach an agreement for a period of time. Thus empty declarations by the employer of willingness to confer with union representatives, offers to adjust individual grievances as they arise, or mere assent to those terms or demands as are found satisfactory, without an understanding as to duration, do not constitute compliance with the statute.

"While the failure to reduce an agreement to writing is not necessarily a violation of the law, the Board has frequently urged that this section be taken, as consistent with business expediency, common sense, and the general purpose of the statute to stabilize industrial relations upon a basis clearly expressed and mutually agreed upon. And the insistence by an employer that he will go no farther than to enter into an oral agreement may be evidence, in the light of other circumstances in the case, of a denial of the right of collective bargaining. Again, while the breach of a collective agreement is not in itself a violation of the statute, the Board has held illegal the wholesale discharge of employees in violation of an implied term of such agreement or understanding without exhausting the processes of

and to make every reasonable effort to reach an agreement."[89] Few employers in 1934 could accept the board's judgment that "collective bargaining . . . is simply a means to an end" and that "the end is an agreement . . . . [having] to do with wages, hours and basic working conditions."[90] The NLRB's forceful rejection of employer expressions of concern for the rights of minority groups and individual employees and the board's heavy emphasis on the *collective* as opposed to the *individual* aspects of labor-management relations were, in great part, a response to the total labor situation in 1934:

> . . . it was one in which unions as a whole were in a very inferior, weak, and rather precarious position. Industry was by and large antiunion and open shop and the unions were not well organized and the whole idea of the legitimacy of a union representing employees was not accepted so that the unions were constantly fighting for their lives. And in that kind of an atmosphere, it became even more necessary to subordinate whatever rights of the individual might be involved to the rights of the union. I don't recall that we thought very far ahead particularly, but I suppose implicit in what we were thinking was that if the union ever did get to a point where the unions were accepted and the employers were not fighting their very existence, then you could bring back into the picture more rights of individuals or minority groups and so forth, you'll start to adjust the balance. But the total picture

---

collective bargaining, since the employer is obligated to bargain collectively before modifying or terminating an agreement, arrangement or understanding. The Board has proscribed the activities of so-called 'run away employers' who sought by the transfer of their business to other localities to avoid their prior agreements or understandings and to defeat the right of their employees to bargain collectively." NLRB files, "Report of the President by the National Labor Relations Board for the Period December 10, 1934 to January 9, 1935, Inclusive," January 1935, pp. 7–9. For specific case references, see Lorwin and Wubnig, *op. cit.*, pp. 312–313. See also Richard Ulric Miller, "The Enigma of Section 8(5) of the Wagner Act," *Industrial and Labor Relations Review*, vol. 18, no. 2 (January 1965), pp. 173–179.

89. *Decisions of the NLRB-I, op. cit.*, vol. I, p. 35.
90. *Ibid.*

at that time was such that it simply would have meant no union strength at all if you'd done it the other way.[91]

The board, moreover, convinced that "majority rule [was] opposed because collective bargaining [was] opposed,"[92] saw industry's anxiety over minority and individual rights as merely a device to prevent unionism and to avoid collective bargaining. Francis Biddle, who replaced Lloyd Garrison as NLRB chairman on November 16, 1934, confirmed in his autobiography that he and Garrison shared that point of view.

The [role of minority groups] was a highly practical consideration which could not be solved on a theoretical and basically misleading plane of the "rights of the minority"— a plane upon which employers argued for the "rights" of men whom they did not represent and whose interests they liked to reduce to the manageable proportions of complacent company unions formed and dominated by management. . . .

"I am tired of hearing theoretical arguments about the rights of the minority", wrote Lloyd Garrison. "I have never seen a case in which these arguments were advanced by a bona-fide minority group genuinely concerned with negotiating a collective bargaining agreement applying to all."[93]

The *Houde* decision, however, was not without problems for organized labor. Under the principle of exclusive representation, it was necessary for the board to determine the grouping of

91. Oral history interview with Thomas I. Emerson, March 19, 1970, pp. 39–40, on file in the Labor Management Documentation Center, ILR, Cornell. In the *Houde* decision, minority employees "were given the right to present grievances, to make their wishes known." See Garrison, *op. cit.*, p. 145.

92. NA, RG25, Francis Biddle address, St. Louis, April 15, 1935, p. 6. Records of NLRB II, office of the secretary, Region XII, correspondence relating to regional offices, 1934–1937.

93. Francis Biddle, *In Brief Authority* (Garden City, N.Y.: Doubleday & Company, 1962), pp. 23–24. According to NLRB member Edwin S. Smith, "Much of the idealistic talk about the rights of minorities in collective bargaining has, I fear, a much more practical basis in the employer's sub-conscious mind." NLRB files, address by Edwin S. Smith before the New England Conference, Boston, Massachusetts, November 23, 1934, p. 15.

employees (or bargaining unit) most appropriate for collective bargaining before a representation election could be conducted. The bargaining unit problem had not been "too difficult a question" for the NLB since that board was "responding to strikes, and wherever there was a strike, that more or less defined the unit. . . ."[94] Because the craft-dominated AFL had little reason to feel threatened by the NLRB in 1934, the federation did not protest when the board assumed to itself the authority to make bargaining unit determinations.[95] Yet, long before the craft-industrial union issue would split the labor movement, the desire to avoid any "precedent which will encourage minority groups to spring up and demand recognition, thus endangering majority rule,"[96] led many inside the NLRB to advocate "majority rule on the basis of a clearly defined *industrial unit* . . . as the axiom of collective action."[97] As one NLRB attorney put it, "this [the approval of more than one bargaining unit in a single plant or

94. Oral history interview with M. Handler, *op. cit.*, p. 38.
95. The board in the *Houde* case asserted that "The question of the proper unit or units must be left for determination according to the circumstances of particular cases as they arise." *Decisions of the NLRB-I*, vol. I, p. 44. The NLRB's six-month report to the president summarized the board's decisions concerning the appropriate units for collective bargaining: "Often the question of what industrial unit should be recognized as appropriate presents difficulties which require careful consideration. Plant representation may be the proper unit; or an industrial, as against a craft, union. The organization of the business, the community of interest, geographical convenience, prior bargaining relations, functional coherence—all these considerations should be taken into account. This is peculiarly an administrative matter which has been determined flexibly by the Board, having in mind the growth and nature of labor unions, without laying down too rigid general principles. The Board has sought wherever possible to avoid dictating labor union policies or being drawn into deciding union jurisdictional disputes." For specific case references, see Lorwin and Wubnig, *op. cit.*, pp. 314–315.
96. NA, RG25, informal files, memorandum from Thomas W. Holland to the National Labor Relations Board, October 18, 1934, p. 1, *The Board of Street Railway Commissioners of the City of Detroit* case.
97. NA, RG25, informal files, memorandum, undated and unsigned, p. 3, *The Board of Street Railway Commissioners of the City of Detroit* case.

company] would amount to encouraging separation, whereas we want to encourage labor solidarity."[98]

As far as the board was concerned, "majority rule is the law and all of our decisions are guided by the principle of majority rule."[99] When Lloyd Garrison (who had agreed to serve as chairman only long enough to "set the board up and get it going")[100] returned to his job as dean of the University of Wisconsin Law School late in October 1934, he sought to protect the board's majority rule position by proposing as his successor Philadelphia attorney Francis Biddle who "was in full sympathy" with what the board had been doing.[101]

According to Lloyd Garrison,

> One of the things that I promised Miss Perkins I would do before leaving would be to help her and the president find a successor for myself so as not to leave the board in the lurch and so there could be a transition in which the work could be carried on without any interruption at all. I spent quite a lot of time canvassing in my own mind the possibilities for the chairmanship and just by accident, one weekend toward the end of the summer, I renewed my acquaintance with Francis Biddle. I'd had only a speaking acquaintance with him earlier and I can't really remember when I first met him, but I scarcely knew him. But it just so happened that on a weekend when I was visiting my family, he was there visiting some other people, and I had a chance to have a long talk with him about life in general and government and the things I was

98. NA, RG25, informal files, memorandum from T. W. Holland to the National Labor Relations Board, *op. cit.*, p. 1.
99. NA, RG25, informal files, letter from B. Wolf to Charles W. Hope December 28, 1934, *Willapa Harbor Lumber Mills* case.
100. Oral history interview with L. K. Garrison, *op. cit.*, p. 3.
101. *Ibid.*, p. 14. Biddle was "a member of one of the oldest and best known families in America." He had attended the Groton School when President Roosevelt was a student there. At the time of his appointment, he was engaged in the practice of corporation law. William Green opposed his appointment "based on the ground that he had been an attorney for the Pennsylvania Railroad, the Great Atlantic & Pacific Tea Company and other corporations." *The New York Times*, November 17, 1934, p. 2, col. 7.

doing, and he immediately struck me very favorably as a potential chairman of the board.[102]

Biddle recalled:

For four years we had rented a summer house at Black Point, near New London. I saw Garrison there occasionally. And when . . . we went back there to spend a night . . ., I saw him again. We lay on the sand for nearly an hour before swimming . . . and he told me about the Labor Board and its problems. I was at once interested. . . . I can still remember my excitement as I asked him questions. This was something new. He had been pioneering in a field where there was little experience and no body of clearly developed doctrine to guide him. The fight was not only for recognition of the function of organized labor but also for its role in American society. [103]

On November 16, 1934 when his appointment was announced, Biddle expressed his intention to follow the interpretation of Section 7(a) "as conceived by Dr. Lloyd K. Garrison"[104] and made clear his belief in the majority rule principle.[105] There were also indications that the New Deal administration supported the board's majority rule doctrine. After Charles Wyzanski, counsel for the Labor Department, talked with Mr. Biddle about the chairmanship, for example, the new chairman became convinced that "it was essential from their [Mr. Wyzanski's and Miss Perkins'] point of view that the new chairman should agree with the Board's interpretation of the principle of majority rule."[106] Furthermore, Charles Wyzanski reported that, while discussing the chairmanship of the NLRB, President Roosevelt said that "We must have a man of real courage. The Board has been courageous. It certainly took great courage to make that Houde decision. That's the sort of thing we want."[107]

102. *Ibid.*, pp. 11–12.
103. Biddle, *op. cit.*, p. 8.
104. *The New York Times*, November 17, 1934, p. 2, col. 7.
105. Biddle, *op. cit.*, pp. 23–24.
106. *Ibid.*, p. 9.
107. NA, RG25, letter from H. A. Millis to L. K. Garrison, October 27, 1934. Board members, records of Harry A. Millis concerning the organization and personnel of the NLRB, 1934–1935.

The Houde Company's defiance of the NLRB, however, demonstrated how unsure the administration actually was and how thoroughly confused the majority rule issue had become. President Roosevelt had approved the principle of majority rule in his executive order of February 1, 1934. Two days later, Messrs. Johnson and Richberg, speaking for the NRA, flatly denied the majority rule principle as developed later in the *Houde* case and told employers that bargaining with minority groups was consistent with Section 7(a). The NLB then ignored the NRA's interpretation by applying the majority rule doctrine in the *Denver Tramway* case in March 1934. Then, before the end of March, President Roosevelt, in announcing the settlement of the automobile strike, found that minority representation was provided for in the "plain language" of Section 7(a).[108]

The confusion was compounded after the demise of the NLB when the Automobile Labor Board continued to apply the principle of minority representation, the National Steel Labor Relations Board (one of the four special boards created by the president under Public Resolution Number 44) was instructed by an executive order of the president's to certify "the choice of the majority" as the bargaining representative[109] and the NLRB began to operate under Public Resolution Number 44 which contained no mention of either majority or minority representation. The issue remained in doubt after the NLRB's *Houde* decision. Francis Biddle recalled that

> Three days after I [Biddle] had been sworn in [as chairman of the NLRB] Richberg told a meeting of the Associated Grocery Manufacturers that it was a mistake to say that "representatives selected by a majority . . . must be accepted as the exclusive representative of all employees—the right of self-organization certainly included the right of each man to decide for himself with what man he desires to be associated." No one had ever been authorized to herd employees into a voting unit and compel them to select their representatives by a majority rule. He doubted whether, legally, anyone could be given such authority. This was an interpretation flatly in contradiction with the *Houde* case, and the often

108. For a discussion of these events, see Chapter II, pp. 61–64.
109. Lorwin and Wubnig, *op. cit.*, p. 337.

repeated views of Garrison. The battle was on, one of those fierce internecine struggles which, to the special joy of newspapermen in particular and to the public generally, broke out so frequently in the undisciplined ranks of the New Deal.[110]

The chairman of the Philadelphia Regional Board told the NLRB sarcastically that Richberg's explanation of the NLRB's *Houde* opinion was "so clear . . . that one metropolitan paper captioned the speech: 'Richberg Calls Houde Decision Sound', and another paper: 'Richberg Has Dealt A Blow to Majority Representation'."[111]

The NLRB had supported its interpretation of Section 7(a) in the *Houde* case by citing "similar interpretations of similar provisions" made by the National War Labor Board of 1918 and the Railroad Labor Board[112] and by arguing that the practical effect of the Houde Company's policy would be "rivalry, suspicion and friction between the leaders of the committees" and confusion among the employees, calculated "to maintain a permanent and artificial division in the ranks."[113]

The NLRB reasoned that, since an election "would be futile" if an employer were required to deal with each group of his employees regardless of their numerical strength, "Congress in expressly providing for elections *necessarily* rejected plural bargaining, and *almost as certainly* endorsed majority rule."[114] Those who disagreed with the board's *Houde* decision maintained that it was equally reasonable to presume that the imposition of the ideas of a majority on an "unwilling minority" would "easily result in discontent, discord and friction among the employees."[115] Opponents of majority rule, moreover, rejected the board's

110. Biddle, *op. cit.*, p. 24.
111. NA, RG25, address of Dr. Billikopf, Philadelphia Board first anniversary luncheon, November 23, 1934, p. 4. Records of NLRB II, office of the secretary, Region IV, Philadelphia, correspondence relating to regional offices, 1934–1937.
112. *Decisions of the NLRB-I, op. cit.*, vol. I, pp. 40–41.
113. *Ibid.*, p. 39.
114. *Ibid.*, pp. 42–43. (emphasis added).
115. Minier Sargent, "Majority Rule In Collective Bargaining Under Section 7(a)," *Illinois Law Review*, vol. 29, no. 3 (November 1934), p. 296.

reading of congressional intent by reasoning that "had Congress intended to provide for majority rule . . . provision would have been made for determination of the unit for the selection of representatives"[116] and by concluding that the silence of Public Resolution Number 44 indicated congressional opposition to majority rule:

> Furthermore, the Wagner Labor Disputes Bill, which was considered by Congress and for which the Joint Resolution was substituted, contained an express provision adopting the principle of majority rule. The fact that the Bill for which the Joint Resolution was substituted contained such an express provision, coupled with the fact that the Railway Labor Act, which was passed at practically the same time as the Joint Resolution, contained a similar express provision, must lead to the conclusion that when Congress failed to make such an express provision in the Joint Resolution it intended that majority rule should not apply in the industries subject to the N.I.R.A.[117]

The conflict and confusion surrounding the *Houde* decision demonstrated the growing need for a clear statement of a national labor policy "one way or the other," either by executive action, court decision, or legislation.[118] As was the case in the crisis of the NLB, however, the administration remained unwilling to make a firm commitment to the labor policy emerging from NLRB decisions. Chairman Biddle believed, moreover, that the board's "consistency was doubtless irritating to the President"[119] whose short-term view and empirical approach to economic recovery required that he be sensitive to the "incidence of power," ready to compromise—and flexible about majority rule.[120] The NLRB, therefore, was vulnerable to challenges to its authority and to its independence.

116. *Ibid.*, p. 280.
117. *Ibid.*, p. 285.
118. NA, RG25, informal files, memorandum from Heber Blankenhorn to the NLRB, October 17, 1934, p. 5, *Houde Company* case.
119. Biddle, *op. cit.*, pp. 38–39.
120. *Ibid.*, pp. 39–40.

A Question of Independence: Conflict with the Department of Labor

Secretary of Labor Frances Perkins posed one such challenge when she attempted to increase her control over the NLRB. Miss Perkins' position had always been that labor boards such as the NLB and the NLRB should not be "independent office[s] of the Government, but should be located in the Department of Labor."[121] The secretary told Congress that "only in a regular department of the Government, a permanent department of the Government, one which has an officer, who has a place in the Cabinet of the President," would the board receive "that attention, that prestige and that continual cultivation . . . that it deserves."[122] Later, according to Chairman Biddle, she told the president that giving the Labor Department control over the NLRB would help to counter the uncoordinated spread of New Deal agencies and would relieve the president of a load from "his overburdened back, a responsibility the intricacies of which, she hinted, he knew little about and cared for not much more so long as there was sufficient peace to allow due progress for the plight of the Blue Eagle under the National Recovery Act."[123]

When the president created the NLRB on June 29, 1934, "in connection with" the Department of Labor, he directed the board to make its reports to the president through the secretary of labor, prohibited the duplication of the Labor Department's mediation and statistical work, and expected the Department of Labor to aid the board in the performance of its duties.[124] The NLB offices (which had been in the Department of Commerce building where the NRA was located) were turned over to the NLRB and were eventually relocated in the newly constructed Department of Labor building at 14th Street and Constitution Avenue. (One NLRB employee recalled that "it was the newest and handsomest building in Washington at that moment and . . . space was set aside for the National Labor Relations Board—

---

121. U.S. Congress, Senate, Committee on Education and Labor, *Hearings on S.2926, op. cit.*, p. 24.
122. *Ibid.*
123. Biddle, *op. cit.*, p. 14.
124. See Executive Order Number 6763 in *Decisions of the NLRB-I, op. cit.*, vol. I, pp, vii–ix and vol. II, pp. vii–x.

[Miss Perkins] wanted very much to have the Labor Board in her building.")[125]

Although Miss Perkins never did more than express her preferences while Senator Wagner was chairman of the NLB, she moved quickly when Lloyd Garrison became chairman of the NLRB to claim authority over the NLRB's budget and the appointment of board personnel. Garrison understood that such an arrangement "would give the secretary of labor virtually a veto over the board's activities because," as he later said, "if we were a mere agency of the Department then through the device of budgetary vetoes, the secretary of labor could dictate to the board what it should and shouldn't do."[126] According to Garrison, the negotiations between the NLRB and the Department of Labor never reached the point where Miss Perkins "thought she had to lay down the law" because he and the secretary "personally got along together extremely well" and because Miss Perkins "knew that we [the NLRB] would never agree in any formal way to a subordination of authority and I don't think she wanted to make an issue of it at that time."[127] Chairman Garrison and Miss Perkins reached an "understanding"[128] under which the NLRB retained "sole control over the hiring and discharging of its employees, and the expenditures of its funds," but agreed to use the Department of Labor symbol, to have its accounting and budgetary employees "work in the Department of Labor, if space [was] available," and to "consult the Secretary of Labor with respect to all major appointments."[129] Miss Perkins disliked this

125. Oral history interview with Herbert Glaser, March 18, 1969, pp. 7–8, on file in the Labor Management Documentation Center, ILR, Cornell.
126. Oral history interview with L. K. Garrison, *op. cit.*, p. 37.
127. *Ibid.*, pp. 38–39.
128. *Ibid.*, p. 38.
129. NLRB files, "Suggested Bookkeeping Arrangement Between the Department of Labor and the National Labor Relations Board," July 16, 1934. Herbert Glaser, who did auditing and accounting for the NLRB in 1934, recalled that prior to being located in the Department of Labor's new building, the NLRB was temporarily housed in the Mills Building at 17th and Pennsylvania Avenue—"We were scattered around in different floors of that building"—across the street from the old Labor Department building. Oral history interview with H. Glaser, *op. cit.*, p. 6.

"consultative, good-will arrangement," however, but she "put up with it" until Francis Biddle became NLRB chairman and then she renewed more vigorously her efforts to place the board under the control of the Labor Department.[130]

On November 13, 1934, two days before Biddle was to go to Washington to be sworn in as chairman, he received a telegram from board members Smith and Millis asking him to be certain to talk with them before the ceremony. Later, Biddle described this event:

> They were very disturbed, were ready to resign—a suggestion not very encouraging to a new chairman just as he was taking over. Had I seen the order appointing me [Executive Order No. 6905]? I had not. The second section, they told me, stripped me of the power of appointment and of budget control, and placed the Board under the Secretary of Labor. Hitherto the Board had been independent, and Millis and Smith were fiercely jealous of their freedom, which Garrison had been able to sustain in spite of occasional differences between him and the Secretary.
>
> Miss Perkins talked with me for half an hour when I called on her the next day, a copy of the order in my pocket, before asking me whether I was ready to be sworn in? I was not, I told her, producing the order. There had evidently been a misunderstanding. Lloyd Garrison, telling me about my work, [had] assured me that part of its attraction was that I should run my own show, reporting to no one but the President, working of course in close cooperation with her—a cooperation from which he had greatly profited—but that I should in fact be my own master in matters of policy and personnel. I was sorry. I had come assuming that such would be the case. Since it was not the case I could not accept the appointment. I stood up and held out my hand. Miss Perkins, taken by surprise, was angry.[131]

After a telephone conversation with the president, who was cruising in the Caribbean at that time, Biddle and Miss Perkins

---

130. Oral history interview with L. K. Garrison, *op. cit.*, pp. 39–40.
131. Biddle, *op. cit.*, p. 12.

agreed that, although the executive order[132] would not be with-drawn, it would be "held in abeyance" until the president re-turned.[133] After Biddle accepted the appointment as chairman, the full board met with Miss Perkins on December 18, 1934[134] after President Roosevelt had suggested to Biddle and Miss Perkins "that a memorandum be executed clarifying the relation-ship between the Board and the Department of Labor."[135] Chair-man Biddle informed Secretary Perkins shortly after that meeting that "it seems clear to us that our difference of opinion on the function and status of the Board is a fundamental one, which cannot be clarified by further conferences." [136]

The NLRB took the position throughout its dispute with the secretary of labor that in order to administer "an act of Congress laying down a specific policy," the board needed to keep free of arrangements that would inevitably tend "to conform" the policies of the NLRB "to the policies of the particular administra-tion in power." [137] As Chairman Biddle put it during the delibera-tions over the Wagner Act,

> The value and success of any quasi-judicial board dealing with labor relations lies first and foremost in its independence

132. Executive Order Number 6905, which was never discussed with the NLRB prior to its issuance, reads in part, "Sec. 1. Francis I. Biddle is hereby appointed as Chairman of the National Labor Relations Board at a salary of $10,000 a year, vice Lloyd K. Garrison of Wisconsin, resigned. Sec. 2. In appointing and retaining officers and employees, and in incurring financial obligations the National Labor Relations Board, created by Executive Order No. 6763, dated June 29, 1934, shall act only with the approval of the Secretary of Labor; but this section shall not be construed to give the Secretary of Labor any authority to review the findings or orders of the National Labor Relations Board in specific cases subject to its jurisdiction." NLRB files, Executive Order No. 6905, November 15, 1934.

133. NLRB files, letter from F. Biddle to F. D. R., December 29, 1934, p. 3.

134. NLRB files, letter from F. Biddle to F. Perkins, December 28, 1934, p. 1.

135. NLRB files, letter from F. Biddle to F. D. R., op. cit., p. 1.

136. NLRB files, letter from F. Biddle to F. Perkins, op. cit., p. 1.

137. NLRB files, letter from F. Biddle to William P. Connery, Jr., May 17, 1935, p. 2.

and impartiality. After all, although the bill deals with the rights of labor, for the success of the machinery contemplated by the act it must in the long run have the confidence of industry and of the public at large. In our view it is in derogation of such independence and such impartiality to attach the Board to any department in the executive branch of the Government, and particularly to a department whose function in fact in the public view is to look after the interests of labor.[138]

Despite Biddle's pleas to the president that "the members of the Board [were] unanimous in their conviction that they cannot usefully operate under such a restriction,"[139] the issue remained unresolved until late in January 1935. At that time, Secretary of Labor Perkins agreed to observe her agreement with Lloyd Garrison "in view of the fact that Congress will shortly give consideration to legislation affecting the establishment and functioning of your Board."[140] At the same time that the board was trying to ward off the Department of Labor, it decided to challenge Donald Richberg and the NRA by asserting jurisdiction in the case of the *San Francisco Call-Bulletin and Dean S. Jennings.*

138. *Ibid.*
139. NLRB files, letter from F. Biddle to F. D. R., *op. cit.*, p. 3.
140. NLRB files, letter from F. Perkins to the NLRB, January 25, 1935. Biddle had suggested this arrangement to the secretary of labor as early as December 28, 1934 and, in frustration, Biddle had written to Lloyd Garrison on December 29, 1934 claiming that "what her ladyship now wishes to do is to put our nice new little Regional Boards into her Department and run them entirely." NLRB files, letter from F. Biddle to F. Perkins, *op. cit.*, and, letter from F. Biddle to L. K. Garrison, December 29, 1934, p. 1.

4 The Old NLRB and a National Labor Policy

On June 18, 1934 the NLB had instructed its San Francisco Regional Labor Board to take jurisdiction over Dean Jennings' claim that he had been compelled to resign as a rewrite man for the San Francisco *Call-Bulletin* because of his "activities in promoting the American Newspaper Guild."[1] After the demise of the NLB less than two weeks later, the newspaper companies refused to consent to the NLRB's jurisdiction and refused to attend a hearing held by the board's regional office on October 5, 1934. Counsel for the *Call-Bulletin*, however, did appear at a subsequent NLRB hearing in Washington on November 13, 1934 to argue that the Code of Fair Competition for the Daily Newspaper Publishing Business, approved by the NRA and the president, gave exclusive jurisdiction to that Code's Newspaper Industrial Board (NIB) and that "the newspaper business is a thing apart because of the publishers' 'trusteeship of the people's right to have a free press.' "[2]

The three members of the NLRB, Chairman Biddle, Harry Millis, and Edwin S. Smith, deliberated the consequences of going forward. Lloyd Garrison remembered Millis as an "immensely experienced student of labor relations [who had] excellent judgment" and who "was full of common sense" and as a man "a good deal older" whom he "admired and leaned on . . . very heavily."[3] Garrison found Edwin Smith to be a "bright and useful member of the Board but temperamentally very, very pro-labor and not perhaps as balanced and dispassionate in his views as Millis."[4]

1. *Decisions of the NLRB-I, op. cit.*, vol. II, p. 8.
2. *Ibid.*, pp. 2–3.
3. Oral history interview with L. K. Garrison, *op. cit.*, pp. 44–45.
4. *Ibid.*

Chairman Biddle "liked the other two members of the Board."[5]
He was particularly fond of Millis who "educated me [Biddle] in
the background and history of the labor movement, and made me
realize the changes that were taking place in its present evolu-
tion":

> He was cautious, thoughtful, patient; profoundly con-
> scious of the injustices that had been done labor's attempt to
> organize, although at the same time aware of the dangerous
> weaknesses in a good deal of labor leadership: not only the
> racketeering and the feather-bedding, but the lack of imagi-
> nation, the insistence on improved wages and hours as the
> sole end, the petty jurisdictional jealousies and squabbles. . . .
> Thus he would talk, with his feet up on his desk, puffing away
> at his pipe; an endless worker, doing a lot of dull reading of
> reports and statistics and articles, with a certain dour satis-
> faction that to get anywhere you had to drudge; wise, cheer-
> ful, courteous; old-fashioned, correct, a little formal in
> personal relationship—it was almost always "Biddle and
> Millis"; serene enough if he could have the feeling of too
> much work—and play nine holes of golf every other week.[6]

Edwin S. Smith "was very different in outlook and tempera-
ment" in Biddle's opinion. Chairman Biddle saw him as "kindly,
but seeing more of the evil than good in the society" and as "dissenting constantly in spirit," if not on paper, with the judgment of
his fellow board members—"his 'mission' to change and alter
society, a conscious and steadily held effort, a vision which
explained his thinking in terms of the mass rather than of the
individual."[7]

The board, with some reluctance, decided that a showdown
with the NRA was necessary to expose the confused and contra-
dictory state of the national labor policy and to force the administration to take a definite stand. Chairman Biddle recalled that
in these deliberations:

> Millis was worried, saw a row coming, and would have
> avoided the decision if possible. He was liberal and progres-

5. Biddle, *op. cit.*, p. 19.
6. *Ibid.*, pp. 19–20.
7. *Ibid.*, pp. 20–21.

sive in point of view, but cautious in approach. I agreed there would be a row, but rather relished the idea. I felt the weakness of our setup, and thought that a showdown would clear the air, emphasize the inconsistencies, the contradictions, the wearying slowness and vagueness of the way labor disputes were being handled. We decided to take the case.[8]

On December 3, 1934 the NLRB held that the federal Constitution conferred no immunity from regulation upon the newspaper industry, that "no genuine issue of freedom of the press can be fabricated out of the Executive Order giving the National Labor Relations Board authority 'to hold hearings and make findings of fact regarding complaints of discrimination against or discharge of employees or other alleged violations of Section 7(a),' " and that the newspaper code did not grant exclusive jurisdiction of 7(a) cases to the Newspaper Industrial Board.[9] The board maintained that Section 4(c) of Executive Order Number 6763 "by necessary implication reaffirms the Board's discretionary power . . . to take jurisdiction of 7(a) cases even where the code for the industry involved has set up an industrial board."[10] The NLRB also took the position that it would defer to such boards "unless the machinery established in the code is not adequate to give redress or is not functioning in a fair or impartial manner; or unless a decision is rendered by such board contrary to a correct interpretation of Section 7(a)."[11]

Although the board did not discuss the work of the Newspaper Industrial Board in its decision, Messrs. Biddle, Millis, and Smith knew that the newspaper board, made up of four publisher members and four members representing newspaper industry employees, had deadlocked on most of the important issues before it concerning substantive law and the NIB's own powers, procedures, and jurisdiction—including whether a representation election should be conducted by secret ballot and "whether the representatives designated by the majority of the employees in an appropriate unit should represent all for the purpose of collective

8. *Ibid.*, p. 32.
9. *Decisions of the NLRB-I, op. cit.*, vol. II, pp. 4–5.
10. *Ibid.*, p. 1.
11. NLRB files, "Proposed Statement by National Labor Relations Board Defining its Jurisdiction," January 21, 1935.

bargaining."[12] Once past the jurisdictional questions in its decision, the NLRB concluded, finally, that the San Francisco *Call-Bulletin*, by its treatment of Dean Jennings, had "interferred with the self-organization of its employees in violation of Section 7(a)."[13]

On December 6, 1934 the NRA "in the person of Blackwell Smith [acting general counsel of the NRA] but with the voice of Donald Richberg"[14] asked that the San Francisco *Call-Bulletin* case be reopened. Donald Richberg supported the newspaper industry's position in a confidential memorandum to the NLRB on December 6, 1934 and advised the NLRB that "in the final analysis" the board should not be interested in "close legal arguments as a possibility of finding a legal justification for its action" since "the Board is an administrative agency of the government, *charged with acting in concert with, and not in opposition to, other administrative agencies.*"[15] Despite the fact that the NLRB had months before transformed itself into a quasi-judicial body, Richberg expressed his belief that, since "*the only*

12. The NIB had also failed to complete the selection of a panel of five impartial chairmen required by the Newspaper Code and had decided only 3 of the 22 Section 7(a) cases before it. The NLRB would later report to the president that the NIB had deadlocked on other questions such as "Whether the Board has authority to act on the application of one party without the consent of the other, and to make decisions binding on all parties to the controversy; whether a party bringing a case before the Board agrees to accept the decision of the Board as final; . . . whether a case should be submitted on the record for decision by a ninth member chosen from the panel of impartial chairmen; . . . whether the Board should be free to direct either party to produce any records or to express its complete willingness to accept any records that either party voluntarily produced; whether the Board should request the publisher to furnish such figures as to payroll and financial status as may enable the Board to judge whether a claim of economy in the discharge of an employee is justified by the facts; . . . ." NLRB files, letter from F. Biddle to F.D.R., March 15, 1935, pp. 1–2.
13. *Decisions of the NLRB-I, op. cit.*, vol. II, p. 8.
14. "The Press Takes Its Stand," *The Nation*, vol. 139, no. 3624 (December 19, 1934), p. 699.
15. NLRB files, memorandum from Donald R. Richberg to the National Labor Relations Board, December 6, 1934, p. 4 (emphasis added).

reason and purpose for the establishment of the NLRB . . . is to bring about the peaceful adjustment of labor disputes," the board ought to know what was behind the guild activity.[16] He then proceeded to detail his opinion of Robert Buck, a vice-president of the American Newspaper Guild, "who practically controlled the activities of the Guild . . . . who [had] frequently expressed his belief that a rebel is the highest type of human being . . . [and who had] done everything in his power to make peaceful relations between the publishers and newspaper employees difficult":

> To show my knowledge of this situation, I may explain that I helped to place two women in the NRA at Mr. Buck's request. One is his daughter and another woman closely associated with him and these two were among the leading spirits in the organization of the NRA Union who have made just about all the trouble possible for a group of over-worked persons desperately trying to build up an emergency organization. You know that I believe in labor organization and collective bargaining, but I recognize that today the entire labor movement is infiltrated with people who scorn and oppose any efforts at the peaceful adjustments of labor relations and whose sole desire is to keep labor relations in constant turmoil.[17]

Richberg also maintained that a public hearing was an inappropriate way to have the NRA bring certain facts to the board's attention ("the participation of active newspaper men doubly emphasizes, to my mind, the wisdom of avoiding any such procedure") and suggested instead that "the administrative agencies of the government can properly consult each other and cooperate in the enforcement of administrative policies."[18]

Francis Biddle recalled that on December 4, 1934, one day after the NLRB's decision and two days before Richberg's correspondence with the board, "Donald Richberg, even more excited than the press itself, [had] rushed over" to see the board—"He hinted at a secret 'understanding' with the newspapers—an understanding

16. NLRB files, letter from D. R. Richberg to F. Biddle, December 6, 1934, p. 2 (emphasis added).
17. *Ibid.*
18. *Ibid.*, p. 1.

reaching very high up indeed."[19] (The NLRB had noted that Elisha Hanson, counsel for the American Newspaper Publishers Association, had testified at the November 13 hearing that "in the course of drafting the Newspaper Code he and Mr. Richberg had 'exchanged memoranda' which would sustain [the newspaper industry's] understanding of what the code meant."[20] The board "supposed" that these memoranda constituted the "secret understanding.") The board recounted for Richberg (and later for President Roosevelt) the extraordinary steps it had taken prior to the issuance of the San Francisco *Call-Bulletin* opinion in order "not to cross any wires with the National Recovery Administration":

> . . . Mr. Magruder, our General Counsel, on November 26 wrote to you [Richberg] informing you of the proposed decision in the Call-Bulletin case; stating the conclusions we had reached respecting the meaning and effect of the Newspaper Code; calling your attention to Mr. Hanson's claim that memoranda had been exchanged; asking to be permitted to examine such memoranda, if any existed; and requesting a conference on the subject. In response, your secretary replied by telephone that you had referred the matter to Mr. Smith, who would communicate with us. Later we were informed by Mr. Smith's secretary that a search of the files had failed to reveal any such memoranda as described by Mr. Hanson. On November 28, Mr. Magruder called on Mr. Smith and Mr. Tate, the Deputy Administrator of the Newspaper Code, with a draft of the opinion setting forth our conclusions on the points upon which our jurisdiction was challenged. Mr. Smith, Mr. Tate and Mr. Magruder went over the draft in detail. No information was conveyed at that conference or at any time prior to the publication of the decision that it contained anything contrary to the understandings of the National Recovery Administration as to the meaning of the Newspaper Code.[21]

Chairman Biddle, however, "thought if there had been a deal

19. Biddle, *op. cit.*, p. 33.
20. NLRB files, letter from F. Biddle to F.D.R., December 6, 1934, p. 2.
21. NLRB files, F. Biddle to D. R. Richberg, December 6, 1934, pp. 3–4.

[the NLRB] had better bring it to the surface."[22] Biddle agreed to reopen the San Francisco *Call-Bulletin* case to give the NRA "an opportunity to present [its] views to the Board prior to final action," but he rejected Richberg's suggestion that the issue be resolved by an exchange of memoranda or further conferences between the board and the NRA.[23] The NLRB chairman told Donald Richberg that "anything you might wish to bring before the Board must be made a matter of record" at a hearing with notice given "to all the parties to the controversy. . . ."[24] The newspaper guild was furious that the case was to be reopened and told Richberg that "the working newspaper men of the nation will not be satisfied until you disclose what happened between Monday evening [December 3] and Tuesday evening [December 4]—Who saw or telephoned you? With whom did you consult? What was said? What did you tell the NLRB?"[25]

As the NRA-NLRB confrontation was building, the board received assessments of the situation from Heber Blankenhorn, a labor relations expert, who conducted "special investigations" as a member of the NLRB's research staff.[26] On November 28, 1934

22. Biddle, *op. cit.*, p. 33.
23. NLRB files, F. Biddle to D. R. Richberg, *op. cit.*, pp. 1–2.
24. *Ibid.*, p. 2.
25. NLRB files, letter from Robert M. Buck to D. R. Richberg, December 13, 1934, pp. 2–3. Biddle remembered that Heywood Broun, president of the American Newspaper Guild, "intimated that there was something evil and surreptitious about our conferring privately with Richberg. . . ." Biddle, *op. cit.*, p. 35.
26. Heber Blankenhorn's job description was not formalized until the Wagner Act was passed in 1935: "Generally to study current developments in the field of labor relations which bear upon problems confronting the Board in handling cases. . . . to plan and carry on complex and intricate investigations into industrial labor conditions . . . [and] to conduct researches respecting industrial labor, and to submit reports and analyses as to suggested policies to be pursued by the Board. . . ." Blankenhorn had been a political reporter for the *New York Evening Sun* for seven years and for five years he had been a labor researcher for the Bureau of Industrial Research in New York City. While with the Bureau of Industrial Research, Blankenhorn supervised the Inter-Church World Movement's inquiry into industrial conditions in the United States,

Blankenhorn told the board that it was "moving on the News-paper Guild cases at the right time . . . . Last night, half a dozen reporters asked me: 'What's your Board going to do? Pass the buck again? Or does this new Chairman mean something? . . . I said: 'He means business quick and fast.' " [27] According to Blankenhorn, on December 6, 1934 "the question all over town" was "Will Biddle stand up to Richberg? i.e. will independent adjudication of labor law stand up to NRA-employer dictation?" [28] He advised the board that inside the NRA the Labor Advisory Board was "lining up" to support the Newspaper Guild:

> Hillman: sick of Richberg . . .; Green: anxiously awaiting the chance of coming to grips with Richberg publicly (But timid as always); Lewis: after long experience of Richberg will seize any opportunity; Howard: swears he will 'not submit anything more to futile Newspaper Board' and will support getting rid of Richbergism. [29]

He informed the board that the American Newspaper Guild's decision to protest Richberg's interference in the San Francisco *Call-Bulletin* case by withdrawing from the NRA's December 5, 1934 public hearing on the wages and hours of news department workers "seems to be acquiring considerable support." [30] Just before the hearing was reopened on December 7, 1934, Blanken-horn told Biddle that "against you" were:

> Administration fears of "prematurely precipitating a fight with industry" based on—
> 1. *Rubber* owners taking election into courts;
> 2. *Steel* owners' threat to do the same as soon as Steel

particularly into the steel strike of 1919. He had also been a cor-respondent for *Labor*, the publication of the Railway brotherhoods. See U.S. Congress, *House of Representatives, Special Committee, Hearings to Investigate the National Labor Relations Board*, 76th Cong., 3d Sess., (Washington: GPO, 1940), vol. XX pp. 4251–4254 and 4309–4310 (hereinafter cited as *Smith Committee Hearings*).

27. NLRB files, "Newspaper Guild Cases," memorandum from H. B. Blankenhorn to F. Biddle, November 28, 1934.
28. NLRB files, memorandum from H. B. Blankenhorn to F. Biddle, December 6, 1934, p. 1.
29. *Ibid.*
30. *Ibid.*

Board orders election (Iron and Steel Institute fought all Monday in New York with Steel Board and stood on the ground "courts of this country have always supported the right of employers to fire a man for any cause"—therefore they will take Section 7(a) to court.)
3. *Auto* lawyers sat with Steel owners.
4. *Textile* owners threatening same attitude.
5. *N.A.M.* offer to "recover" the country if Administration will damp down N.R.A. enforcement of Section 7(a).[31]

Blankenhorn told the board that newspaper reporters had said to him, "Your white hope has fallen on his face," and that he replied, "Biddle will stick. Wait."[32] The board did reaffirm its jurisdiction over the newspaper industry when Blackwell Smith (who represented the NRA at the December 7 hearing when Donald Richberg refused to attend) presented "no new evidence . . . throwing any light on the meaning of the Code."[33] Chairman Biddle recalled the hearing:

Smith reargued the case and added nothing. . . . Richberg's activity in trying at all costs to get us to drop the case was perhaps accounted for by the fact that, with or without the nod of his chief, he had induced the newspapers to come into the code by assuring them that complaints from the Guild would go to the code board. If the President had dropped such an assuring word, obviously that could not be revealed; and perhaps Richberg was merely taking the rap, as all of us were glad to take it from time to time, if we weren't rapped too hard, merely made to look like fools. But Richberg did not take any rap, and he did not appear before us. His case would have been greatly strengthened if he had publicly testified that he had assured the newspapers that their own board would be exclusive. . . . I suppose if he had testified to an "understanding" it would have further separated labor from NRA. These special boards in most cases were distrusted. That the administration had made a deal with the publishers would not

31. *Ibid.*, p. 2.
32. *Ibid.*, p. 3.
33. *Decisions of the NLRB-I, op. cit.*, vol. II, p. 9.

have looked very nice. . . . The President had deep if simple convictions. I doubt whether Donald Richberg had any . . . . he changed, when ambition touched him, from a supporter of liberal labor policies to an instrument to prevent their success. I could not trust him, and I do not think that his influence on the President was healthy.[34]

"Hell broke loose"[35] after the NLRB's decision was announced as all parties began maneuvering to apply the maximum political pressure on the administration. The newspaper publishers called a convention of the 1,200 code newspapers for January 28, 1935 "with a strong intimation that they would resign from the code."[36] Donald Richberg (who by the end of December 1934 "could hardly contain himself about the NLRB") sent a series of handwritten notes to the president in which he accused the board of "arrogant self-assertion" and recommended that—since the board "is today doing much more harm than good—It's [sic] power for mischief should be curbed."[37] The four labor members of the NIB called for a convention of their own "to have the support of labor leaders in getting the compliance machinery to work in the Jennings case."[38]

After the NLRB had transmitted the San Francisco *Call-Bulletin* case to the Compliance Division of the NRA, the board tried, without success, to talk with the president about that case as well as about its relations with the Labor Department. When Edwin Smith was able to arrange a meeting for December 31, 1934 with Louis Howe, the president's chief secretary, Chairman Biddle suggested to Smith that he "bear in mind" "that the NRA has no business to pass on this Board's jurisdiction or its discretion in exercising it" and that he tell Howe *confidentially* that the convention called by the labor members of the NIB had "the support of the A.F. of L. and of several of the big Internationals. . . ."[39] (The NRA had stepped up the pressure by refusing to re-

34. Biddle, *op. cit.*, pp. 34–35.
35. *Ibid.*, p. 35.
36. *Ibid.*
37. Schlesinger, *The Coming of the New Deal, op. cit.*, p. 399.
38. NLRB files, "Conference Called By Labor Members of the Newspaper Industrial Board," July 18, 1935, p. 80.
39. NLRB files, memorandum from F. Biddle to Edwin S. Smith, Decem-

move the *Call-Bulletin*'s Blue Eagle and by sending the case to the NIB "asking for counsel and advice.")[40] Edwin Smith, in his conference with Howe and in subsequent telephone conversations with him, indicated that the board was willing to conduct a hearing for all interested parties before deciding whether to assume jurisdiction in a code industry, but that otherwise he and the other board members "felt that we had gone as far as we should in our statement [on jurisdiction]."[41] During a January 9, 1935 telephone conversation with Smith, Howe declared that the board's attitude left "things just the way they were before" and at that point Howe "said pleasantly, 'All right, thank you' and hung up the receiver."[42]

That was the last the NLRB would hear from the administration until January 22, 1935, when President Roosevelt, one week before the newspaper publishers convention, "stepped in on the side of the newspapers against the Board."[43] The president "requested" that in "the very small number—probably less than five—" of codes which provide for the "final adjudication of complaints of violation of labor provisions," the NLRB "refuse to entertain any such complaint, or to review the record of a hearing thereon, or to take any other action thereon."[44] Although the board was entitled to investigate the merits of charges that the code tribunal was unqualified, the president denied the NLRB the authority to determine its own jurisdiction in such cases. The NLRB could

ber 29, 1934, p. 1. The larger international unions that were present at the conference included the United Textile Workers, the Mine Workers, the International Ladies Garment Workers Union, the International Brotherhood of Electrical Workers, and the International Association of Machinists. See NLRB files, "Conference Called By . . .," *op. cit.*, pp. 1–3.

40. Lorwin and Wubnig, *op. cit.*, p. 303, fn. 36.
41. NA, RG25, "Conversation between E. E. Smith and Mr. Louis Howe . . .," memorandum from E. S. Smith to Messrs. Biddle and Millis, January 9, 1935, pp. 1–2. Board members, records of Harry A. Millis, correspondence, memoranda, and other records on industrial relations boards, July 1934–May 1935.
42. *Ibid.*
43. Biddle, *op. cit.*, p. 36.
44. NLRB files, letter from F. D. R. to Chairman Biddle, January 22, 1935, p. 1.

only submit its recommendations to the president.[45] Chairman Biddle considered the president's letter "a curious document, half casual, half peremptory. It had the earmarks of having been written hastily to avoid a crisis. It was clumsy and lacked frankness. The stated facts were wrong. . . ."[46] The Washington correspondent of the *Nation* believed that the president's letter "was drafted chiefly by Mr. Richberg"[47] and Biddle felt that "the way the incident had been handled bore the marks of Richberg's uninspired manipulation."[48]

The board met with the president on January 24, 1935. The day before, Biddle, Smith, and Millis had agreed that they would try to "make the President understand that in the opinion of the Board its usefulness and authority have largely been destroyed (1) by the Executive Order of November 15, and (2) by his letter taking away [the board's] jurisdiction over code boards."[49] As revealed in Biddle's memorandum to the file at the time, they intended

to make him realize that we are in grave doubt as to whether we should continue . . . . [to suggest] that the [second] paragraph of his Executive Order of November 15 be revoked . . . . [to suggest] that he direct the N.R.A. to remove the Blue Eagle in the Jennings case; [to persuade him] to agree that we make to him a detailed report on the newspaper situation, praying that he remove all 7(a) cases from [the NIB's] jurisdiction, and that this report be given publicity after he has

45. *Ibid.*
46. Biddle, *op. cit.*, p. 36. Although there were five *special boards* which had been established by executive or administrative order in the automobile, steel, longshore, petroleum, and textile industries, there were twenty-six, not five, industrial relations boards handling labor complaints including the bituminous coal, construction, trucking, daily newspaper, motion picture, and shipbuilding industries.
47. "The Letter to Mr. Biddle," *The Nation*, vol. 140, no. 3631 (January 6, 1935), p. 144.
48. Biddle, *op. cit.*, p. 37. Arthur Schlesinger wrote that "With relish, Richberg called up Biddle, who had not been consulted, to inform him of the presidential decision." *The Coming of the New Deal, op. cit.*, p. 400.
49. NLRB files, "Memorandum of Talk With President," memorandum from F. Biddle to the files, January 23, 1935, p. 1.

had an opportunity of considering it; [and to ask] him to state to us whether or not we may expect that our jurisdiction will in the future be interfered with by the issuing of Executive Orders or letters dealing with our rights and authority.[50]

Although Smith and Millis reinforced their expressions of concern and frustration by submitting their resignations to the president,[51] the board members settled for much less than their objectives of January 23 when they had their conference with the president the next day. Biddle, who "did not think that [the president's] blandishments would carry much weight with Millis and Smith," recalled that the president was more than "moderately sympathetic" during their conference—"stroking down their angry feathers, showing sympathy . . . at his best, as he always was when he had to smooth over a prickly situation—and was having his way."[52]

The president "immediately stated that he entirely agreed with us, that our view of the law in the Jennings case was correct, indicating that his action in limiting our jurisdiction was necessary but that he intended to make the newspapers behave."[53] At Biddle's suggestion, the president did agree to write another letter to the board ("in order to restore some of the morale of the Board, which had largely been destroyed by his last letter") authorizing the board to report to him on the work of the NIB and "stating that he did not propose to interfere with our jurisdiction any longer."[54] According to Biddle, the president "immediately asked whether there were any 'special' boards which we had in mind" and "indicated very clearly that he did not wish us to get into the automobile situation. . . . It [was] very evident that he [did] not want us to get into that."[55] (Biddle speculated later that the

---

50. *Ibid.*, pp. 3–4.
51. NLRB files, letter from E. S. Smith to F. D. R., January 23, 1935; *The New York Times*, January 24, 1935, p. 9, col. 1; and Biddle, *op. cit.*, p. 37.
52. Biddle, *op. cit.*, p. 37.
53. NLRB files, memorandum from F. Biddle to files, January 24, 1935, p. 1.
54. *Ibid.*, p. 2.
55. *Ibid.* The AFL had withdrawn from the Automobile Labor Board at this time and the continuation of the code was being negotiated.

president's decision in the *Call-Bulletin* situation might have been influenced by a statement which he made "too impulsively" indicating that the NLRB would assume jurisdiction in the automobile industry "if circumstances made it seem advisable.")[56]

Although the president in a January 28 letter did ask the board to report on the "history and status" of the NIB and did mention that the "arrangements made in the case of this and a small number—two or three other codes—" were exceptions to the general authority of the NLRB,[57] Steve Early, who handled the president's press relations, told Biddle that "the President under no circumstances would permit the letters being given to the press."[58] The president, moreover, ended the San Francisco *Call-Bulletin* incident on February 7, 1935 by telling Biddle that it was "highly inadvisable that any publicity be deliberately given out— We have all of us been altogether too much in the public press of late!"[59]

The Failure of Section 7(a)

The president had revealed that he was still not prepared to support a public policy of collective bargaining as defined by the NLRB. The NRA had prevailed once again at the White House and the president in his settlement of the *Call-Bulletin* dispute had created "a method under which industries might free themselves from jurisdiction of the Labor Board."[60] The NIB deadlocked on the Jennings issue[61] and no decision was ever reached in that case.

See "Richberg Misinforms the President," *The Nation*, vol. 140, no. 3631 (January 6, 1935), p. 157.

56. Biddle, *op. cit.*, p. 39.
57. NLRB files, letter from F. D. R. to F. Biddle, January 28, 1935.
58. NLRB files, memorandum from F. Biddle to the files, February 1, 1935. See also NLRB files, letter from F. Biddle to F. D. R., February 4, 1935.
59. NLRB files, letter from F. D. R. to F. Biddle, February 7, 1935.
60. *The New York Times*, January 23, 1935, p. 1, col. 4.
61. NLRB files, "Meeting of the Newspaper Board at Washington, January 28–29, 1935," memorandum from H. K. Brunck to F. Biddle,

The NLRB and organized labor were now convinced that Section 7(a) "could not and would not" be enforced.[62] Biddle, however, did not resign (and prevailed upon his colleagues to reconsider their decision)[63] because he had placed his faith in a new Wagner bill then in preparation:

> But I was against resigning. . . . The action would not have led anywhere. Labor was weak, was badly organized in the great industries like steel and rubber and automobiles. NRA was breaking down. Section 7-a was but an affirmation of a right, something would have to take its place if the right was to be protected by law. And the statute had been drafted, was almost ready. Bob Wagner, with whom I had been working on the draft, begged me to stay, to hold the Board together. A new fight was on the horizon. Let us keep what we had, as we affirmed our position. Labor would back us unanimously, there was a chance to win. . . .[64]

The NLRB and the NLB had pioneered in the creation and development of a common law of labor relations—or as the chairman of the NAM put it, the NLRB "has 'enacted' the Wagner bill [the Labor Disputes Act] which Congress refused to legislate"[65]— but it was clear from the complete collapse of compliance procedures that this unenforceable common law had to be made into an enforceable statutory authority. The board had tried to enforce Section 7(a) by obtaining the removal of an employer's Blue Eagle, the NRA's symbol of compliance,[66] by negotiating an arrangement under which the government Contract Compliance Division

---

February 11, 1935. See also NLRB files, letter from F. Biddle to F. D. R., March 15, 1935, pp. 1–2.

62. Biddle, *op. cit.*, F. D. R., p. 41.

63. *Ibid.*, p. 37. Secretary Perkins also urged Edwin Smith to reconsider his resignation. See Louis Stark, "Wagner Seeks To Outlaw Company-Promoted Union; Bill For Majority Rule," *The New York Times* February 15, 1935, p. 1, col. 1.

64. Biddle, *op. cit.*, p. 37.

65. Robert L. Lund, "Labor Organizing by the Congress and Lawmaking by the Labor Board," *The Annals*, vol. 178, March 1935, p. 105.

66. According to historian Arthur Schlesinger, "One day, after talking with Henry Wallace about thunderbirds, the General sketched a figure modeled on the old Indian ideograph. Suitably retouched by a

of the NRA agreed to cancel the government contract of any company found by the board to be "in continuing violation of Section 7(a)"[67] and by attempting to "secure certain and swift action" in the courts through Department of Justice prosecution of 7(a) violators.[68] All three approaches failed. Whereas the removal of the Blue Eagle by the NRA made "absolutely no difference" to most employers in most industries[69] (the Houde Company, for example, sold automobile parts to the automobile manufacturers), it was theoretically, at least, a "destructively successful" punishment when applied to employers who sold

professional, this grew into the Blue Eagle. Bearing the legend, "We Do Our Part," it became NRA's symbol of compliance. . . . 'In war, in the gloom of night attack,' as the President explained in his broadcast, 'soldiers wear a bright badge on their shoulders to be sure that comrades do not fire on comrades. On that principle, those who cooperate in this program must know each other at a glance." Schlesinger, *The Coming of the New Deal, op. cit.*, p. 114.

67. At an executive meeting on October 8, 1934, the board "decided to send to the Government Contracts Division, N.R.A. all decisions it issues with a covering letter stating that the company is in continuing violation of Section 7(a). Mr. Healy will then investigate to see if the company has any Government contracts. If the company does not comply with the decision of the Board at the end of the compliance period we will inform Mr. Healy of this fact and request him to take steps to cancel any existing Government contract or prevent the company from securing any Government contracts. Mr. Healy will then, through the Division of Procurement of the Treasury, circularize the various departments of the Government and inform them that the company is in violation of the Code. If the company has any Government contracts Mr. Healy will take steps to have those contracts cancelled." NLRB files, minutes of the meeting of the board, October 8, 1934, p. 56. There is evidence that Healy, who was the chief of the NRA's Government Contracts Division, also instructed the Reconstruction Finance Corporation to withhold funds from "violators." See NA, RG25, informal files, letter from Frank Healy to C. H. Marfield, May 29, 1935, *Eagle Rubber Company* case.

68. NLRB files, "Suggestions For Testimony Before Senate Committee On Enforcement of Section 7(a)," report from Thomas I. Emerson to the National Labor Relations Board, March 8, 1935, p. 1.

69. NLRB files, F. Biddle, "Statement Before the Senate Finance Committee," n.d., p. 8.

labeled goods or who had substantial government contracts.[70] This potential effect was never realized, however, because of numerous injunction proceedings restraining the removal of Blue Eagles,[71] because customers became increasingly less likely to boycott an employer who had been deprived of his Eagle as the public's enthusiasm for the NRA diminished in late 1934[72] and because the NRA "in several cases where large companies were concerned" refused to hold up government contracts and restored a company's Blue Eagle without consulting the NLRB.[73]

In the board's opinion, however, the enforcement of Section 7(a) depended "ultimately" upon the prosecution of violators in the courts and in this regard the experience of the NLB and the NLRB revealed "a breakdown that [was] virtually one hundred percent."[74] An internal study of the board's case statistics, for example, showed that between July 9, 1934 and March 2, 1935 the NLRB had found a violation of Section 7(a) in 86 of its 111 decisions and that compliance had not been obtained in 52 of these 86 cases.[75]

Although the board sent a total of 33 of these noncompliance cases to the Department of Justice, the Justice Department had taken only one case to court (the *Houde Company* case which the board had wanted judicially affirmed as soon as possible) and that

70. *Ibid.* See also Harry A. Millis' comment in National Labor Relations Board, *Legislative History of the National Labor Relations Act* (Washington: GPO, 1949), vol. I, p. 1562.

71. NLRB files, "Report to the President by the National Labor Relations Board for the Period December 10, 1934 to January 9, 1935, Inclusive," January 1935, p. 19.

72. Lorwin and Wubnig, *op. cit.*, p. 326. See also Schlesinger, *The Coming of the New Deal, op. cit.*, p. 166.

73. Biddle, *op. cit.*, p. 26. In the most publicized of these cases, the National Industrial Recovery Board (which was appointed to administer the NRA in place of General Johnson) returned the Blue Eagle to the Colt Patent Fire Arms Manufacturing Company and permitted the company to continue its government contracts. See NA, RG25, informal files, *Colt Patent Arms Manufacturing Company* case.

74. NLRB files, "Suggestions for Testimony Before Senate Committee on Enforcement of Section 7a," report from T. I. Emerson to the National Labor Relations Board, March 8, 1935, pp. 3–4.

75. *Ibid.*, p. 1.

case was still pending when the NIRA was declared unconstitutional in May 1935. Moreover, in the two years in which Section 7(a) had been in effect, only one case had been tried in the courts—the *Weirton Steel Company* case which was filed when the NLB was in operation.[76] Technically, the problem was caused in great part by the Justice Department's insistence that "the cases referred to it by the Board for prosecution should be fully and completely prepared in all legal details."[77]

Since the NLRB had no power "to order the production of witnesses and documents," the board found this requirement "practically impossible to accomplish,"[78] particularly since experience had indicated that "when the Department says that further investigation is necessary it means that [the board] must present to them a case that is virtually 100% air-tight before they will even send it out to the District Attorney for prosecution."[79] Board attorney Thomas Emerson commented on the situation in a memorandum to Biddle:

> Take for example a situation which frequently arises. A complaint of violation of Section 7(a) is made to one of the regional boards. The regional board schedules a hearing on the complaint and requests the employer to attend. The employer refuses to appear. There is no method of forcing his attendance and the regional board is compelled to procede [sic] without hearing the employer's side of the case. The regional board then issues findings of fact and a decision. The employer refuses to comply with the decision and the record is

76. *Ibid.*, p. 3. Seven of these cases had been referred to the local district attorney "on the understanding that further evidence must be secured," in nine cases the Justice Department had advised the board that further investigation was necessary before they could be sent to the local district attorneys, in three cases the Department of Justice decided that no suit was justified, and in thirteen cases the department had "various other reasons for not proceeding." *Ibid.*, pp. 1–3.
77. *Ibid.*, p. 4. For an analysis of these "serious investigative defects," from the point of view of the Justice Department, see NLRB files, letter from Homer Cummings to F. Biddle, February 28, 1935.
78. NLRB files, letter from T. I. Emerson to F. Biddle, March 8, 1935.
79. NLRB files, "Pending Cases in the Department of Justice," memorandum from T. I. Emerson to F. Biddle, March 8, 1935.

forwarded to the National Labor Relations Board for further action. The National Labor Relations Board ordinarily prepares tentative findings of fact based upon the findings of the regional board and sends a notice to the employer that a hearing will be held at which he will be given an opportunity to show cause why the tentative findings of fact should not be made final. The employer then again refuses to attend the hearing and the National Labor Relations Board makes its tentative findings of fact final. If this case should be brought to court possibly the employer, being forced to appear, could produce facts throwing a different light on the controversy. The Department of Justice therefore feels that before directing the local District Attorney to proceed with the case it must have further facts. The Board is unable to supply them. Thus after months of delay no action is taken.[80]

In an attempt to offset these weaknesses and "to strengthen the records, eliminate unnecessary material, and bring out the essential issues,"[81] Biddle, Smith, and Millis visited many of the regional boards in February, March, and April 1935.[82] Despite

80. NLRB files, "Suggestions For Testimony Before Senate Committee on Enforcement of Section 7a," report from T. I. Emerson to the National Labor Relations Board, March 8, 1935, pp. 4–5.
81. NA, RG25, memorandum from F. Biddle to Elinore Herrick and Ben Golden, New York Regional Board, March 18, 1935, p. 2. Records of NLRB II, office of the secretary, Region II, New York, correspondence and reports relating to regional offices, 1934–1937.
82. Biddle visited NLRB offices in Cincinnati, Cleveland, and Detroit; Edwin S. Smith went to the Atlanta, Fort Worth, and New Orleans districts; and Harry A. Millis inspected the Milwaukee, Minneapolis, and Chicago regional boards. Benedict Wolf, NLRB secretary, also spent two weeks observing the New York Regional office. See NA, RG25, letter from F. Biddle to Mrs. Elinore Herrick, February 11, 1935, p. 1. Records of NLRB II, office of the secretary, correspondence and reports relating to regional offices, Region II, New York, 1934–1937; memorandum from H. A. Millis to the board, April 8, 1935, National Archives, Record Group 233, records of the United States House of Representatives, files of the Special Committee to Investigate the NLRB, 76th Congress, Box No. 129; and NA, RG25, memorandum from B. Wolf to the board, March 7, 1935, Records of NLRB II, office of the secretary, Region II, New York, correspondence and reports relating to regional offices, 1934–1937.

subsequent personnel changes and a series of instructions from the board,[83] many defects and irregularities in the handling of cases remained. Biddle found in one case handled by the New York region, for example, that, contrary to the NLRB's "pamphlet of instructions," the company had received "little information regarding the nature of the issue to be heard," that the regional board had improperly placed the burden of proof on the company to show that it was not guilty of the alleged violation, that the company had not been told "that the hearing might affect the company's right to the Blue Eagle" (a statement which the NRA considered essential), that the hearing had been conducted in the absence of the employer members of the panel, and that a regional board member had given the appearance of having prejudged the case and had antagonized the company by making remarks concerning the company's guilt prior to hearing the facts of the case.[84]

Biddle stressed the "seriousness of the errors" and told the regional board that "were this case to be forwarded to the NRA for removal of the Blue Eagle, the points which [he had stressed] could be argued, with force before N.R.A. or in restraining proceedings, to show that the company had not had a fair hearing."[85] Such "irregularities" did not always favor unions, however. Biddle also criticized the Pittsburg regional board for "getting the reputation of representing industry, so that unions are no longer filing complaints. . . ."[86]

Despite these major defects in the existing machinery, the board was convinced privately that "the real reason for our failure to get anywhere is . . . not only our lack of power but the extreme

83. See, for example, NA, RG25, memorandum from B. Wolf to E. Herrick, February 27, 1935. Records of NLRB II, office of the secretary, Region II, New York, correspondence and reports relating to regional offices, 1934–1937.
84. NA, RG25, informal files, letter from F. Biddle to the Regional Labor Board, Second District, March 27, 1935, pp. 1–2, *Claire Knitting Mills* case.
85. *Ibid.*, p. 2.
86. NA, RG25, letter from F. Biddle to John J. Kane, February 14, 1935, p. 1. Records of NLRB II, office of the secretary, Region IV, Pittsburg, 1934–1937.

reluctance of the Department of Justice to push the cases. . . ."[87] The Department, before its reorganization in mid-March 1935, was described by a member of the board's legal staff as unsympathetic, lax, and "in many cases" incompetent:[88]

> . . . [it was] the most political branch of the administration, and in its early days had political attorney generals and even political solicitor generals, and its staff was filled with people who were more or less failures as lawyers or else ancient bureaucratic types. . . . They were just completely out of sympathy with Section 7(a) [but] even if the Department of Justice had been filled with enthusiasts for our position, it would have been difficult for them because they wouldn't have been expert on it.[89]

Biddle maintained that the board's failure to obtain enforcement of its decisions amounted "to a complete nullification of the law"[90] and had resulted in "increasing unrest in labor circles" due to a "belief on the part of labor that the Government is not interested in enforcing the law on their behalf, and a belief on the side of employers that the law cannot be enforced."[91] (The NLRB, in its final report to the president, emphasized that compliance had been obtained in only 46 of the 158 cases in which compliance had been directed.)[92] The board held that without enforcement, Section 7(a)

87. NLRB files, letter from T. I. Emerson to F. Biddle, March 8, 1935.
88. NLRB files, "Pending Cases in the Department of Justice," memorandum from T. I. Emerson to F. Biddle, March 8, 1935.
89. Oral history interview with T. I. Emerson, *op. cit.*, pp. 46–48. Arthur Schlesinger noted that the Department of Justice was "stuffed with second-rate political appointees." See Schlesinger, *The Politics of Upheaval, op. cit.*, p. 261. See also Richard Cortner, *The Wagner Act Cases* (Knoxville: University of Tennessee Press, 1964), p. 67.
90. National Labor Relations Board, *Legislative History of the National Labor Relations Act, op. cit.*, vol. I, p. 1472.
91. NLRB files, letter from F. Biddle to Harold M. Stephens, February 12, 1935.
92. NLRB files, "Report To The President By The National Labor Relations Board for the Period From July 9, 1934 to August 27, 1935, Inclusive," August 1935, p. 21.

was merely a "pious wish"[93] and it called on Congress to take a definite stand.

Section 7(a), unenforceable as it now is in actual practice, is merely the expression of a paper right, a sort of innocuous moral shibboleth. Such paper rights raise hopes, but when they are shattered the reaction is far worse than if they had never been written in the statute books. It is surely more intellectually honest to face the situation squarely, and either pass an adequate bill or refuse to pass any.[94]

A National Labor Policy: The Wagner Act

Weeks before Senator Wagner introduced his National Labor Relations Act in the Senate on February 21, 1935, Biddle made a speaking tour of the major industrial centers of the East and Middle West outlining for groups of businessmen and union officials "what from our experience seemed to be the necessary features of any new legislation."[95] The board wanted Congress to state clearly the obligation of the employer to bargain collectively, endorse and define the principle of majority rule, create a judicial and administrative agency "wholly independent of any executive branch of the government," provide for vigorous and prompt enforcement of the board's rulings, grant the board "the widest scope . . . to permit it to build up a constructive body of labor law," and apply the legislation to all workers in all industries engaged in interstate commerce "irrespective of the codes."[96]

When Senator Wagner decided in the fall of 1934 to revise his

93. NLRB files, F. Biddle, "Statement Before the Senate Finance Committee," p. 11.
94. *Ibid.*, p. 13. See also n.d., *The New York Times*, April 12, 1935, p. 8, col. 1.
95. Biddle, *op. cit.*, p. 42.
96. NLRB files, "Report To The President By The National Labor Relations Board For The Period December 10, 1934, To January 9, 1935, Inclusive," January 1935, pp. 20–21. See also Biddle, *op. cit.*, p. 42.

labor disputes bill, Chairman Biddle directed the board's legal staff, particularly General Counsel Calvert Magruder, Philip Levy, and Philip G. Phillips, to work closely with Leon Keyserling, Senator Wagner's legislative counsel, in the preparation of the new legislation.[97] The board became "very busy in developing its ideas with reference to needed changes in the law."[98] Harry Millis told one of the board's regional directors in mid-December 1934 that "we have had long sessions with Senator Wagner and we are going to have still further sessions before we come to the end of a redraft of his [labor disputes bill]."[99]

Philip Levy, who succeeded Leon Keyserling as Senator Wagner's legislative counsel in 1937, recalled that, although Senator Wagner insisted that the ultimate decisions concerning the legislation and the final drafting of the bill's provision be carried out in his office under his personal direction, "the Board through its staff was by far the largest outside contributor to the development of the details [of the Wagner Act] on both procedure and substance."[100] The AFL through its counsel, Charlton Ogburn, "constantly consulted" with Keyserling and the board's legal staff but "was content to leave the preparation [of the bill] in their hands."[101]

Senator Wagner and his advisors excluded the Department of Labor ("as a consequence of earlier differences") and "did not seek the advice of the NRA [or] approach the White House until the bill was ready for introduction."[102] Although, as the drafting developed, many portions of the Senator's new bill could be traced to the Norris-LaGuardia Act, the Railway Labor Act, and to earlier efforts by congressional and presidential commissions to resolve issues of national labor policy, the "great difference" in the National Labor Relations Act was what Levy called the "vital

97. Bernstein, *The New Deal Collective Bargaining Policy, op. cit.,* p. 88. See also oral history interview with Philip Levy, *op. cit.*
98. NA, RG25, letter from H. A. Millis to Gordon Wagenet, December 19, 1934. Board members, records of Harry A. Millis concerning the organization and personnel of the NLRB, 1934–1935.
99. *Ibid.*
100. Oral history interview with P. Levy, *op. cit.*
101. Bernstein, *The New Deal Collective Bargaining Policy, op. cit.,* p. 88.
102. *Ibid.*

added factor"—the participation and the experience of the NLB and the NLRB.[103]

The draftsmen wrote all but one of the "necessary features" suggested by the NLRB into the national labor relations bill, S.1958.[104] The legislation provided for an impartial board of three members as "an independent agency in the executive branch of the government"[105] empowered to enforce rights rather than to mediate disputes. The board's legal staff insisted that "there should be no compromise," particularly with the Department of Labor, on the necessity for NLRB independence[106] and the board's jurisdiction was tied to interstate commerce rather than to NRA codes.

The drafters of the bill also established the NLRB as a "'Supreme Court' to eliminate the confusion [caused] by the diversity of interpretation by a multiplicity of [industrial relations boards]."[107] There was no provision for partisan membership "since it has generally come to be recognized that such membership impairs the impartial action of the Board as a quasi-judicial body and leads to compromise and adaptation on questions of law. . . ."[108]

The board's lawyers working with Senator Wagner and Keyserling also felt that "a board larger than three for the present time at least seems to be unnecessary and unwieldy and to invite dissension and compromising among the membership."[109] Be-

103. Oral history interview with P. Levy, op. cit.
104. For a detailed description of the legislative history of the Wagner Act, see Bernstein, The New Deal Collective Bargaining Policy, op. cit.
105. National Labor Relations Board, Legislative History of the National Labor Relations Act, op. cit., vol. I, p. 1348. This language was taken from the 1934 Raiîway Labor Act. See NA, RG25, series of memoranda from Philip Levy on each provision of S.1958, "Section 3(a)," n.d. Records of NLRB II, Legal Division, office of the general counsel, Calvert Magruder, Wagner bill file.
106. NA, RG25, series of memoranda from P. Levy on each provision of S.1958, "Section 3(a)," op. cit.
107. Bernstein, The New Deal Collective Bargaining Policy, op. cit., p. 88.
108. National Labor Relations Board, Legislative History of the National Labor Relations Act, op. cit., vol. I, p. 1348.
109. NA, RG25, Series of memoranda from P. Levy on each provision of S.1958, "Section 3(a)," op. cit.

cause the success of the NLRB's work depended heavily upon the quality of the regional boards, the NLRB insisted that S.1958 contain a provision giving the board full control over its regional system and took the position that it was important that this provision not be "tampered with."[110]

The draftsmen also broadened the NLRB's administrative discretion "by employing general enabling language" especially in regard to the finding of unfair labor practices, to the determination of the appropriate unit for collective bargaining, and to the board's power to provide remedies.[111] Section 7 of the bill, for example, was simply a "verbatim recital" of the rights of employees under Section 7(a) of the NIRA[112] and was to "be read in connection with Section 8(1)"[113] of S.1958 (also taken from 7(a)) which made it an unfair labor practice for an employer "to interfere with, restrain, or coerce employees in the exercise of the rights guaranteed in Section 7."[114]

The board attorneys felt it "essential that the Act contain a blanket provision lest the courts emasculate specific provisions or employers find practices not specifically covered which impede the progress of self organization."[115] The blanket provisions were designed not only to make the precedents of the NLB and the NLRB available to the new board but also to "permit [the new board] to prevent activities for which the old [agencies'] experience provided no precedent."[116]

110. NA, RG25, series of memoranda from P. Levy on each provision of S.1958, "Section 4(a)," n.d., *op. cit.*

111. Bernstein, *The New Deal Collective Bargaining Policy, op. cit.*, p. 88.

112. National Labor Relations Board, *Legislative History of the National Labor Relations Act, op. cit.*, vol. I, p. 1350.

113. NA, RG25, series of memoranda from P. Levy on each provision of S.1958, "Section 7," n.d., *op. cit.*

114. Bernstein, *The New Deal Collective Bargaining Policy, op. cit.*, p. 94.

115. NA, RG25, series of memoranda from P. Levy on each provision of S.1958, "Section 7," n.d., *op. cit.* See also National Labor Relations Board, *Legislative History of the National Labor Relations Act, op. cit.*, vol. I, p. 1352. Irving Bernstein lists the following practices which were not specifically outlawed: espionage, blacklisting, agreements in violation of the act, hostile statements, and strikebreaking. Bernstein, *The New Deal Collective Bargaining Policy, op. cit.*, p. 94.

116. Bernstein, *The New Deal Collective Bargaining Policy, op. cit.*, p. 94.

Although "none of the draftsmen . . . foresaw the cleavage in the union movement that appeared later in 1935," the board was given wide latitude in the determination of the appropriate unit for collective bargaining so that—despite criticism of this provision by AFL leaders—the NLRB could "sanction" industrial as well as employer plant and craft units.[117] Biddle told the Senate Committee on Education and Labor that "to lodge this power of determining this question with the employer would invite unlimited abuse and gerrymandering [and] would defeat the aims of the statute" and to allow employees to decide the appropriate unit (what Philip Levy called "Richberg's last stand on this point")[118] would "defeat the practical significance of majority rule" by permitting workers to splinter into small groups that "could make it impossible for an employer to run his plant."[119] (When Senator LaFollette remarked that the board could do that as well, Biddle agreed but added, prophetically, that "you have to take a chance to an extent on your Board.")[120]

The board was also empowered to order a violator to cease and desist and "to take such affirmative action, including restitution, as will effectuate the policies of the Act."[121] The broad terms, "affirmative action" and "restitution," were used "to take in the host of varied forms of reparation which the National Labor Relations Board has been making in its present decisions, to suit the needs of every individual case."[122]

The procedure which the board was to follow in unfair labor practice cases was "drafted principally after the Federal Trade Commission Act but draws upon the best features of other statutes."[123] Since S.1958 provided that the rules of evidence would not be controlling at an NLRB hearing, the board was willing to subject to judicial review the "conduct of the case as to due

117. *Ibid.*, p. 96.
118. NA, RG25, letter from P. Levy to Calvert Magruder, April 6, 1935, p. 5. Records of NLRB II, Legal Division, office of the general counsel, Calvert Magruder, memoranda and miscellaneous file.
119. National Labor Relations Board, *Legislative History of the National Labor Relations Act, op. cit.,* vol. I, p. 1458.
120. *Ibid.*
121. *Ibid.*, p. 1302.
122. *Ibid.*, p. 1360.
123. *Ibid.*, p. 1359.

process of law in connection with notice of hearing, introduction of evidence, amendments to complaints, etc."[124] The drafters, however, stripped the Department of Justice and the NRA of their control over compliance procedures by providing for the review and enforcement of NLRB orders in the circuit courts of appeals. The circuit courts were preferred over the district courts by the NLRB because (1) other statutes such as the Federal Trade Commission Act provided for this approach, (2) the circuit courts were "in the habit of dealing with administrative business and know the problems," (3) "such courts are too busy to read elaborate records and are therefore more likely to acquiesce in the findings of fact by the Board," (4) if the district courts were used, there would be no saving of time "in the cases of particularly recalcitrant employers," since the district court decisions could be appealed to a circuit court, and (5) "decisions by the circuit courts of appeals would in most cases be final, since the Supreme Court will be too busy to grant certiorari in all but a few cases."[125]

Because the NLRB's election orders under Public Resolution Number 44 had been involved in "endless court litigation which [destroyed] the whole purpose of the election provision," however, S.1958 did not provide for appeals from NLRB election orders.[126] The board took the position that an election order was simply a method of ascertaining a certain fact and should not be subject to court review until the results "have been made the basis . . . of an order relative to an unfair labor practice. . . ."[127]

In order to increase the NLRB's ability to influence the enforcement of its own decisions, board findings of fact (if supported by evidence) were to be conclusive, "otherwise there would be constant reiteration of the same issues of fact and the entire purpose of establishing an administrative body with experience to deal with the facts and the operation of a particular statute, would

124. NA, RG25, series of memoranda from P. Levy on each provision of S.1958, "Section 10(c)," *n.d., op. cit.*
125. NA, RG25, series of memoranda from P. Levy on each provision of S.1958, "Section 10(f)," *n.d., op. cit.*
126. NA, RG25, series of memoranda from P. Levy on each provision of S.1958, "Section 9(d)," *n.d., op. cit.*
127. National Labor Relations Board, *Legislative History of the National Labor Relations Act, op. cit.,* vol. I, p. 1357.

be entirely nullified."[128] (Under Public Resolution Number 44, board proceedings in court had to be commenced *de novo* by the Justice Department, "despite the hearings held, the record compiled, and the decision announced" by the NLRB.)[129] The draftsmen of S.1958 also made certain that the NLRB would no longer be denied access to essential information by empowering the board to issue subpoenas "requiring the testimony of witnesses and the production of evidence."[130]

Although the controversial principles of majority rule and exclusive representation were established conclusively in S.1958,[131] the bill, unlike Senator Wagner's 1934 labor disputes bill,[132] contained no reference to the refusal to bargain in good faith as an unfair labor practice. Because Senator Wagner and Leon Keyserling doubted that a good faith requirement could be cast in satisfactory statutory language,[133] they took the position before the Senate Committee on Education and Labor that "such a duty [was] clearly implicit" in the bill's provisions protecting the employees' right to organize for the purpose of collective bargaining[134] and they trusted that "the board would establish the obligation on a common law basis as its predecessors had under similar circumstances."[135] This approach was unacceptable to the board:

128. *Ibid.*, pp. 1362–1363.
129. NLRB files, "Suggestions For Testimony Before Senate Committee On Enforcement Of Section 7(a)," report from T. I. Emerson to the National Labor Relations Board, March 8, 1935, p. 4.
130. Bernstein, *The New Deal Collective Bargaining Policy, op. cit.*, p. 98.
131. See S.1958, Section 9(a), National Labor Relations Board, *Legislative History of the National Labor Relations Act, op. cit.*, vol. I, p. 1300.
132. Section 5(2) of S. 2926 provided that it would be an unfair labor practice for an employer "to refuse to recognize and/or deal with representatives of his employees, or to fail to exert every reasonable effort to make and maintain agreements with such representatives concerning wages, hours, and other conditions of employment." U.S. Congress, Senate, Committee on Education and Labor, *Hearings on S.2926, op. cit.*, p. 2.
133. Bernstein, *The New Deal Collective Bargaining Policy, op. cit.*, p. 95.
134. National Labor Relations Board, *Legislative History of the National Labor Relations Act, op. cit.*, vol. I, p. 1419.
135. Bernstein, *The New Deal Collective Bargaining Policy, op. cit.*, p. 95.

It seems that in many ways the duty to bargain collectively is the crux of the whole bill and the omission might prove very serious. . . . We feel that it is quite possible for a court to say that the duty to bargain collectively is not spelled out in Section 8(1) when read in connection with Section 7. Under the decisions of this Board we feel that the best that can be made out of the present bill is that it invalidates bargaining with minority groups or individuals when the representatives of the majority have been designated and have approached the employer for the purpose of collective bargaining. . . . At present, the majority rule in the Bill really stands out as a solemn declaration with no conceivable way of enforcing it and with no particular legal significance attached to it . . . . it may be urged that some employers will refuse to bargain at all since their duty in this respect is not clearly prescribed by law. In any case, it is perfectly clear that the bill fails to meet the cause of about 75% of the strikes and will undoubtedly increase the number of such strikes. At best, it can be said that under the bill the duty to bargain collectively is doubtful.[136]

Senator Wagner was particularly concerned that an explicit good faith bargaining requirement in S.1958 would intensify and strengthen attacks on the bill by making it more vulnerable to charges that the law would require an employer to reach an agreement with a union and that the agreement be written—that is, a kind of compulsory arbitration.[137] (At one point in the drafting of the bill, the NLRB had urged that the "necessity of a written agreement [be] specifically included in collective bargaining."[138]) The proponents of the Wagner bill were also apprehensive over the "sources of danger" inherent in disagreements within their own ranks:[139] not only over Biddle's insistence on a

---

136. NA, RG25, series of memoranda from P. Levy on each provision of S.1958, "Section 8 (1)," *n.d. op. cit.*
137. Oral history interview with P. Levy, *op. cit.* See also NLRB files, H. A. Millis, "Princeton Conference On Industrial Relations, 1935: The Government and Industrial Relations," September 20, 1935, pp. 14–15.
138. NLRB files, "Proposed Wagner Bill," memorandum from P. Levy and Philip Phillips to the National Labor Relations Board, n.d.
139. NA, RG25, letter from H. A. Millis to Roy C. Jacobson, March 19,

duty to bargain provision, but also over the AFL's support of the secretary of labor in her continuing efforts to place the Board under her authority, and the federation's distress over the appropriate unit section and its preference for a tripartite board "in order to gain a voice in its operations."[140]

The opposition (essentially "the business community in virtually solid phalanx")[141] took up the same arguments that had been used against the Senator's labor disputes bill one year earlier: the bill was an unconstitutional exercise of the commerce power, it violated due process, Section 7(a) was sufficient, the NLRB would gerrymander units to give the AFL an advantage that would eventually lead to an AFL monopoly, and the bill violated the principle of equality before the law by imposing "responsibilities upon management without corresponding duties for unions."[142] Senator Wagner sought to exploit the outcome of the congressional elections of 1934 by choosing to have the first confrontation with this opposition take place in the Senate:

> The congressional elections of November, 1934, were no less influential than the board in laying the foundation for the enactment of comprehensive legislation the following year. The brake exercised by anticipation of an electoral test

1935. Records of NLRB II, office of the secretary, Region XIV, Colorado, 1934–1937.

140. Bernstein, *The New Deal Collective Bargaining Policy*, op. cit., pp. 105–106 and 125–126. The AFL also proposed several other amendments "characterized by concern over application of majority rule and a desire to retain procedural initiative in its own hands. Unions should be permitted to enter closed shop agreements even when not representing majorities, while the right of individuals to present grievances should be eliminated. . . ." *Ibid.*, p. 106.

141. *Ibid.*, p. 100. Throughout March and April 1935, the NLRB tried to find employers who would be willing to testify in favor of the Wagner bill. The regional boards reported "almost unanimous" employer resistance. NA, RG25, letter from F. Biddle to R. Gordon Wagenet, March 4, 1935. Regional board records, Region XVI, San Francisco, "Labor Legislation Correspondence, 1935." See also NLRB files, letters from Stanley Mathewson to F. Biddle, April 16, 1935; F. J. Miller to F. Biddle, March 8, 1935; and Robert H. Cowdrill to F. Biddle, March 7, 1935.

142. Bernstein, *The New Deal Collective Bargaining Policy*, op. cit., pp. 106–111.

was swept away. As the results came in, the *New York Times* declared, "The President and his New Deal . . . won the most overwhelming victory in the history of American politics. . . ." The election for practical purposes eliminated the right-wing of the Republican Party. Hence the legislature was prepared to entertain more progressive measures. The realignment of the two chambers was equally significant. In the 73rd the House had been the more progressive body, but in its successor the Senate occupied that position, a factor weighed in planning legislative strategy.[143]

Despite an anti-Wagner bill campaign that *United States News* called "the greatest ever conducted by industry regarding any Congressional measure,"[144] the Wagner forces remained in "effective control of the legislation" at all times,[145] even to the extent that Senator Wagner and his assistant, Leon Keyserling, wrote the Senate Education and Labor Committee's favorable report on S.1958.[146] Senate Education and Labor Committee Chairman David I. Walsh's decision to give that responsibility to Senator Wagner provided the senator and his supporters with "a key opportunity to break with the 1934 Report [a Labor Department draft written by Charles Wyzanski and offered by Senator Walsh as a substitute for Senator Wagner's labor disputes bill in 1934][147] and, more important, to state congressional intent for the guidance of the board and the courts."[148] The committee unanimously reported S.1958 on May 2, 1935 with only one important change: the NLRB, "through the persuasiveness of Biddle, Garrison and others,"[149] had prevailed upon Senator Wagner to include a duty to bargain section in the bill.[150] Actually, Lloyd Garrison recalled

143. *Ibid.*, p. 88.
144. *Ibid.*, p. 110.
145. Oral history interview with L. Keyserling, *op. cit.*, p. 22.
146. *Ibid.* See also Bernstein, *The New Deal Collective Bargaining Policy, op. cit.*, p. 112.
147. See National Labor Relations Board, *Legislative History of the National Labor Relations Act, op. cit.*, vol. I, p. 1070.
148. Bernstein, *The New Deal Collective Bargaining Policy, op. cit.*, p. 112.
149. Miller, *op. cit.*, p. 180.
150. Section 8 (5) read: "It shall be an unfair labor practice for an employer to refuse to bargain collectively with the representatives of his employees, subject to the provisions of Section 9 (a)." National

that he might not have been as enthusiastic about this provision had not the need for a united front seemed so great at the time:

> When I appeared before the Senate Committee to support the Wagner Act, I was very much tempted to suggest a provision . . . to make it clear that the duty to bargain collectively would be satisfied by a requirement that the employer should meet with the union whenever requested at reasonable times but I was, however, persuaded that at the late stage at which I appeared before the Senate Committee that any proposal by a supporter of the bill to change the bill would be a complicating factor and would quite possibly be seized on by opponents of the bill to set it back; that the main thing was to get it enacted and then, if it needed amendment later, it could always be amended.[151]

The NAM, convinced that the situation was desperate in that Senator Wagner's bill would "undoubtedly pass" if it came to a vote, decided to "divert" the bill by amendment.[152] The NAM hoped that an amendment prohibiting the coercion of employees by other employees and unions "would appeal to many Senators who would vote for the bill in its entirety [and that] the AFL would then object so strenuously . . . as to prefer no legislation at all."[153] Robert Wagner was also certain that his bill could not be defeated if brought to a vote in the Senate.[154] When Senate Majority Leader Joseph Robinson and "the very influential" Senator Pat Harrison "took Wagner down to the White House to convince him and the President that if the bill came up for a vote it couldn't pass" and to persuade the senator to withdraw his bill, Wagner

---

Labor Relations Board, *Legislative History of the National Labor Relations Act, op. cit.*, vol. II, p. 2290.

151. Oral history interview with L. K. Garrison, *op. cit.*, pp. 50–51.
152. Bernstein, *The New Deal Collective Bargaining Policy, op. cit.*, p. 114.
153. *Ibid.* The potential popularity of this proposal was indicated by the support it received from a special committee of the Twentieth Century Fund (otherwise a strong supporter of the Wagner bill) including, among others, William H. Davis, William M. Leiserson, Sumner H. Slichter, and John G. Winant. See NLRB files, "Findings and Recommendations of the Special Committee on Government and Labor of the Twentieth Century Fund, Inc.," February 26, 1935.
154. Oral history interview with L. Keyserling, *op. cit.*, p. 52.

urged the president not to intervene again and told Roosevelt, "all I want is a vote." The president, although offering no support, agreed not to impede the Senate's consideration of the bill.[155]

Senator Wagner formally presented S.1958 to the Senate on May 15, 1935 and debate began the next day. Once the Education and Labor Committee's revisions were accepted without objection,[156] only two problems remained to trouble the proponents of S.1958: the NAM's amendment to prevent "coercion-from-any-source" which was introduced by Senator Tydings of Maryland and Senator Walsh's persistent reassurances that the bill was simply "misunderstood." (According to Philip Levy, this was "the kind of thing that Walsh did too much of in the legislative history. He was always making speeches about what the law did not do. By the time he got through saying all the things it did not do there wasn't a hell of a lot left for it to do.")[157]

The board opposed the NAM amendment as a "joker" that would "defeat the very objectives of the bill."[158] Philip Levy told the NLRB's general counsel, Calvert Magruder, that "our knowledge of the . . . restricted economic view of many of our federal judges, and of the animus of the employers' associations, should be sufficient warning of the grave danger in having terms of this type in the Wagner Bill."[159] He warned that

. . . employers all over the country would be rushing to the Board and its agents with complaints against all the labor unions which attempt to organize their plants. Organized

155. *Ibid.*, p. 31. Keyserling claims that Joe Robinson "didn't want to embarrass the members of the Senate with having to declare themselves" on Senator Wagner's bill. *Ibid.*, pp. 31–32. On this incident, see also Leon Keyserling, "The Wagner Act: Its Origin and Current Significance," *The George Washington Law Review*, vol. 29, no. 2 (December 1960), p. 202 and Bernstein, *The New Deal Collective Bargaining Policy, op. cit.*, p. 114.

156. Bernstein, *The New Deal Collective Bargaining Policy, op. cit.*, p. 115.

157. Oral history interview with P. Levy, *op. cit.* For the more familiar comments of Senator Walsh, see National Labor Relations Board, *Legislative History of the National Labor Relations Act, op. cit.*, vol. II, pp. 2372–2374 and 2391–2396.

158. NLRB files, memorandum from Laurence A. Knapp to the NLRB, n.d., p. 1.

159. NA, RG25, memorandum from P. Levy to Calvert Magruder, April

activity by the various employers' associations in this respect is well-nigh inevitable. The Board will have to exercise its subpoena power and may well have to probe into the internal affairs of labor union[s] . . . . a wealth of litigation on complaints of this type is to be expected. On the other hand, if the Board should become unfavorable to organized labor, because of unfortunate appointments or of a hostile administration, the power vested in the Board under the bill to prevent this particular unfair labor practice would constitute the Board the most dangerous instrumentality for the suppression of labor activity that I can conceive of under our present system of Government. We have had an example in the automobile industry of the operation of a settlement which prohibits "coercion from any source", reduces these vital economic struggles to gentlemanly discussions about ice water and annual picnics, and imposes by force of Government a particular form of labor organization.[160]

Levy proposed that, "if a substitute is essential as a face-saving device," the board "write into the statute the practice now pursued by this Board, and refuse a vote in elections or reinstatement to former positions to employees who have been guilty of violence as found by the Board."[161] No face-saving was necessary, however. The Tydings amendment was defeated by a vote of fifty to twenty-one. The Senate one hour later that same day,[162] May 16, 1935—only one day after Senator Wagner had brought his bill to the floor—passed S.1958 by a vote of sixty-three to twelve. Irving Bernstein has analyzed these Senate debates in his authoritative study of the legislative history of the Wagner Act:

> The speed with which the debate proceeded, the feebleness of the opposition, and the preponderance of the vote exceeded Wagner's expectations. . . . The influence of labor was at its height and Senators who had little enthusiasm for S.1958 feared to face the AFL at the polls with a negative vote on

6, 1935, p. 4. Records of NLRB II, Legal Division, office of the general counsel, Calvert Magruder, memoranda and miscellaneous file.

160. *Ibid.*, p. 5.

161. *Ibid.*, p. 6.

162. J. Joseph Huthmacher, *Senator Robert Wagner: And the Rise of Urban Liberalism* (New York: Atheneum, 1968), p. 196.

their records. The White House, moreover, no longer blocked the way. Second, many Senators, convinced that the bill was unconstitutional, shifted the onus of its defeat to the Supreme Court. While gaining labor's political support, they felt certain that the measure would not take effect since employers would withhold compliance until the court declared it void.

In view of the large issues at stake, the "debate" in the Senate was a disappointment. This was due, first, to the fact that the bill had been discussed for more than a year in Congress, in the press, and over the radio and had been the subject of a flood of congressional mail. When the Senators entered the chamber they already knew how they would vote. Since this was recognized by both sides, neither sought needless debate. The second factor was that the opposition lacked a champion.[163]

The hearings before the House Committee on Labor "were only a pale reflection of those held by the Senate and the arguments were echoes."[164] On May 20, 1935 the House Committee reported the Wagner bill (numbered HR.7978 in the House) exactly as the Senate had passed it except that, after consulting with President Roosevelt "in reference to this,"[165] Committee Chairman Connery (described by Leon Keyserling as being highly responsive to Secretary of Labor Perkins)[166] induced his committee to place the board under the control of the Department of Labor.

On May 24, 1935 President Roosevelt called Senator Wagner, Miss Perkins, Donald Richberg, Assistant Attorney General Harold Stephens, William Green, Sidney Hillman, and John L. Lewis to a White House conference[167] during which "Wagner and Richberg debated the measure."[168] At this conference, possibly because of the impending Supreme Court decision in the *Schechter*

163. Bernstein, *The New Deal Collective Bargaining Policy, op. cit.*, pp. 116–117.
164. *Ibid.*, p. 117.
165. National Labor Relations Board, *Legislative History of the National Labor Relations Act, op. cit.*, vol. II, p. 3206.
166. Keyserling, *op. cit.*, p. 207.
167. Bernstein, *The New Deal Collective Bargaining Policy, op. cit.*, p. 118.
168. Schlesinger, *The Coming of the New Deal, op. cit.*, p. 406.

Poultry Corporation case[169] and possibly because it had become clear to the president "that the bill would be forced to a decision by its sponsor and that it would pass both houses of Congress overwhelmingly whether he endorsed it or not,"[170] Roosevelt "made it at last clear that he wanted the Wagner bill in some form."[171] Three days later, the Supreme Court in its *Schechter Poultry Corporation*[172] decision "knocked down with a series of blunt strokes the entire edifice of the NRA."[173] The New Deal's "Black Monday" brought joy to Justice Brandeis:

> The old Justice had rejoiced in Hughes' opinion; he had noted on the draft, "This is clear and strong—and marches to the inevitable doom." Now he said triumphantly to Corcoran [an advisor to President Roosevelt], "This is the end of this business of centralization, and I want you to go back and tell the President that we're not going to let this government centralize everything. It's come to an end."[174]

The Supreme Court's decision had a shock effect on the proponents of the Wagner legislation and the bill was brought back to the House Labor Committee for reexamination. With the assistance of Philip Levy and Calvert Magruder of the NLRB and Leon Keyserling, the bill's declaration of policy was revised "to emphasize the effect of labor disputes on interstate commerce and to de-emphasize the mere economic effects which had been rejected by the court."[175] After a period of indecision and fear "that legislation on the verge of enactment would be snatched away,"[176] the President announced his post-NRA policy:

169. Bernstein, *The New Deal Collective Bargaining Policy, op. cit.*, p. 118.
170. Keyserling, *op. cit.*, p. 203.
171. Schlesinger, *The Coming of the New Deal, op. cit.*, p. 406.
172. *Schechter Poultry Corporation* v. *United States*, 295 U.S. 495 (1935).
173. Schlesinger, *The Politics of Upheaval, op. cit.*, p. 280.
174. *Ibid.*
175. Oral history interview with P. Levy, *op. cit.* Among other things the Supreme Court had found that "The NRA attempt to fix hours and wages in this intrastate business was an invalid exercise of the commerce power over transactions with only an indirect effect upon interstate commerce." Bernstein, *The New Deal Collective Bargaining Policy, op. cit.*, p. 120.
176. Bernstein, *The New Deal Collective Bargaining Policy, op. cit.*, p. 121.

In place of the NRA, the President now recommended a program looking, not to central control of the economy, but to the patrolling of separate sectors by separate laws. Speaking with a decisiveness new that session, he called for [among other things] the passage of the Wagner bill to replace Section 7(a) . . . .[177]

The House Labor Committee issued its second report incorporating the new policy section on June 10, 1935. The opposition to the bill, although slight, was centered on four issues: constitutionality, the location of the board in the Department of Labor, the "coercion from any source" amendment, and the appropriate bargaining unit question. In Philip Levy's opinion, the *Schechter* decision persuaded most lawyers and most members of Congress that the Wagner bill was unconstitutional so that "the opposition just folded up."[178] After Representatives Robert Ramspeck of Georgia and Vito Marcantonio of New York (whose minority report on the House Labor Committee had been prepared by Leon Keyserling)[179] objected to the board being placed in the Department of Labor and, after it became apparent that William Green's support of the secretary of labor was merely a "tactical gesture,"[180] the House voted 130 to 48 to make the NLRB an independent agency.[181] The "coercion from any source" amendment was then defeated without a roll call vote.[182]

Over the objections of Chairman Connery, Representative Ramspeck then introduced an amendment to bar the NLRB from ordering a multiemployer unit.[183] Although the NLRB's general counsel preferred to maintain the board's wide discretion on unit

177. Schlesinger, *The Politics of Upheaval, op. cit.*, p. 290.
178. Oral history interview with P. Levy, *op. cit.*
179. Oral history interview with L. Keyserling, *op. cit.*, p. 22 and Keyserling, *op. cit.*, p. 207.
180. Oral history interview with L. Keyserling, *op. cit.*, p. 23.
181. Bernstein, *The New Deal Collective Bargaining Policy, op. cit.*, p. 124.
182. *Ibid.*
183. The original language of the Wagner bill read: "The Board shall decide in each case whether, in order to effectuate the policies of this Act, the unit appropriate for the purposes of collective bargaining shall be the employer unit, craft unit, plant unit, or other unit." (See National Labor Relations Board, *Legislative History of the National Labor Relations Act, op. cit.*, vol. II, p. 2291.) Representative

determination under the bill, he concluded that, since "the Board has gotten along two years without having prescribed a unit larger than the employees of a single employer," the Ramspeck amendment was hardly fatal to the bill.[184] He recommended that "the amendment certainly should not be thrown out if . . . the passage of the bill would thereby be endangered."[185] Senator Wagner had said that the bargaining unit section of the bill had given the drafters "more trouble than any other" and that "neither he nor the board derived much satisfaction from it."[186] Employers were not alone in their fear of the appropriate unit provisions of the Wagner bill: "The craft leaders of the AFL, harassed by emerging industrial unionism that was later to erupt into the CIO, were similarly distraught lest an unsympathetic board join these forces against them."[187] Senator Wagner felt obliged to reassure the executive council of the AFL on June 6, 1935 that his bill would not destroy craft organizations.[188] Under these circumstances, the House adopted the Ramspeck amendment 127 to 87.[189] The Wagner bill was then passed without a roll call vote on June 19, 1935.

By June 26, 1935 the House and Senate had resolved their disagreement on the amendments to the Wagner bill[190] and the

---

Ramspeck's amendment added the proviso "that no unit shall include the employees of more than one employer." Ramspeck did not intend to interfere with those situations where multiemployer bargaining was preferred but he did want to prevent the Board "from ordering it." Bernstein, *The New Deal Collective Bargaining Policy, op. cit.,* p. 125.

184. NLRB files, analysis of House amendments to S.1958, Calvert Magruder, n.d., p. 7.

185. *Ibid.*

186. Bernstein, *The New Deal Collective Bargaining Policy, op. cit.,* p. 125.

187. *Ibid.*

188. *Ibid.,* p. 126.

189. *Ibid.*

190. Representative Ramspeck stated that "we have worked out a compromise to [his] amendment which accomplished, in my opinion, exactly the object I had in mind, which is to limit the jurisdiction of the Board in setting up units appropriate for collective bargaining, to plant units, craft units, or employer units, the employer unit being the largest unit constituted." The compromise was to substitute the words "or appropriate subdivision thereof" for the words

President Roosevelt signs the National Industrial Recovery Act. Senator Wagner is second from left. (United Press International)

General Hugh S. Johnson, U.S.A. (Ret.), Administrator of the NRA, gives his views to a group of prominent business leaders in June 1933. (Wide World Photos)

Donald Richberg, NRA General Counsel. (United Press International)

Insignia for NRA followers. Charles T. Coiner of Philadelphia, Pa., creator of the Blue Eagle. (Wide World Photos)

Milton Handler, General Counsel of the National Labor Board. (Photograph c. 1974.)

Labor strife threatens the Recovery program: Pennsylvania National Guardsmen watch the movements of soft-coal strikers after six strikers were shot in labor disturbances in August 1933. (Wide World Photos)

The National Labor Board after six months. Seated (from left): Louis Kirstein, Chairman Wagner, Dr. Leo Wolman. Standing (from left): William Green, George Berry, Pierre S. du Pont, Father Francis J. Haas. (Wide World Photos)

Ernest Weir and Senator Wagner after an October 1933 strike-ending agreement that was soon repudiated by the company. (United Press International)

Recovery trouble, March 1934. (United Press International)

The old National Labor Relations Board confers with the directors of its regional boards. Seated in front is the national board: Chairman Lloyd Garrison (center) with Harry A. Millis (left) and Edwin S. Smith (right). (United Press International)

Francis Biddle, who replaced Lloyd Garrison as Chairman of the old National Labor Relations Board. (United Press International)

Budd workers vote in Philadelphia in March 1934 in an NRA-directed election under President Roosevelt's automobile settlement allowing for proportional representation—a serious blow to the authority of the NLB. (Wide World Photos)

The Schechter Brothers test the NRA. From left: Joseph Schechter, Joseph Heller (attorney for the Schechters), and Martin, Aaron, and Alexander Schechter. (Wide World Photos)

Senator Wagner, William Green, and Frances Perkins at the Senate Labor Committee hearings on the Wagner Bill, 12 March 1935. (Wide World Photos)

Labor at the barricade:
After NRA, June 1935.
(United Press International)

Philip Levy, NLRB attorney who was a major contributor to the substantive provisions of the Wagner Act.
(Recent photograph courtesy
of Mrs. Philip Levy)

The Wagner Act NLRB. From left: Edwin S. Smith, Donald Wakefield Smith, J. Warren Madden. (Courtesy of the NLRB)

Heber Blankenhorn, the NLRB's "professional detective" who "practically single handed" led the drive for a civil liberties investigation by LaFollette as another way to establish the constitutionality of the Wagner Act. (Courtesy of Gerhard Van Arkel)

John M. Carmody, a member of the first Wagner Act NLRB testifying before the LaFollette Committee on 11 April 1936 concerning "rumors" that "the Ford Company is shot through with labor spies." (Wide World Photos)

The Justices of the Supreme Court. From left: Justices Cardozo, Stone, Sutherland, Van-Devanter, Chief Justice Hughes, Brandeis, Butler and Roberts. Justice McReynolds is absent. (Wide World Photos)

Sitdown strikers at the Chevrolet plant in Flint, Michigan, in December 1936 at the start of a 43-day strike of auto workers. (Wide World Photos)

Charles Fahy, General Counsel of the NLRB and the board's chief legal strategist in the constitutional cases. (United Press International)

David Saposs, Chief of the NLRB's Division of Economic Research. (Photograph courtesy of Harry Brickman)

NLRB Conference in Washington, D.C., 15 November 1938. (Photograph courtesy of Owsley Vose and George Turitz)

key to above.

1. Thomas Emerson
2. Unidentified
3. Robert Watts
4. Charles Fahy
5. Donald Wakefield Smith
6. J. Warren Madden
7. Edwin S. Smith
8. Nathan Witt
9. Beatrice Stern
10. George Pratt
11. William Ringer
12. Earl Bellman
13. Towne Nylander
14. Unidentified
15. Gerhard Van Arkel
16. David Persinger
17. William Walsh
18. Fred Mett
19. Samuel Zack
20. Unidentified
21. Unidentified
21a. David Saposs
22. Katherine Ellickson
23. Elizabeth Bliss
24. Paul Nachtman
25. Miriam Camp
26. Unidentified
27. Richard Perkins
28. Sara Gamm
29. Eugene Thorrens
30. Charles Whittemore
31. Charles Persons
32. Thomas Wilson
33. Webster Powell
34. Anne Freeling (Schlesinger)
35. Henry Kent
36. George Koplow
37. Charles Douds
38. Jack Krug
39. Joseph Hoskins
40. Jack Dorsey
41. Alice Nelson
42. Virginia Leary
43. William Aicher
44. Unidentified
45. Jacob Blum
46. Edward Schneider
47. Alice Rosseter
48. Bennett Schauffler
49. Harry Jones
50. W. G. Stewart Sherman
51. Robert Rissman
52. Garnett Patterson
53. Elinore Herrick
    (Tentative Identification)
54. William Seagle
55. Alvin Rockwell
56. Frank Bowen
57. Daniel Harrington
58. William Consedine
59. Unidentified
60. Martin Wagner
61. Unidentified
62. Ralph Winkler
63. Unidentified
64. Alan Perl
65. Howard Friedman
66. Bernard Alpert
67. Lewis Gill
68. Unidentified
69. Joseph Robison
70. Margaret Farmer
71. Robert Burstein
72. Richard Salant
73. Unidentified
74. Frank Bloom
75. Edna Loeb (Friedman)
76. Lester Asher
77. Harry Brown
78. David Rein
79. Jack Kaufman
80. R Marsden
81. William Stix
82. David Shaw
83. John Lindsay
84. Ray Compton
85. Guy Farmer
86. Philip Phillips
87. Unidentified
88. Unidentified
89. Unidentified
90. Unidentified
91. George Turitz
92. Francis Hoague
93. Solaman Lippman
94. Charles Logan
95. Unidentified
96. Unidentified
97. James Paradise
98. Tilford Dudley
99. Edward Grandison Smith
100. Horace Ruckel
101. Harold Cranefield
102. Henry Winters
103. Nathaniel Clark
104. David Morse
105. Charles Graham
106. Aaron Warner
107. Unidentified
108. Ida Klaus
109. Paul Kuelthau
110. A. Howard Myers
111. Drexel Sprecher
112. Leonard Bjork
113. Unidentified
114. Warren Woods
115. Edwin Elliott
116. Wallace Cohen
117. Arnold Cutler
118. Malcolm Mason
119. Louis Libbin
120. Unidentified
121. Unidentified
122. Martin Raphael
123. A. Bruce Hunt
124. Robert Kleeb
125. David McCalmont
126. Marcel Mallet-Prevost
127. Howard Lebaron
128. Warren Sharfman
129. Lawrence Broadwin
130. Henry Lehman
131. Mary Schleifer
132. Abraham Kaminstein
133. Selma Rice (Rein)
134. Lyle Cooper
135. Bernard Freund
136. Victor Pascal
137. Gustaf Erickson
138. Alan Rosenberg
139. Russel Packard
140. Unidentified
141. Fannie Boyls
142. Bliss Daffan
143. Frank Paone
144. Sylvester Garrett
145. George Rose
146. Carol Agger (Fortas)
147. Herbert Glaser
148. Robert Cowdrill
149. Owsley Vose
150. Walter Nolte
151. Unidentified
152. Margaret Holmes
153. Wesley McCune
154. Jack Karro
155. Harry Cooper
156. Martin Kurasch
157. Andrew Toth
158. Harry Roberts
159. Sol Davison

president signed the National Labor Relations Act on July 5, 1935. The act had passed, however, with only a "tepid public blessing"[191] from the president—presidential behavior which Leon Keyserling described as "almost inexplicable and in all respects extraordinary."[192] What is certain is that the NRA had been in a condition of "weariness and irresolution" since mid-1934.[193] The partial economic recovery of 1934 had reduced the sense of national crisis which had provided the incentive for cooperation with the NRA:

So long as the sense of emergency gave the public interest a chance to win out over special interests, NRA worked. With a touch of recovery, the sense of emergency receded, and private interests came to the fore . . . . [and] tempted private groups to concentrate on what each could get for itself. In the end, NRA foundered on the problem of asserting a vague public interest against the specific and well-focused demands of self-serving private interests.[194]

Although President Roosevelt seemed to be pursuing a pro-business policy early in 1935 ("perhaps because he had no better ideas of his own"),[195] organized business was one of the most important private interest groups which had asserted "a revised self-confidence and a renewed mistrust of Washington."[196] The split between the president and business became apparent in the spring of 1935.

The New Deal, he [the president] believed, had saved the position and the profits of the businessmen. He had forgiven their errors of the past and their lack of ideas for the future. And now organized business was assuming what he regarded

"other unit" in the original language. *Ibid.*, p. 127. For Ramspeck's comment, see National Labor Relations Board, *Legislative History of the National Labor Relations Act, op. cit.*, vol. II, p. 3265. For the complete conference report see *ibid.*, pp. 3252–3258.

191. Keyserling, *op. cit.*, p. 203.
192. *Ibid.*, p. 202.
193. Schlesinger, *The Coming of the New Deal, op. cit.*, p. 166.
194. *Ibid.*, p. 176.
195. Schlesinger, *The Politics of Upheaval, op. cit.*, p. 213.
196. Schlesinger, *The Coming of the New Deal, op. cit.*, p. 471.

147

as a posture of indiscriminate, stupid, and vindictive opposition.[197]

The administration, moreover, was convinced that the courts were bent on a "judicial nullification" of the New Deal.[198] But it was the Supreme Court, ironically, that delivered the president from the "NRA mess"[199] and his dependence on the cooperation of business and left him with little but the Wagner bill to meet the challenge of labor unrest.[200] Events imposed policy on the president and forced the New Deal to stop viewing "the governmental process as an exercise in conversion and cooperation" and to start seeing it as an "exercise in litigation and combat."[201] It was a shift that numbered General Johnson and Donald Richberg among its casualties and that placed the NLRB in control (if only an uneasy control) of the new national labor policy. The work of the pre-Wagner Act labor boards was now complete.

197. Schlesinger, *The Politics of Upheaval, op. cit.*, p. 273.
198. *Ibid.*, pp. 448 and 452.
199. *Ibid.*, p. 289.
200. Bernstein, *The New Deal Collective Bargaining Policy, op. cit.*, pp. 128 and 131.
201. Schlesinger, *The Politics of Upheaval, op. cit.*, pp. 264 and 395.

5 The Wagner Act NLRB
and the Constitutional Test

Few people were anxious to serve on the NLRB in 1935 since the record of the Supreme Court in passing judgment on New Deal legislation, particularly the *Schechter Poultry Corporation* case,[1] left little doubt in most minds that the Wagner Act would not survive the inevitable Supreme Court test. Almost two months passed after the signing of the Wagner Act before President Roosevelt named the members of the new labor board[2]: Joseph Warren Madden, chairman, John M. Carmody, and Edwin S. Smith, a holdover from the old NLRB. In the opinion of *Business Week*, "the feeling is that the President had to hunt a long time and drop down below the upper bracket to find anyone who would

---

1. *Schechter Poultry Corporation* v. *United States*, 295 U.S. 495 (1935).
2. The appointments of the three board members were confirmed by the Senate on August 24, 1935 and became effective on August 27, 1935. Chairman Madden's appointment was for five years, Carmody's for three, and Smith's for one. *The New York Times*, August 24, 1935, p. 5, col. 4 and August 25, 1935, p. 27, col. 1. In June 1935 Secretary of Labor Perkins prepared the following list of "Possible Appointments for the Labor Relations Board" for President Roosevelt with a few personal observations: "1. Frank Murphy of Detroit; 2. Ray Stevens—late of Siam; 3. Raymond Ingersoll, of Brooklyn, New York; 4. Robert Bruere—an extremely good negotiator—New York State; 5. Sara Wambaugh—expert on plebiscites and taking of elections. Comes from Ohio—very solid, substantial, authoritative and calming type of person; 6. Harold Stevens—Assistant Attorney General; 7. Thomas Woodward—of the Shipping Board; 8. William Davis—formerly of the N.R.A. in charge of Compliance at one time. Very successful in negotiating and arrangements. Very, very fair but liberal; 9. Lloyd Garrison—good but not so practical as we

take a chance, the past history of labor boards being what it is."[3]

The new chairman certainly had little knowledge of either labor relations or labor law. J. Warren Madden was a professor of law at the University of Pittsburg specializing in the law of property and torts at the time of his appointment to the NLRB.[4] He had what he recalls as only an "intelligent citizen's" understanding of the New Deal and the Wagner Act.

> I didn't have much of an idea of what was in the Wagner Act, but I had the general idea that it had to do with the right

---

thought but has an open mind; 10. George Stocking—now on the Petroleum Board. Has proved very successful—has a fine relationship; 11. Will French—former Industrial Commissioner of California, Republican, liberal, practical; 12. George Bell—great experience as Impartial Chairman of the Men's Clothing Industry; 13. George Alger—New York City—Impartial Chairman in several needle trades—good job—fine man—Republican; 14. Colonel Frank Douglas—of Oklahoma—now on the Textile Labor Relations Board; 15. Josephine Rocke; 16. Jacob Billikopf—has been head of the Philadelphia Regional Labor Board—very successful—nice personality—head of the Jewish Charities; 17. Walton Hamilton—of the N.R.A.; 18. Douglas Brown—now at Princeton and in charge of an organization known as Personnel Management; 19. John Carmody—on the Railway Mediation Board; 20. Lindsay Rogers." Memo from F. Perkins to F.D.R., June 20, 1935. Franklin D. Roosevelt Library, Hyde Park, New York, Official File 716.

3. "Six Whom Business Watches," *Business Week*, no. 313, August 31, 1935, p. 11.

4. Madden was born in Damascus, Illinois on January 17, 1890. He was graduated from the University of Illinois in 1911 and received the degree of Doctor of Jurisprudence from the University of Chicago in 1914. From 1914 to the time of his appointment to the NLRB, Madden was a law professor at the universities of Oklahoma, Ohio State, West Virginia, and Pittsburgh. He was dean of the College of Law at West Virginia University from 1921 to 1927. He was also an advisor to the American Law Institute on the subject of torts and property. He was the author of a textbook and a casebook on the law of domestic relations and was the editor of two casebooks dealing with real property. For a summary of Madden's background, see *Smith Committee Hearings, op. cit.*, vol. 13, pp. 2575–2576. See also oral history interview with J. Warren Madden, October 28, 1968, p. 20., on file in the Labor Management Documentation Center, ILR, Cornell.

of employees to organize unions and join unions and so on. But my ideas about it were very superficial.[5]

When, prior to his appointment to the board, Madden told Secretary of Labor Perkins that he "just didn't know anything about labor law [and] that [he] didn't know anything really about this board and the statute," Miss Perkins reassured him by saying "Well, that is fine. You will not have any preconceptions about it and you can just start it from the ground up and learn it as you go."[6]

Madden had been recommended by the former chairmen of the old NLRB, Lloyd Garrison and Francis Biddle, and by Charlton Ogburn, counsel for the AFL, each of whom had come to know Madden under somewhat fortuitous circumstances. In 1933 Governor Pinchot of Pennsylvania asked a University of Pittsburgh economist to recommend "Pittsburgh lawyers of liberal turns of mind" to serve on a commission to study the use of private police by the coal and steel companies in Pennsylvania. Although the professor was not familiar with any practicing Pittsburgh lawyers, Madden was his next-door neighbor and "just on that basis" Madden was appointed to the commission. One of the other members was Francis Biddle and the two men became "quite well acquainted."[7]

During the summer of 1933, Madden was a visiting professor at the Stanford University Law School where he also became well acquainted with another visiting law professor from the University of Wisconsin, Lloyd Garrison.[8] Later, in 1934, Madden was

5. Oral history interview with J. W. Madden, *op. cit.*, p. 13.
6. *Ibid.*, pp 20–21.
7. This story is recounted in *ibid.*, pp. 13–16. In August 1934, a staff member from the old NLRB recommended Madden to Harry A. Millis for the job of regional director in Pittsburg. This staff member described Madden as liberal, fair-minded, judicial, and as a man of common sense. NA, RG25, memorandum from R. Gordon Wagenet to H. A. Millis, August 29, 1934. Board members, records of Harry A. Millis concerning organization and personnel of the NLRB, 1934–1935. Biddle wanted to appoint Madden to the Pittsburgh regional board in the spring of 1935, referring to him as "an excellent man." NA, RG25, letter from F. Biddle to John J. Kane, February 14, 1935 and memorandum from F. Biddle to the file, March 6, 1935. Records of NLRB, office of the secretary, Region IV, Pittsburg, 1934–1937.
8. Oral history interview with J. W. Madden, *op. cit.*, p. 18.

appointed as the impartial arbitrator of a wage dispute on the Pittsburgh street railway system. He was selected by the company-appointed arbitrator who was a former law student of Madden's and by the union-appointed arbitrator who had served with Madden on the Pinchot commission. Charlton Ogburn "at somebody's suggestion . . . had dropped in at these hearings in Pittsburgh, listened to them for a time . . . and apparently was impressed by them."[9]

The new chairman was sensitive to the disappointment which the staff of the NLRB felt at the appointment of an unknown.

> There was considerable consternation in the staff of the Board. The enactment of the Act had raised their hopes to a high pitch, the delay in appointing the Board had been frustrating, and now, for the office which they regarded as second to none in importance, they got someone they had never even heard of.[10]

Yet, J. Warren Madden, considered at first little more than "a name that was pulled out of a hat,"[11] would be remembered by his staff as the man who dominated the board "intellectually" and "morally."[12] The people who worked with him during the five turbulent years of his chairmanship think of him with affection and respect as an intelligent and able lawyer, but mostly as a completely honest, dedicated, kind, and generous human being.[13] Chairman Madden's basic approach to the Wagner Act and to the operations of the NLRB has been most accurately described as

9. *Ibid.*, pp. 16–18.

10. J. Warren Madden, "The Origin and Early History of the National Labor Relations Board," *The George Washington Law Review*, vol. 29, no. 2 (December 1960), p. 242.

11. Oral history interview with Meta Barghausen, March 19, 1969, pp. 5–6, on file in the Labor Management Documentation Center, ILR, Cornell. (Mrs. Barghausen has been the personal secretary of all the NLRB chairmen from Madden to the present.)

12. Oral history interview with T. I. Emerson, *op. cit.*, March 19, 1970, p. 102.

13. See the oral history interviews with Harry Brickman (retired chief of the NLRB's Operations Analysis Section), March 18, 1969, p. 30; Charles Fahy, July 23, 1968, p. 17; T. I. Emerson, *op. cit.*, p. 102; and Estelle Frankfurter, *op. cit.*, p. 108, all on file in the Labor Management Documentation Center, ILR, Cornell.

that of "a good and sincere civil liberties lawyer."[14] Nathan Witt, a holdover from the old NLRB, who became the secretary of the board in 1937 and who was in the middle of the controversy that raged about the board during the latter years of Madden's chairmanship, has provided a most astute and revealing analysis of Madden as the chairman of the NLRB:

> ... he was more or less in a class by himself ... of the public figures I have known or worked with and known to any substantial extent. He was basically a conservative man but with a strong feel for the decency in what's called liberalism, certainly liberal as far as civil liberties are concerned and certainly a conservative as far as basic economic issues are concerned. And as far as politics go—using the word in the usual sense of knowing your way around, how to maneuver, how to operate with people on the Hill and with the White House, all that—he was certainly at the beginning rather on the naive side, principally because he was so honest and straightforward and direct. So how he got by as long as he did is still a puzzle to me.[15]

Madden's approach to the internal operations of the NLRB did not receive unanimous support from the staff of the board, however. The chairman's belief, for example, that the political views or ideology of a board employee were "none of my [Madden's] business as long as he was working for the objectives of the National Labor Relations Act,"[16] would become a matter of great divisiveness within the NLRB just a few years later when the board came under severe attack because of alleged communist infiltration. (Certain staff members felt that Chairman Madden was "absolutely innocent in the sense that [he was] utterly unsophisticated about what was going on" [and that] "the most important problem that the Board had was its inability to understand what was going on among the staff.")[17]

14. Oral history interview with E. S. Smith, *op. cit.*, p. 20.
15. Oral history interview with Nathan Witt, February 17, 1969, p. 14, on file in the Labor Management Documentation Center, *op. cit.*, Cornell.
16. Oral history interview with J. W. Madden, *op. cit.*, p. 70.
17. Oral history interview with Ida Klaus, February 27, 1969, pp. 17, 39–40, on file in the Labor Management Documentation Center,

Chairman Madden's political inexperience, as well as his personal beliefs, seems to have influenced his attitude toward the board's relations with the White House:

... my [Madden's] attitude with regard to the president was that if the president would let us alone . . . we had better let him alone. That any idea of the chairman of the board making his presence felt in the White House whenever he could was just completely wrong. That if you had that kind of contact with the president, the president would occasionally at least, or perhaps frequently, in reaction to what was being said in the newspapers and the magazines about the board, would say, "I see you're having trouble about this and this. Don't you think you better do that?" And then you're stuck with it. . . . That if the president would let us alone . . . that we would let him alone and not get his undeliberated reactions and then feel as if we had to follow them or be embarrassed by not following them.[18]

John M. Carmody, on the other hand, was less the legal theorist and more the man of action. He was appointed to the NLRB on Senator Wagner's "strong recommendation as a solid man who had his feet on the ground and had a lot of experience in labor relations."[19] Carmody, thought by some to be "untactfully outspoken," had worked as a young man in steel mills and coal mines before becoming superintendent of a clothing factory and, eventually, an industrial engineer. He had been an editor of *Factory* and *Coal Age* magazines, chief engineer of the Civil Works Administration, chairman of the National Bituminous Coal Labor

---

ILR, Cornell. Miss Klaus, who was a board review attorney in 1937 and solicitor when she left the board in 1954, believed that, whereas Madden was honest, "straightforward," and dedicated, he was also "quite naive" and although a good chairman, "he wasn't good enough in this respect." *Ibid.*, p. 40. Another NLRB staff member, Estelle Frankfurter, recalled that "some of us . . . thought that there was too much leeway and too much rope given. . . ." Oral history interview with Estelle Frankfurter, February 4, 1970, pp. 107–108, on file in the Labor Management Documentation Center, ILR, Cornell.

18. Oral history interview with J. W. Madden, *op. cit.*, pp. 163–164.
19. Oral history interview with P. Levy, *op. cit.*

Board, and was serving as a member of the National Mediation Board when he was appointed to the NLRB.[20]

Board member Carmody was committed by his experience to the mediation approach and he "was not particularly sympathetic to what he regarded as a lot of legal rigmarole."[21] Chairman Madden remembered him as an "energetic Irishman" and as an activist who wanted "to go out and crack people's heads together," but "instead of that here we are, cagily planning legal strategy, and he thought it was terrible."[22] Carmody, impatient with the NLRB's preoccupation with legal strategy and with the inability of the board to do much to enforce the Wagner Act until the Supreme Court decisions of April 1937, resigned after one year with the NLRB on August 31, 1936.[23] He was replaced by Donald Wakefield Smith on September 23, 1936.[24] (There are few records available which would reveal D. W. Smith's role in the affairs of the NLRB. Interviews with those who worked with him at the board, however, indicate that he was appointed at the request of Senator Guffey of Pennsylvania whose niece was married to Smith and that he was not equal to the other members of the board in ability but was happy to be in the position and merely went along with the board's decisions, particularly those of Chairman Madden.)[25]

20. See "Six Whom Business Watches," *Business Week*, no. 313, August 31, 1935, p. 11 and *The New York Times*, August 24, 1935, p. 5, col. 4.
21. Oral history interview with P. Levy, *op. cit.*
22. Oral history interview with J. W. Madden, *op. cit.*, p. 95. See also oral history interview with Nathan Witt, *op. cit.*, pp. 36–37.
23. Madden, *op. cit.*, p. 249.
24. Donald Wakefield Smith was born in Homestead, Pennsylvania on November 5, 1899. He received an A.B. degree from the University of Pittsburgh in 1922 and a law degree from Georgetown University in 1925. Smith practiced labor and immigration law in Washington, New York City, and Philadelphia from 1925 to 1936 when he was appointed to the board. The full text of *The New York Times* article announcing his appointment said only that "President Roosevelt today appointed Donald Wakefield Smith, a Washington attorney, as a member of the National Labor Relations Board. He will succeed John M. Carmody who resigned about a month ago to accept an appointment with the Rural Electrification Administration." *The New York Times*, September 22, 1936, p. 8, col. 4.
25. See oral history interviews with Louis Silverberg, March 6, 1970,

The holdover member of the NLRB, Edwin S. Smith, later to become a controversial figure at the board, was already being characterized by a leading business magazine as "an ex-personnel manager who fights big business" and as a man whose "intemperate, radical, public utterances" were being openly criticized as "not in keeping with the character of a semi-judicial government officer."[26]

A Reorganization for the Constitutional Test

Chairman Madden was the only member of the original board and its staff who had not worked for the government under the NIRA and who had "no direct acquaintance with the Government's handling of labor problems."[27] Under the provisions of the Wagner Act, the NLRB had inherited the experienced staff of the old NLRB and a working regional board organization as well. Francis Biddle, chairman of the old NLRB, and his staff had been laying the groundwork for the new NLRB weeks before the Wagner Act was passed. In board meetings and in conferences with regional directors, the old board studied and made recommendations concerning personnel changes, the reorganization of the national board and its regional offices, budgetary requirements, procedures which might be followed under the Wagner bill for hearing board cases and enforcing board decisions, and the need for near perfection in the selection and prosecution of the first test cases to be brought to the courts.[28]

pp. 9–10; Marcel Mallet-Prevost, September 4, 1970, pp. 18–19; Gerhard Van Arkel, op. cit., pp. 10–11; J. W. Madden, op. cit., p. 98; E. S. Smith, op. cit., pp. 69–71; and Nathan Witt, op. cit., pp. 37–38, all on file in the Labor Management Documentation Center, ILR, Cornell.

26. "Six Whom Business Watches," *Business Week*, August 31, 1935, p. 11.
27. J. Warren Madden, "Birth of the Board," in Louis G. Silverberg, ed., *The Wagner Act: After Ten Years* (Washington: BNA, 1945), p. 36.
28. See NLRB files, memorandum from F. Biddle to B. Wolf, B. Stern, and P. Herzog, May 18, 1935; a series of memoranda concerning the

Throughout the summer of 1935, moreover, after the Wagner Act had been passed but before the new board had been appointed, staff members of the old board prepared a series of detailed legal memoranda dealing with the bargaining unit, rules of evidence, administrative findings, the choice of test cases, the use of economic data to establish the constitutionality of the NLRA, and mediation and settlement activities under the new act.[29] The staff of the old NLRB had also made substantial headway in drafting new rules and regulations for the more formal procedure required by the Wagner Act and in preparing instructions for members of the staff detailing their duties under the new procedures and the new law.[30] Because of the organizational work of these experienced staff members and the existence of a complete regional

---

personnel of the regional labor boards, May 21, 1935; a series of memoranda from the administrative staff to the board ("National Labor Relations Board Organization: Suggestions," May 23, 1935, "Regional Board Organization: Suggestions," May 23, 1935, "Procedure," May 21, 1935, and "Washington Staff," n.d.); minutes of a conference with regional directors, June 4, 1935.

29. See NLRB files, "Findings," memorandum from I. S. Dorfman to the general counsel, June 29, 1935. See also NA, RG25, "Memoranda," memorandum from General Counsel Charles Fahy to all attorneys, September 26, 1935. Records of NLRB II, Legal Division, Litigation Section, files of Daniel M. Lyons, senior litigation attorney, legal memoranda file; NA, RG25, "The Bargaining Unit," memorandum from G. L. Patterson to the national labor relations board, July 3, 1935. Records of NLRB II, Legal Division, office of the general counsel, files of Calvert Magruder, Magruder personal file; NA, RG25 "Mediation and Settlement Activities Under the New Act," memorandum from E. S. Smith to Messrs. C. Magruder, B. Wolf, T. Emerson, R. Watts, and N. Witt, August 19, 1935. Records of NLRB II, Legal Division, office of the general counsel, files of Calvert Magruder, Magruder personal file.

30. Madden in Silverberg, *op. cit.*, p. 36. See also NLRB files, minutes of an executive meeting of the board, May 20, 1936 (a reference to the fact that Philip Levy "was busy all summer working on Board Rules and Regulations"); oral history interviews with T. I. Emerson, *op. cit.*, pp. 49–50 and P. Levy, *op. cit.* There is also evidence indicating that Calvert Magruder and Gerhard Van Arkel, general counsel and staff member of the old NLRB, respectively, worked on the new rules and regulations. NLRB files, "Stipulations," memorandum

setup in the field, the new board was ready to begin its work without much delay. In early September 1935, the board called its regional directors to Washington to discuss the new arrangements with them in preparation for the first cases to be filed under the Wagner Act.[31] Their reaction was not favorable.

The preparatory work of the new board and its Washington staff had been directed toward one overriding objective: establishing the constitutionality of the Wagner Act. Consequently, the board's procedural rules and regulations had been drafted "to give the Washington office very substantial control so that it would be able to formulate the litigation strategy."[32] The board, for example, adopted a policy requiring that a regional board obtain Washington approval before issuing a complaint in any case.[33] The NLRB, in addition, assigned a regional attorney to each regional office to advise the regional director, to draft complaints, interview witnesses, make further investigations, prepare cases for trial, present the board's cases at hearings before trial examiners, and prepare legal briefs or any other required legal documents.[34] The regional attorney, who was now arguably "more of a key figure than the Regional Director,"[35] worked under the direction and control of the general counsel and his staff in Washington.[36] The NLRB also instructed regional directors not to attempt mediation or conciliation without direct authorization from the board.[37] The board's desire for constitutionality resulted

from G. Van Arkel to the NLRB, August 2, 1935. See also NA, RG25, memorandum from C. Magruder to T. Emerson, September 12, 1935. Records of NLRB II, Legal Division, office of the general counsel, Calvert Magruder, Magruder personal file.

31. Oral history interview with J. W. Madden, *op. cit.*, p. 25. See also Madden in Silverberg, *op. cit.*, p. 36.
32. Oral history interview with T. I. Emerson, *op. cit.*, p. 51.
33. *Smith Committee Hearings*, *op. cit.*, vol. 24, part II, pp. 5541–5542.
34. Madden in Silverberg, *op. cit.*, p. 36. See also NLRB files, "Tentative Draft, Instructions to Staff Members," August 29, 1935 and "Instructions to Staff Members," September 17, 1935, pp. 1–26.
35. Oral history interview with T. I. Emerson, *op. cit.*, p. 57.
36. Madden in Silverberg, *op. cit.*, p. 36. See also NLRB files, "Instructions to Staff Members," September 17, 1935, pp. 1–12.
37. NLRB files, "Instructions to Staff Members," September 17, 1935, p. 21 and memorandum from E. M. Herrick to office staff, September 25, 1935.

not only in the centralization of authority in the Washington office but also in a decision that the "place of the lawyers on the staff would be much more important than it had been."[38]

The board and its Washington staff had anticipated that the regional directors (only one of whom was a lawyer) would not be "quite in tune with our ideas of a rigorous law enforcement operation rather than a mediation or conciliation operation."[39] One regional director claimed that his work was now "lamed because of the overload of legalistic forms and phraseology" and that his job was now "much more stilted and formal and stiff. . . ." He felt that "keeping the peace by mediating men back into their work places was always more interesting than gathering facts about law violations and assisting in prosecuting the culprits."[40]

Many of these regional board personnel had been with Senator Wagner's National Labor Board when the objective was the preservation of industrial peace and the means were informal and flexible mediation and conciliation. They had long resisted the centralization of authority in Washington and the continual movement toward the judicial approach and the formalization of procedures.[41] Some of the regional directors believed that labor peace was still the basic objective and that the regional personnel were the ones primarily responsible for achieving it.[42] They were

38. Madden in Silverberg, *op. cit.*, p. 36; NLRB files, letter from L. K. Garrison to J. W. Madden, September 13, 1935 and letter from J. W. Madden to L. K. Garrison, September 16, 1935.
39. Oral history interview with T. I. Emerson, *op. cit.*, p. 55.
40. NA, RG25, memorandum from John P. Boland to B. Wolf, October 23, 1935. Records of NLRB II, office of the secretary, Region III, Buffalo, 1934–1937.
41. See Chapter III, pp. 86–87.
42. Oral history interview with George Pratt, March 18, 1970, pp. 80–81, on file in the Labor Management Documentation Center, ILR, Cornell. As of September 12, 1935, the regional directors were Frank Coffee in Atlanta, Bennet Schauffler in Baltimore, Joseph McCartin in Boston, Rev. John Boland in Buffalo, P. A. Donoghue in Chicago, Ralph Lind in Cleveland, Edwin Elliott in Fort Worth, Robert Cowdrill in Indianapolis, George Pratt in Kansas City, Towne Nylander in Los Angeles, Nathaniel Clark in Milwaukee, Charles Logan in New Orleans, Elinore Herrick in New York, Stanley Root in Philadelphia, Clinton Golden in Pittsburgh, Harold Garvey in St. Louis, R. Gordon Wagenet in San Francisco, and Charles W.

convinced that the Washington office, in stripping the regions of "activities and responsibilities that [they] felt were rightfully [theirs]," had demonstrated little understanding of "what actually goes on in the field offices dealing with problems."[43]

George Pratt who, as secretary of the Kansas City Regional Office, attended the Washington conference of regional directors in September 1935, recalled the dissatisfaction of some of the regional officers:

> ... we were all called back to Washington in probably September 1935 ... and there we were called into a conference. We were to be told how the [National Labor Relations Board] was to be organized .... it was then announced that we would consider the rules and regulations that the Board had drafted and tentatively adopted to govern the activities of the board under the National Labor Relations Act. Thereupon, there was passed out to each of us a folder containing the rules and regulations and ... this was the first time that any of us had seen them. We took some time out to read and study the rules and ... there were a number of us who were quite dismayed when we read them because they seemed ... to do basically two things: one, treat each regional director as merely a messenger boy without having any concern for what each of us considered had been our special and unique contribution and our special value because of our knowledge and relationship to the regions we were working in and second, by the same token, reserved all authority, even for the most minor matters, to the office in Washington. With the experiences that each of us had had in the past ... in the preceding year or 15 months, a group of us felt that this way of doing business was quite impossible and would result in nothing more than immense backlogs, traffic jams, and would prevent our actually accomplishing what we all understood to be the major goal—namely, the preservation of labor peace....[44]

Hope in Seattle. See NLRB files, minutes of the board meeting, September 12, 1935.
43. *Ibid.*, pp. 78–79.
44. *Ibid.*, pp. 74–76.

The new chairman knew that the regional directors "were highly skeptical of the new arrangement."

Being laymen of liberal views, they did not have a high opinion of the usefulness of lawyers who seemed only to have succeeded in getting what the Directors regarded as good laws held unconstitutional. They had been doing the interesting and pleasant work of mediation and persuasion, and of arranging the informal hearings before tri-partite panels of important people. They feared they would have lawyers at their elbows, telling them what not to do and how not to do it. They feared that the lawyers would be sent out from Washington, and would not know how to get on with the good people of the regions. Mr. Carmody of the Board gathered from the tone of the conference that the whole enterprise was likely to be a lawyer-ridden one, and regretted, momentarily at least, that he had let himself be enticed away from the National Mediation Board, where there were no lawyers.[45]

Although the "suggestions" made by the regional directors "were given the most considerate attention,"[46] the rules and regulations were published on September 14, 1935[47] and the instructions to the staff were issued on September 17, 1935.[48] The regional directors were expected to adjust themselves to the "new arrangements." As some of the regional officers had anticipated, the board decided to send "practically all members of the Legal Staff" in Washington "temporarily into the field" as acting regional attorneys.[49] These Washington staff attorneys, who

45. Madden in Silverberg, *op. cit.*, p. 37.
46. NLRB files, letter from E. S. Smith to Stanley Mathewson, director regional labor board, 9th District, September 19, 1935.
47. For a summary of the NLRB's new procedures, see National Labor Relations Board, *First Annual Report* for the fiscal year ended June 30, 1936 (Washington: GPO, 1936), pp. 21–28. See also NLRB files, "Rules and Regulations—Series 1," September 14, 1935.
48. NLRB files, "Instruction to Staff Members," September 17, 1935.
49. NLRB files, minutes of the board meeting, September 11, 1935. Stanley Surrey was assigned to Boston, David Moscowitz to New York, Robert Watts to Pittsburgh, Nathan Witt to Cleveland, Daniel Shortal to Buffalo, Gerhard Van Arkel to Philadelphia and Baltimore, Thomas Emerson to Atlanta, Fred Krivonos to Indianapolis, David Shaw to St. Louis, I. S. Dorfman to Kansas City, Louis

reported directly to the board's general counsel, had "access to all the operations that were going on" in the regional offices. They were assigned to recruit a permanent regional attorney and "teach him the ropes," set up and implement the rules and regulations in the regions, get "the operation going," create "new attitudes," and recommend the appointment of new personnel, if necessary.[50] The staff attorneys, moreover, were responsible for "sorting out" the thousands of charges being filed with regional boards around the country to get "the best ones into litigation quickly to decide the constitutional issues. . . ."[51]

The NLRB further tightened its control over field operations by retaining the authority to make all appointments to the regional board staffs (usually upon the nomination of the regional director),[52] ruling that no volunteers (such as those who formed the labor-management panels of the NLB and the old NLRB) would be permitted to work with the regional boards,[53] adopting a plan "for the supervision by Board members of particular regional offices,"[54] instituting a rigorous system of weekly and monthly reports to Washington concerning case work and "general labor trends in the territory,"[55] and enforcing stringent budgetary

Jaffe to Minneapolis, Charles Wood to Chicago and Milwaukee, Philip Phillips to Seattle, San Francisco, and Los Angeles, Garnett Patterson to Detroit, Malcom Halliday to Fort Worth and New Orleans, and Laurence Knapp to Cincinnati.

50. Oral history interview with T. I. Emerson, *op. cit.*, pp. 56–59.
51. *Ibid.*, p. 59.
52. NLRB files, "Instructions to Staff Members," September 17, 1935, p. 24.
53. NLRB files, minutes of the board meeting, September 13, 1935.
54. NLRB files, minutes of the board meeting, December 27, 1935. Madden was assigned New York, Pittsburgh, Cleveland, Cincinnati, St. Louis, Fort Worth, and Los Angeles. Carmody was to supervise Boston, Philadelphia, Atlanta, Detroit, Kansas City, Minneapolis, and San Francisco. Smith was responsible for Baltimore, Buffalo, New Orleans, Chicago, Indianapolis, Milwaukee, and Seattle. See also NLRB files, "Supervision by Board Members of Particular Regional Offices," memorandum from E. S. Smith to J. W. Madden, December 14, 1935 and NLRB files, minutes of the executive meeting of the board, November 4, 1935.
55. NLRB files, "Instructions to Staff Members," September 17, 1935, pp. 22–24.

regulations.[56] This centralization of authority immersed the board in all kinds of administrative work ranging from daily 3:00 p.m. meetings "to discuss reports from the legal staff in the field"[57] to the minutiae of approving the purchase of second hand books for the NLRB law library,[58] appointing file clerks, book-keepers and stenographers,[59] reviewing the floor plans and rents paid by the regional boards,[60] and complaining to the regional boards that "there is no uniformity, at present, in the signs on the doors of the Regional Offices or listings on the boards in the buildings in which the Regional Offices are located."[61]

In the critical area of the conduct of NLRB hearings, the board relieved the regional directors of the "special responsibility" which they had under the old NLRB "to see to it that a full and complete record [was] built up."[62] The NLRB transferred this responsibility to a newly created Trial Examiners Division—a separate division "not connected with the Legal Division and in no way responsible to it."[63] Since the board saw the trial examiners as the representatives of the board in its quasijudicial capacity, it stressed that the separation of the Trial Examiners Division from other board functions "must always be borne in mind and should be apparent to the public."[64] To underscore this separation from the Legal Division, the secretary of the board was given direct supervision over the trial examiners[65] who now had

56. *Ibid.*, pp. 25–26.
57. NLRB files, minutes of an executive meeting of the board, September 24, 1935.
58. NLRB files, minutes of an executive meeting of the board, October 8, 1935 and October 14, 1935.
59. See, for example, NLRB files, minutes of the board meeting, September 9, 1935, September 23, 1935, and September 24, 1935.
60. NLRB files, minutes of an executive meeting of the board, September 21, 1935 and September 24, 1935.
61. NA, RG25, memorandum from B. Wolf to Joseph McCartin, director, Region I, November 14, 1935. Records of NLRB II, office of the secretary, Region I, correspondence and reports relating to regional offices, 1934–1937.
62. See Chapter III, p. 83.
63. NLRB files, "Instructions to Trial Examiners," C-4, p. 22.
64. *Ibid.*, pp. 22–23.
65. *Ibid.*, p. 23. See also the NLRB files, letter from B. Wolf to U.S. Civil Service Commission, November 19, 1936.

"the responsibility of getting into the record all the facts which [they] and the Board will need to enable them to render a fair decision in the case, and which will enable the Courts to sustain the Board *on the evidence in the record.*"[66]

Yet, the trial examiner who found a violation of the act could only recommend "the affirmative steps which the Trial Examiner thinks the respondent should take to effectuate the policies of the Act . . . ."[67] The trial examiner's findings, conclusions, and recommendations were put into the form of an intermediate report which the regional director served upon the parties. If the parties filed exceptions to the trial examiner's report, or if there was no compliance with the report, the case was transferred to Washington where the board itself would "order further testimony, receive briefs, hear oral arguments or decide the case forthwith."[68]

The NLRB, moreover, reserved the right to transfer a case to itself from a regional office before or after a hearing before a trial examiner, in which case the trial examiner prepared only a short informal report for the confidential use of the board.[69] The board retained this authority not only as part of its overall plan to control the litigation strategy on the way to the Supreme Court but also because only a few people in this new field possessed the legal experience, the training in labor relations, or the familiarity with administrative practices before quasijudicial agencies to qualify as an NLRB trial examiner. At the suggestion of board member Carmody, for example, trial examiners were hired at first on a per diem basis ($25.00 per day) "until the Board can determine how effective they will be."[70] Regional directors were asked to recommend former public panel members from the old NLRB regional boards who might qualify and to "communicate also with the Deans of law schools regarding law professors who would be suitable as trial examiners."[71] (During the period ending June 30,

66. NLRB files, "Instructions to Trial Examiners," C-4, p. 9 (emphasis added).
67. *Ibid.*, p. 18.
68. *Ibid.*, p. 1.
69. *Ibid.*, pp. 1 and 22.
70. NLRB files, minutes of an executive meeting of the board, September 25, 1935.
71. NLRB files, minutes of an executive meeting of the board, October 21, 1935. See also NLRB files, letter from J. W. Madden to Dean

1936, for example, 119 of the 145 cases heard by trial examiners were transferred to the board: 65 of these by board order, 45 by exceptions to the intermediate report, and 9 because of the respondent's failure to comply with the trial examiner's report.)[72]

The board tried to compensate for this inexperience and to formalize procedures by issuing a detailed set of instructions to trial examiners covering preparations for a hearing, motions which could be made at the hearing, the conduct of hearings, the rules of evidence, the examination of witnesses, lists of points to be developed in unfair labor practice and representation cases, and the nature and form of the intermediate report.[73] Of all the instructions issued and of all the changes made, however, there was no clearer evidence of the board's decision to reject completely the informal mediation approach than the instruction to the trial examiners that "it is important to read every decision issued by the Board since these are absolutely controlling upon him [the Trial Examiner]. The Trial Examiner must always remember that he can issue no Intermediate Report which is contrary to a principle laid down by the Board in any decision it has made."[74]

The new board, in addition, sought doctrinal continuity with the NLB and the old NLRB.

A study of the decisions of the National Labor Relations Board which was appointed pursuant to Joint Resolution approved June 19, 1934, and which was replaced by this Board, and of the National Labor Board which went out of existence on July 9, 1934, will be of great value. The laws upon which these decisions were based were similar in principle to the National Labor Relations Act, and the interpretations set forth in the decisions of these Boards deserve great weight.

The decisions of these Boards are available in indexed form. As an essential part of the preparation for a hearing, the Trial Examiner should, upon reading the pleadings contained in

---

William H. Spencer, University of Chicago Law School, October 31, 1935 and letter from J. W. Madden to Dean Edward Fraser, University of Minnesota Law School, October 31, 1935.

72. National Labor Relations Board, *First Annual Report, op. cit.*, p. 38.
73. NLRB files, "Instructions to Trial Examiners," C-4, pp. 1–22.
74. *Ibid.*, p. 23.

the formal file, and familiarizing himself with the issues, read the cases of the two previous Boards on similar issues.[75]

The new board was dedicated to formulating a litigation strategy, developing a body of case law interpreting the Wagner Act, and withstanding the inevitable Supreme Court test. As Elinore Herrick, the regional director in New York City, put it:

> We used to be highly informal because we really had no law behind us. We did a lot of things which worked successfully then but which might jeopardize our whole structure now that we have a real law. The day is past when we can enforce the equivalent of Section 7(a) by asking the Mayor to turn off the water in Brooklyn laundries which were refusing to bargain collectively! And I don't know that I regret this change. Prior to passage of the Wagner-Connery Act, we were an emergency organization and used emergency methods to reach our goal. We now have a long range goal so our methods are necessarily different.[76]

The extralegal approach apparently was not uncommon even after the Wagner Act was passed. The board's secretary, Benedict Wolf, complained in May 1936 that in "several instances . . . Regional Directors . . . [had] communicated directly or indirectly with customers of the Respondent in an effort to have these customers apply pressure on the Respondent to get him to comply with the Act."[77] In June 1936, in a case involving an association of Italian bakers, another regional director reported that he had obtained "the cooperation of the State's Attorney's police department" who at the regional's director's suggestion "ordered the company union to disband or he would have an investigation of the Association re price-fixing and compulsory labels on bread."

75. *Ibid.*, pp. 23–24.
76. NA, RG25, memorandum from E. Herrick to B. Wolf, October 26, 1935. Records of NLRB II, office of the secretary, Region II, correspondence and reports relating to regional offices, 1934–1937.
77. NA, RG25, memorandum from B. Wolf to regional directors, May 19, 1936. Records of NLRB II relating to the Smith Committee Investigation, File I-4, instructions to staff which may be questioned by committee.

The director told the board that "they [the Association] settled with the AFL unions."[78]

The NLRB, however, was poorly equipped at the outset to implement its new quasijudicial role. The essentially nonlegalistic mediatory approach of the NLB and of the regional boards of the old NLRB left the new board on September 1, 1935 with only thirteen attorneys in the Washington office and only one attorney in the field.[79] The board needed many more qualified attorneys to staff not only the new Trial Examiners Division but also two new additions to the Legal Division: the Litigation Section and the Review Section (see the figure below). (The Litigation Section represented the board in judicial proceedings, was responsible for the conduct of hearings before the board, and advised the regional attorneys in their conduct of hearings before agents of the board in the field. The Review Section assisted the board in the analysis of the records of hearings conducted before trial examiners in the regions and before the board in Washington.)[80]

The board was anxious to appoint additional attorneys so that it could bring its original staff attorneys back from the regions to Washington and set up "a systematic division of the work and definite assignments among the attorneys, who are now obliged to jump from one thing to another."[81] Yet the board had "a hell of a time building up [its] staff and getting qualified people," not only because most people were "convinced [the NLRB would] be put out of business by the Supreme Court,"[82] but also because the

78. National Archives, Record Group 233, records of the House Special Committee to Investigate the National Labor Relations Board, 76th Cong., 3d Sess. (hereinafter referred to as RG233), memorandum from L. W. Beman to B. Wolf, June 6, 1936.
79. *Smith Committee Hearings, op. cit.,* vol. 13, p. 2728. The board had a total staff of 50 people in Washington (37 administrators and 13 members of the legal staff) and 69 people in the field (20 regional directors, 1 attorney, 16 "examiners," and 32 clerical staff members).
80. National Labor Relations Board, *First Annual Report, op. cit.,* pp. 14–15. See also Benedict Wolf, "Administrative Procedure Before the National Labor Relations Board," *New Jersey Law Journal,* vol. 61, September 8, 1938, p. 311.
81. NLRB files, memorandum from Charles Fahy to J. W. Madden, November 20, 1935.
82. Oral history interview with N. Witt, *op. cit.,* p. 19.

Figure. Organizational Chart of the National Labor Relations Board, 1935

```
                          ┌─────────────────────────────┐
                          │          THE BOARD          │
                          │ Appointed by President to   │
                          │ enforce the National Labor  │
                          │     Relations Act           │
                          │      (49 Stat. 449)         │
                          └─────────────────────────────┘
```

Source: National Labor Relations Board, *First Annual Report,* for the year ended June 30, 1936 (Washington: GPO, 1936), p. 20.

salary range of $3,200 to $4,600 for regional attorneys and comparable legal positions in Washington did "not permit the obtaining of outstanding lawyers of reputation."[83] (It was also difficult to find experienced labor lawyers since there was no "field" of labor law before the New Deal and labor law courses were rarely included in the curricula of the nation's law schools.)

As a result, the board tapped recruitment sources that were most unusual in the 1930s and for which the board was severely criticized in later years. The board turned to young attorneys who were "flocking all over the New Deal" because of their concern with the social issues of the day.[84] Nat Witt, who as assistant general counsel did the hiring for the Review Division, recalled that ". . . we had a remarkable bunch of lawyers. They were young and had to be zealous . . . . zealots in the sense that they believed in what they [were] doing and [were] devoted to the job. . . ."[85] Although Chairman Madden found "this emormous lot of young lawyers" in the Review Division to be overzealous at times and although he was "cautious in listening to their presentation of cases" because he thought "they might very well be coloring the thing a bit,"[86] he concluded that their zeal was a great advantage to the board.

> I think if we had been cagey about whom we hired and had tried to screen out the people who were overzealous, we probably would not have gotten as effective a staff as we did. I think we got an awful lot for our money. Just by the fact of the zeal that was put into the work.[87]

The board also hired a large number of women attorneys, particularly in the Review Division where, in 1939, 13 percent of

83. NLRB files, memorandum from C. Fahy to J. W. Madden, October 1, 1935.
84. Oral history interview with N. Witt, *op. cit.*, p. 20.
85. *Ibid.*, pp. 20 and 113–114. Charles Fahy wanted regional attorneys who had an interest in progressive legislation such as the NLRA and who were "interested in this general character of legislation and the philosophy behind it." NLRB files, memorandum from C. Fahy to J. W. Madden, October 1, 1935.
86. Oral history interview with J. W. Madden, *op. cit.*, pp. 125–126.
87. *Ibid.*, p. 299.

the attorneys were women.[88] The board, in addition, offered jobs to Jewish law graduates who faced discrimination in private practice:

> ... if we were going to get the most legal ability for our meager salary, the place to get it was to hire these young Jews and we hired a great many of them. I mean, they were the most for the money and that was just because they weren't having the opportunities in private practice that high ranking Gentile boys were having.[89]

The NLRB, of course, did hire some experienced people, particularly for supervisory positions. Chairman Madden felt, for example, that the board "could not possibly have been luckier" than when Charles Fahy agreed to become general counsel.[90] Fahy, who was recruited by Calvert Magruder, general counsel of the old NLRB, and by Tom Emerson, a member of the old board's staff, had been involved in the earliest litigation under the New Deal while serving on the Petroleum Administrative Board as the ranking member of the solicitor's staff in the Interior Department.[91] He enjoyed "universal respect and admiration" within the NLRB as a very able, thorough, patient, and careful lawyer.[92] Gerhard VanArkel, who served under Fahy at the board, and who himself became the board's general counsel in 1946, characterized Fahy as

88. The author was unable to locate figures for earlier years. There were 91 review attorneys in 1939 and 12 of these attorneys were women. These figures were compiled from a list of the names of those working in the Review Division in 1939. See *Smith Committee Hearings, op. cit.*, vol. 1, pp. 158–180.

89. Oral history interview with J. W. Madden, *op. cit.*, p. 124.

90. *Ibid.*, p. 28.

91. Oral history interview with C. Fahy, *op. cit.*, pp. 3–7. Fahy graduated from Georgetown University Law School in 1914 and remained in private practice until going to work with the Department of the Interior in 1933 where he was first assistant solicitor in 1933, vice chairman of the Petroleum Administrative Board in 1934 (which administered the Petroleum Code under the NIRA) and chairman of that board in 1935. Judge Fahy believes that it was Paul Herzog who suggested his name to Magruder. Letter from Judge Fahy to the author, July 21, 1972.

92. Oral history interview with N. Witt, *op. cit.*, p. 15.

... a very hard taskmaster. Usually he was the essence of politeness and cordiality, but, if you got out of line, he could get madder than any human being I've ever seen and express himself in the most scathing terms . . . . but when he bawled you out, he had reason to do it, it was fair and merited. He had the great respect of the board . . . . Madden and Fahy were intimately close friends . . . and Madden, I think, was certainly more swayed by Charlie Fahy's views than that of any other single person . . . . I thought that he really left his very strong mark on the board.[93]

The Work Begins and the Opposition Responds

Now that the key appointments had been made, the board and its regional system reorganized, and the rules and regulations issued, Fahy was able, on October 14, 1935, to instruct his attorneys in the field to "start sending in their cases."[94] The board set its first hearing for October 22, 1935 in what "looked like a good test case,"[95] *Pennsylvania Greyhound Lines, Inc.*, and decided to conduct that hearing themselves in Pittsburgh.[96]

But events had not waited for the NLRB to become prepared. The powerful and successful opponents of the NLB and the old NLRB, the steel and automobile industries, again laid down their challenges to the new board and Ernest T. Weir, "having successfully thumbed his nose at Section 7(a) stated that he would ignore

93. Oral history interview with G. Van Arkel, *op. cit.*, pp. 29–30.
94. NLRB files, minutes of an executive meeting of the board, October 14, 1935.
95. NLRB files, minutes of an executive meeting of the board, September 25, 1935.
96. NLRB files, minutes of an executive meeting of the board, October 8, 1935. See also NA, RG25, memorandum from B. Wolf to E. Herrick, October 17, 1935. Records of NLRB II, office of the secretary, Region II, correspondence and reports relating to regional offices, 1934–1937. *In the Matter of Pennsylvania Greyhound Lines, Inc.* became 1 NLRB 1.

the Wagner Act."[97] On September 5, 1935, only nine days after the members of the board had been appointed, the National Lawyers Committee of the American Liberty League (an organization of the leading manufacturers in the country) issued, *pro bono publico*, a 132-page statement concluding that "in the light of our history, the established form of government, and the decisions of our highest Court . . . [the Wagner Act] . . . is unconstitutional and that it constitutes a complete departure from our constitutional and traditional theories of government."[98] *The New York Times* identified the chairman of the League's Lawyers Committee as Raoul Desvernine, "who has appeared in Washington many times lately as counsel for the steel industry," and the chief draftsman of the committee's report as Earl F. Reed, "chief counsel for the Weirton Steel Company in its fight against the original National Labor Relations Board . . . ."[99] The full committee consisted of 58 lawyers from virtually all of the major cities in the country and, as Chairman Madden realized, "every one of those named was recognized in his area as a lawyer of distinction and success."[100]

The board saw the report as "a deliberate and concerted effort by a large group of well-known lawyers to undermine public confidence in the statute, to discourage compliance with it, to assist attorneys generally in attacks on the statute, and perhaps to influence the courts."[101] According to Chairman Madden,

> . . . when the principal organization of manufacturers in the country pronounced to its members the unconstitutionality and invalidity of the act, it created an enormous problem for the Board, whose duty it was to enforce the act. It put

97. Bernstein, *Turbulent Years, op. cit.*, p. 349.
98. U.S. Congress, House of Representatives, Committee on Labor, *Hearings On Proposed Amendments To The National Labor Relations Act*, 76th Cong., 1st Sess. (Washington: GPO, 1939), vol. 8, pp. 2242–2245. The names of the members of the National Lawyers Committee, the summary of the committee's conclusions, and the full text of the committee's report are found in *ibid.*, pp. 2241–2287.
99. *The New York Times*, September 19, 1935, p. 1, col. 3. See also *The New York Times*, September 13, 1935, p. 1, col. 3 and September 20, 1935, p. 13, col. 4.
100. Madden, *op. cit.*, pp. 242–243.
101. National Labor Relations Board, *First Annual Report, op. cit.*, p. 47.

the enterprises which were subject to the act in a rebellious mood, a mood where they thought that their duty to their fellows really required them to repudiate this law, and that obedience to it or acquiesence in the administration of it was really, from their standpoint, an unpatriotic act, and the consequence, of course, was that while the act might have moved into smooth administration and general obedience, this kind of incitation to disobedience made that impossible.[102]

Confronted with the Liberty League report and the bitter opposition of employers, the board was convinced that there was no possibility that it could function as Congress intended until the Wagner Act was approved by the Supreme Court. Constitutionality was the key to obtaining compliance from hostile employers whose attorneys, inspired by the National Lawyers Committee, would not be engaging in what Chairman Madden called "a holy crusade with pay."[103] The board also needed the approval of the Supreme Court to secure the cooperation of unions "whose custom was either to organize employees through the employer or strike, [not] to campaign among workers in a peaceful Board election"[104] and whose experiences with Section 7(a) of the NIRA had made them skeptical of the new law.[105] Constitutionality, moreover, would help the board to gain the understanding and support of the public by overcoming the NLRB's "almost unanimously unfriendly press. . . ."[106]

The Constitutional Strategy

Since the prospects for the constitutionality of the Wagner Act were only as good as the connection between strikes and interferences with interstate commerce, the NLRB, as early as August

102. *Smith Committee Hearings, op. cit.,* vol. 13, 2580. See also oral history interview with J. W. Madden, *op. cit.,* pp. 29–33.
103. Madden, *op. cit.,* p. 243.
104. Bernstein, *Turbulent Years, op. cit.,* p. 351.
105. Madden in Silverberg, *op. cit.,* p. 37.
106. Bernstein, *Turbulent Years, op. cit.,* p. 351.

1935, began to consider "definite plans" for the organization of "industrial economic research."[107] Four days after the appointment of J. Warren Madden as the first chairman of the Wagner Act NLRB, Edwin S. Smith, a nonlawyer member of the board, told him that the board needed

> an "industrial economist" thoroughly versed in the history of labor relations in various industries in this country. He should be a man capable of presenting his material adequately both in writing and as a witness. It would certainly be a full-time job, and a busy one. . . .[108]

Harry A. Millis, a member of the pre-Wagner, Public Resolution Number 44 board, and Francis Biddle, successor to Lloyd Garrison as that board's chairman, recommended David J. Saposs for the job.[109] It is clear from Saposs's recollections of his first interview with Chairman Madden that the board had neither formulated any "definite plans" for economic research nor even decided that it could be useful:

> I telephoned Mr. Madden [and] made an appointment. When I got there he was exceedingly friendly and very polite, but the first thing he told me [was] "I haven't the slightest idea what you can do in the board or for the board." Well, I began explaining to him what I thought could be done, but actually I myself wasn't very clear at that time as to what could be done, but I had certain notions of a general nature. "Well," he said, "Millis and Biddle have recommended you; you're hired." So I started working.[110]

On the NLRB organizational chart, at least, the Division of Economic Research attained status equal to that of the Legal Division, the Trial Examining Division, and the Division of

107. NLRB files, "Work of the Industrial Economist," memorandum from E. S. Smith to John Carmody, September 20, 1935.
108. NLRB files, "Industrial Economist," memorandum from E. S. Smith to J. W. Madden, August 31, 1935.
109. Oral history interview with David J. Saposs, July 22, 1968, p. 4, on file in the Labor Management Documentation Center, ILR, Cornell.
110. *Ibid.*, p. 5.

Publications.[111] But the lawyers in the NLRB did not see it that way; an economist who worked in the Division of Economic Research remembered: "As usual, in those days before computer technology enabled the government economist to draw even with lawyers in salary and status, the lawyers were running the show: 'After all it *is* a law which is being enforced.'"[112] A lawyer's attitude toward the economist was reflected as late as 1940 when Chairman Madden explained the relatively low salaries of the board's economist to a House Appropriations Committee: "it happens also that you can turn out economists more or less *en masse*. I mean you can take almost any kind of individual and if you put him through a certain type of education he can do this kind of work."[113] Saposs, by his own description a stubborn and "impudent"[114] person, had been preparing for the kind of work he was able to do at the NLRB ever since John R. Commons introduced him to institutional economics and the "Brandeis technique."[115] He set out to convince the board's lawyers that the NLRB did need an economist.[116]

111. *Smith Committee Hearings, op. cit.,* vol. 24, part II, p. 5112.
112. Morris Weisz in Jack Barbash, ed., "Research as a Tool of Administration: The Contribution of David J. Saposs," *The Labor Movement: A Re-Examination* (Madison: University of Wisconsin Press, 1967), p. 101.
113. U.S. Congress, Senate, *Hearings on H. R. 10539 Before the Subcommittee of the Senate Committee on Appropriations,* 76th Cong., 1st Sess., part I, (Washington: GPO, 1940), p. 578.
114. Oral history interview with D. Saposs, *op. cit.,* p. 11.
115. *Ibid.,* p. 3. The "Brandeis technique" is a reference to the economic brief filed by Louis Brandeis in *Muller* v. *Oregon,* 208 U.S. 412 (1908). Saposs was born in the Russian Ukraine and came to the United States when he was nine years old. Prior to his appointment as chief economist at the NLRB, he had worked for the U.S. Commission on Industrial Relations, the New York State Department of Labor, the Carnegie Corporation Americanization Study, the Inter-Church World Movement, The Twentieth Century Fund, and the U.S. Department of Labor. He had taught at the University of Wisconsin, the University of Toledo, and Brookwood Labor College; had been the education director of the Amalgamated Clothing Workers; and had written many books and articles in the field of labor relations.
116. *Ibid.,* pp. 10–11.

Saposs staffed the Economics Division with persons of diverse backgrounds—an agricultural statistician, a political scientist, an historian, a journalist, a monetary theorist, a social worker, an attorney, and "occasionally even a labor economist"—requiring only that they share "Saposs' desire to study the 'actual experience' of labor relations and his sympathetic understanding of the labor movement."[117]

The staff of the Economics Division carried on two interrelated types of work: it gathered economic material as evidence for use by the board in particular cases and it made general studies of labor relations problems to guide the board in its formulation of policy. The current case work of the division ranged from the provision of assistance in drafting complaints (usually restricted to advising the board regarding its jurisdiction through investigations of corporate organization and descriptions of interstate operations and properties) to the preparation of materials for use at board hearings or for inclusion in appellate court briefs.[118] These materials included

> extracts from official sources or authoritative writings on the economics of the respondent's industry or operations; extracts from authoritative writings in the field of labor economics on a general question of labor relations, such as the significance of union recognition in collective bargaining; authenticated copies of governmental reports on an aspect of respondent's labor relations;[119]

and expert testimony given by the chief economist concerning such labor relations problems as "written agreements, independent unions, employer labor policies and activities, and the

---

117. Weisz in Barbash, *op. cit.*, p. 102.
118. The Division's work is summarized in each of the first five NLRB annual reports: *First Annual Report, op. cit.*, pp. 60–66; *Second Annual Report* for the fiscal year ended June 30, 1937 (Washington: GPO, 1937), pp. 41–47; *Third Annual Report* for the fiscal year ended June 30, 1938 (Washington: GPO, 1938), pp. 245–253; *Fourth Annual Report* for the fiscal year ended June 30, 1939 (Washington: GPO, 1939), pp. 152–157; and *Fifth Annual Report* for the fiscal year ended June 30, 1940 (Washington: GPO, 1940), pp. 124–130.
119. NLRB, *Third Annual Report* for the fiscal year ended June 30, 1938 (Washington: GPO, 1938), p. 249.

history of the respondent's labor policy."[120] In the *Berkshire Knitting Mills* case,[121] for example, in which the company was charged with sponsoring a company union and interfering with its employees' right to join the American Federation of Hosiery Workers, Saposs testified about the historical development of employer antilabor policies and activities, the revelations of the LaFollette Committee, and the findings of a Division of Economic Research analysis of eighty-five "independent" unions.[122] The Economic Research Division also analyzed employment records, primarily to investigate section 8 (3) charges[123] and to secure compliance with back pay and reinstatement orders.[124]

The Economic Division also prepared research memoranda[125] ("The Structure of AFL Unions," "The Role of Supervisory

120. *Ibid.*, pp. 249–250.
121. *Berkshire Employees Association* v. *NLRB*, 121 F. 2d 235 (3d Cir. 1941).
122. NLRB files, Division of Economic Research, "Statistical Analysis of 85 'Independent' Unions and Readapted Company Unions," Research Memorandum Number 1, March 1938; " Subject Matter Covered in Testimony at the Berkshire Knitting Mills Hearings," memorandum from D. J. Saposs to J. W. Madden, E. S. Smith, D. W. Smith, C. Fahy, and R. Watts, January 6, 1938; *The New York Times*, January 6, 1938, p. 8, col. 4 and January 5, 1938, p. 14, col. 1.
123. For example, when an employer was charged with having discriminated against his employees through a reduction in work force, allegedly necessitated by business conditions, employment records would be searched to check out seniority plans, merit rating systems, employee production records, and so forth. See the NLRB files, Division of Economic Research, "Investigation and Analysis of Employment Records and Personnel Policies in Connection with 8(3) Cases," August 24, 1939.
124. See NLRB files, Division of Economic Research, "The Functions of the NLRB Division of Economic Research," April 13, 1940, p. 6.
125. See, for example, NLRB files, D. J. Saposs, "Statistical Analysis of 85 'Independent' Unions and Readapted Company Unions," Research Memorandum Number 1, March 1938 (mimeographed); D. J. Saposs, "Digest of Testimony at Hearing in Case of Inland Steel Company and Steelworkers' Organizing Committee," Research Memorandum Number 2, April 1938 (mimeographed); D. J. Saposs, K. P. Ellickson, and B. W. Stern, "Role of Supervisory Employees in Spreading Employer Views," Research Memorandum Number 3, November 1938 (mimeographed); Lyle Cooper, "Union-Employer

Employees in Spreading Employer Views"), research outlines[126] ("Effective Collective Bargaining," "Employer Labor Policies and Activities"), and printed bulletins[127] (*Written Trade Agreements in Collective Bargaining, Governmental Protection of Labor's Right to Organize*) for use in future cases, for the information of the board, and for general policy planning. The bulletin, *Written Trade Agreements in Collective Bargaining*, is typical of this aspect of the division's work. This bulletin was an expansion of the economic materials prepared for the board in the *Inland Steel* case,[128] which involved a question of whether the company's refusal to enter into a written agreement with the union was a violation of the NLRA. The division made a detailed study of the theory and practice of collective bargaining, the historical development of the written trade agreement, the forms and content of the trade agreement, and the prevailing practice concerning the written agreement in a selected group of industries. The study concluded that a written trade agreement signed by both the employer and the union was an integral part of collective bargaining, helping to reduce industrial unrest, provide a constitution for industrial democracy, and "[institutionalize] the whole collective bargaining process."[129] The published bulletin informed employers and unions of the board's attitude toward written collective bargaining contracts and provided documen-

---

Responsibility," Research Memorandum Number 4, January 1939 (mimeographed); D. J. Saposs, "Structure of AFL Unions," Research Memorandum Number 8, May 1939 (mimeographed).

126. See, for example, NLRB files, D. J. Saposs, "Employer Labor Practices and Activities," Research Outline Number 6, March 1938 (mimeographed); D. J. Saposs and L. Cooper, "Effective Collective Bargaining," Research Outline Number 7, December 1938 (mimeographed.)

127. See, for example, NLRB files, *Governmental Protection of Labor's Right to Organize*, Bulletin Number 1, August 1936; *The Effect of Labor Relations in the Bituminous Coal Industry*, Bulletin Number 2, June 1938; *Collective Bargaining in the Newspaper Industry*, Bulletin Number 3, October 1938; and *Written Trade Agreements in Collective Bargaining*, Bulletin Number 4, 1939.

128. *Inland Steel Co.* v. *NLRB*, 109 F. 2d 9 (7th Cir. 1940).

129. NLRB files, *Written Trade Agreements in Collective Bargaining*, Bulletin No. 4, November 1939, pp. xii, 251, 256.

tary support for the board's position in future cases involving this issue.[130]

Economic labor relations data helped build the case records on which the Supreme Court sustained the constitutionality of the Wagner Act in 1937. A few years later, J. Warren Madden would tell the Smith Committee that the NLRB's development of the records in these cases was "a masterful job," "a perfectly splendid job," and that "a better piece of legal work has not been done."[131] He might have added that there was no better illustration of the potency of a coordinated effort by the board's legal departments and the Division of Economic Research.

The legal strategy was the core of the effort.[132] The board believed that the Supreme Court's decision in *Texas and New Orleans RR.* v. *Brotherhood of Railway and Steamship Clerks*[133] had established that the portions of the act that pertained to the protection of self-organization were "reasonable means of carrying out a legitimate end" and were not arbitrary or capricious. Although the provisions concerning collective bargaining (particularly majority rule) were less certain to be upheld, "the danger of an unfavorable ruling on this [due process] issue [was] not great."[134] The act was much more vulnerable on the question of the commerce power and on this point the choice of legal arguments and the selection of test cases became most critical. The Supreme Court in its *Schechter* decision[135] had already rejected arguments based upon the more intangible obstructions to commerce mentioned in section 1 of the NLRA,[136] such as the depressing effects on the market of wage competition and inadequate

130. NLRB files, "Bulletin on Written Trade Agreements," memorandum from D. J. Saposs to J. W. Madden, E. S. Smith, and D. W. Smith, September 23, 1937.
131. *Smith Committee Hearings, op. cit.*, vol. 13, p. 2710.
132. For an interesting discussion of the legal strategy in each of the Wagner Act cases, see Cortner, *op. cit.*, pp. 89–194.
133. 281 U.S. 548 (1930).
134. NLRB files, "Selection of Test Cases Under the National Labor Relations Act," memorandum (M410) from T. I. Emerson, G. Van Arkel, Charles Wood, and Garnet Patterson, July 9, 1935, p. 1.
135. *Schechter Poultry Corp.* v. *United States*, 295 U.S. 495 (1935).
136. Section 1 of the NLRA reads: "The denial by employers of the right of employees to organize and the refusal by employers to accept the

purchasing power[137] or the alleged expansionary effects on commerce of the increased income resulting from an equalization of bargaining power between employer and employee. The board decided that the foundation would be the other congressional

procedure of collective bargaining lead to strikes and other forms of industrial strife or unrest, which have the intent or the necessary effect of burdening or obstructing commerce by (a) impairing the efficiency, safety, or operation of the instrumentalities of commerce; (b) occurring in the current of commerce; (c) materially affecting, restraining, or controlling the flow of raw materials or manufactured or processed goods from or into the channels of commerce, or the prices of such materials or goods in commerce; or (d) causing diminution of employment and wages in such volume as substantially to impair or disrupt the market for goods flowing from or into the channels of commerce.

"The inequality of bargaining power between employees who do not possess full freedom of association or actual liberty of contract, and employers who are organized in the corporate or other forms of ownership association substantially burdens and affects the flow of commerce, and tends to aggravate recurrent business depressions, by depressing wage rates and the purchasing power of wage earners in industry and by preventing the stabilization of competitive wage rates and working conditions within and between industries.

"Experience has proved that protection by law of the right of employees to organize and bargain collectively safeguards commerce from injury, impairment, or interruption, and promotes the flow of commerce by removing certain recognized sources of industrial strife and unrest, by encouraging practices fundamental to the friendly adjustment of industrial disputes arising out of differences as to wages, hours, or other working conditions, and by restoring equality of bargaining power between employers and employees.

"It is hereby declared to be the policy of the United States to eliminate the causes of certain substantial obstructions to the free flow of commerce and to mitigate and eliminate these obstructions when they have occurred by encouraging the practice and procedure of collective bargaining and by protecting the exercise by workers of full freedom of association, self-organization, and designation of representatives of their own choosing, for the purpose of negotiating the terms and conditions of their employment or other mutual aid or protection."

Act of July 5, 1935, ch. 372, § 1, 49 Stat. 449.

137. Despite its mention in section 1, Charles Wyzanski, who presented oral arguments on behalf of the NLRB in the *Associated Press* case,

finding contained in section 1: that employer unfair labor practices lead to strikes and industrial unrest, which physically obstruct the flow of commerce.

Mere declarations by the legislature, however, would not be enough to justify the exercise of federal power. The legislative findings had to be supported by facts if the Supreme Court was to give weight and "great respect" to congressional conclusions. A review of the Supreme Court cases dealing with the weight to be given to legislative findings indicated that the "independent examination of the facts by the Court is without boundaries and may lead anywhere. Resort may be had to the facts known judicially to the Court . . ., to the evidence considered by Congress . . ., to facts argued before the Court, etc."[138] It was recommended that factual evidence supporting the congressional findings of section 1 should be introduced into the case records and "should not be limited to the reports of the Congressional Committees and the record before these Committees, but should contain in addition other facts and material."[139]

The statute as a whole was to be justified by the introduction of certain general proofs: that interstate commerce was involved in the particular case, that the employer did commit a specific unfair labor practice, that such illegal acts have led or tend to lead to industrial unrest which obstructs interstate commerce, and "that the remedy adopted [was] in general an appropriate one."[140] The

---

told the Supreme Court that "the demoralization of the wage structure, may have something to do with the reasonableness of the regulation, but it is not the foundation or the source of congressional power." Arguments in Senate Document Number 52, *Cases Arising Under the Railway Labor Act and the National Labor Relations Act Before the Supreme Court of the United States*, 75th Cong., 1st Sess. (Washington: GPO, 1937), p. 72. J. W. Madden said in his oral argument in the *Jones and Laughlin* case that "I could imagine that there might be a sufficient connection between the wages and the labor troubles thereby stopping the flow of commerce, but I see no such intimate connection whatever as there is between strikes and the flow of commerce." *Ibid.*, p. 115.

138. NLRB files, "The Relevance and Importance of the Congressional Findings Contained in the National Labor Relations Act," memorandum by Stanley S. Surrey, September 30, 1935, pp. 25–26.

139. *Ibid.*, p. 27.

140. *Ibid.*, pp. 25–26.

board was advised, however, that it would be dangerous to stop with a general argument that might prove too much (by seeming to place all labor relations under the supervision of the federal government) rather than to go on to the specific case before the Court "and the effect of the unfair labor practice in *that* case upon interstate commerce."[141] The case-by-case approach was tactically designed in part, to anticipate any desire of the Supreme Court "to narrow a favorable decision to prevent it from being too strong a precedent in favor of the regulation of labor relations."[142] The board was also reminded that the Court had shown great interest in the business transactions of the Schechter Poultry Corporation.[143]

The best test case, therefore, would be one in which the general congressional findings of section 1 were clearly and concretely verified by its particular facts: a case where the employer's unfair labor practices had caused his employees to strike and to shut down the plant. In weaker cases, where the effect of the unfair labor practice was not so clear, the board would have to rely on the tendency of such practices to lead to labor disputes that obstruct commerce. The question in that type of case was "one of probability and the findings of Congress [were] relevant to show what the probabilities [were]" moreover, the "history of past labor disputes in which the employer was involved [was] relevant to show what probably might occur in a future case. The labor relations experience of the industry [was] likewise relevant."[144]

In September 1935 an outline was drawn up detailing the kinds of economic data needed to support the legal strategy. The significant tests of the interstate nature of the respondent's business and industry included the products produced, the relative size of the business and the industry, the capital invested, sources of raw materials and manufactured parts, markets for finished products, the amount and value of production shipped out of state, advertising in other states, and the use of the products of other businesses and industries engaged in interstate commerce. The company's and the industry's histories were to be searched

141. *Ibid.*, p. 4 (emphasis added).
142. *Ibid.*, pp. 3–4.
143. *Ibid.*, p. 3.
144. *Ibid.*, p. 5.

for strikes or threats of strikes (particularly those caused by employer unfair labor practices) and the effects of a stoppage on interstate commerce. It was also considered important to develop general labor relations facts that did not pertain directly to the specific business or industry, such as the causes of strikes in general, the removal of the causes of strikes by forbidding unfair labor practices, and the advantages of "friendly adjustment through the machinery provided by the Act."[145]

The Choice of Test Cases

The board's tactics in the field were no less important than the strategy in Washington. Since the Wagner Act had stripped the Department of Justice of its control over NLRB litigation,[146] the new board was able to pick its cases, hold administrative hearings, determine violations, make decisions and findings of fact, and take its own cases to court.[147] The board moved quickly, "resolved" to get to the Supreme Court "with cases as impressive as possible"[148] rather than with the "sick chicken" kind of case which had invalidated the National Industrial Recovery Act.

The Board, advised by the general counsel and his staff, was always conscious of the strategic problems of the litigation which was bound to come in due course. Its orders to cease and desist from unfair labor practices, when such orders would be made, would be subject to review in the United States Circuit Courts of Appeals, and their decisions would be reviewable, by writ of certiorari, in the Supreme Court of the United States. The Board was resolved that the cases which reached the Supreme Court should, if possible, be

145. NLRB files, "The Use of Economic Data to Support the Constitutional Basis of the Wagner Labor Relations Act," memorandum (M411), September 17, 1935, pp. 10–13.
146. See Chapter IV, pp. 123–127.
147. Oral history interview with T. I. Emerson, *op. cit.*, p. 45.
148. Oral history interview with J. W. Madden, *op. cit.*, p. 44.

impressive cases which involved important and significant enterprises. One reason why we were sensitive on that question was that the *Schechter* case, in which the Supreme Court had nullified the National Industrial Recovery Act, had involved the poultry code and the selection of chickens from crates, eliminating diseased chickens. Those who rejoiced at the decision referred contemptuously to the Government's case as the "sick chicken case". Among our early hearings were those of companies named Kiddie Cover, a manufacturer of children's overalls, and Infant Sox. We had a dread of finding ourselves in the Supreme Court with such cases.[149]

Consequently, from September 1935 to January 1936, regional directors were required to submit all cases to the board in Washington for its approval before any complaints were issued.[150] The board advised its regional directors that in cases which were "not the kind we would like to put forward in the early stages of litigation, it should be possible in most instances to explain why the friends of the law would not select that case for the establishment of the law, and why it is advisable that a complaint should not be issued immediately."[151] The board, however, incurred the criticism of organized labor for telling unions "in the face of a flat and direct violation of the law [that they] had no remedy and must wait until the law had been further approved,"[152] for

149. Madden, *op. cit.*, p. 244.
150. NLRB files, memorandum from B. Wolf to Ralph A. Lind, January 15, 1936. See also *Smith Committee Hearings, op. cit.*, vol. 24, pp. 5541–5542. Section 3(d) of the Taft-Hartley Act gave the general counsel of the board "final authority, on behalf of the Board, in respect of the investigation of charges and issuance of complaints under Section 10. . . ."
151. NA, RG25, letter from B. Wolf to E. Herrick (sent to all regional directors), October 17, 1935. Records of NLRB II, office of the secretary, Region II, correspondence and reports relating to regional offices, 1934–1937.
152. NLRB files, address of J. W. Madden at the 57th Annual Convention of the American Federation of Labor, October 5, 1937, p. 2 (mimeographed). See also *Report of the Proceedings of the 57th Annual Convention of the American Federation of Labor* (Washington: Judd & Detweiler, 1937), pp. 231–236.

"holding up its decision in cases in which the Trial Examiner had made a report favorable to the union,"[153] and for not moving "immediately" to compel employers to obey its orders.[154] The board was urged to hold hearings, decide cases, and enforce its orders in order to encourage beleaguered unions and raise their morale,[155] support regional board offices in antiunion towns,[156] and complement union organizing drives and "strike preparedness."[157] Heber Blankenhorn, a carry-over from the old NLRB and a special investigator for the new board, told Chairman Madden that the "NLRB can still thunder from the pulpit and excommunicate from the congregation of the righteous. That comforts the flock, disconcerts the heathen, and marks down the latter against the day of wrath to come."[158] He pleaded with the board to "relegate metaphysics to the Supreme Tribunal, and to get on with good works."[159]

The NLRB, however, never altered its basic position that the board's control of the test cases which would be the first to get to the circuit courts and to the Supreme Court was "much more important than issuing a decision in any particular case, because it [was] undoubtedly better to put up with some discontent on the part of the unions than to have the Board, in order to avoid such discontent, find itself in the Supreme Court with a case which is

153. NA, RG233, memorandum from Charles Hope, regional director, 19th Region, to B. Wolf, June 12, 1936, p. 3, Box 157.
154. NA, RG233, memorandum from Stanley Root, regional director, 4th Region to the National Labor Relations Board, March, 1936, Box 125.
155. NA, RG25, "Atlanta Woolen Mills," memorandum from Mortimer Kollender to C. Fahy, September 9, 1936 and "Conference with Mr. Constangy, Attorney for the Georgia State Federation of Labor on August 11th," memorandum from J. W. Madden to the file, August 14, 1936, *Atlanta Woolen Mills* case.
156. NA, RG25, informal files, "Columbian Enameling & Stamping Co.," memorandum from Robert H. Cowdrill to B. Wolf, April 1, 1936, *Columbian Enameling & Stamping Company* case.
157. NLRB files, "Curtailment of Board Hearings," memorandum from H. Blankenhorn to J. W. Madden, J. Carmody, and E. S. Smith, June 16, 1936. See Chapter IV, pp. 115–116, fn. 26, for a biographical sketch of H. Blankenhorn.
158. *Ibid.*
159. *Ibid.*

not particularly strong. . . ."[160] Although the board attempted to placate disgruntled unions by reassuring them that favorable court decisions would "increase the possibility of securing compliance . . . even in cases which [were] not taken into the Circuit Courts,"[161] the NLRB was emphatic that "the question of how we shall conduct our litigation must be determined by ourselves and our legal staff, and cannot be controlled by others who have no responsibility for the success of our law."[162]

The board gave first preference to cases arising in those industries where the employees were actually *in* interstate commerce, such as interstate transportation and communication. The next best industries were those which the Supreme Court had already designated as being in the flow of interstate commerce, such as stockyards, packing houses, grain elevators, and milling companies. Although rated third best and "generally less desirable," test cases in manufacturing could not be delayed since they constituted the bulk of the NLRB's potential jurisdiction.[163]

The board brought along an interstate bus case (*Washington, Virginia and Maryland Coach Co.*), an interstate communication case (*Associated Press*), and three interstate manufacturing operations (*Jones and Laughlin Steel Corp., Fruehauf Trailer Co.,* and *Friedman-Harry Marks Clothing Co.*).[164] The board took this

160. NA, RG25, "Decisions in Cases," memorandum from B. Wolf to E. Herrick, March 12, 1936. Records of NLRB II, office of the secretary, Region II, correspondence and reports relating to regional offices, 1934–1937.

161. NA, RG25, informal files, letter from B. Wolf to Maurice J. Nicoson, Esq., April 24, 1936, *Columbian Enameling & Stamping Company* case.

162. NA, RG25, informal files, letter from J. W. Madden to Honorable Robert Ramspeck, March 11, 1936, *Atlanta Woolen Mills* case.

163. NLRB files, "Selection of Test Cases Under the National Labor Relations Act," memorandum (M410) from T. I. Emerson, G. Van Arkel, Charles Wood, and Garnet Patterson, July 9, 1935.

164. *Washington, Virginia & Maryland Coach Co.* v. *NLRB*, 301 U.S. 142 (1937); *Associated Press* v. *NLRB*, 301 U.S. 103 (1937); *NLRB* v. *Friedman-Harry Marks Clothing Co.*, 301 U.S. 58 (1937); *NLRB* v. *Fruehauf Trailer Co.*, 301 U.S. 49 (1937); *NLRB* v. *Jones & Laughlin Steel Corp.*, 301 U.S. 1 (1937). The board's first case, the *Pennsylvania Greyhound Lines, Inc.*, remained undecided in the third Circuit

varied set of cases, representative of the broad scope of the NLRB's potential jurisdiction, into four circuit courts of appeals[165] for review that would provide the Supreme Court with "a range of thinking of circuit court judges about the statute. . . ."[166] Ironically, it was because the NLRB lost all of its manufacturing cases in the circuit courts that it was able to hold these more doubtful cases until they could be accompanied to the Supreme Court by the strong interstate transportation and communication cases.[167]

The NLRB also chose carefully the kinds of unfair labor practices which it wanted to bring to the Supreme Court. The board intentionally avoided presenting the Court with the "touchy" and more doubtful questions of the duty to bargain and majority rule, both of which had been "tough" issues in the history of the NLB and the old NLRB—a toughness which was reflected in the legislative history of the act. It was no accident, therefore, that the alleged unfair labor practices in all of the Wagner Act test cases consisted of the "simple issues" of discharges for union activity or other interferences with self organization.[168] (The duty to bargain and majority rule questions were raised, however, in the *Virginian Railroad Company* case[169] which arose under the Railway Labor Act and was argued before the Supreme Court on the day before the Court heard the NLRB cases. The *Virginian* case was a "welcome addition" to the board cases because "congressional authority over labor relations in the railroad industry

---

Court of Appeals through February 1936, so the board had to proceed with other cases.

165. *Associated Press* and *Friedman-Harry Marks* were taken to the Second Circuit, *Jones & Laughlin* to the Fifth Circuit, *Fruehauf Trailer* to the Sixth Circuit, and *Washington, Virginia & Maryland Coach Co.* to the Fourth Circuit.

166. Oral history interview with C. Fahy, *op. cit.*, p. 21.

167. Cortner, *op. cit.*, p. 137.

168. Oral history interview with P. Levy, *op. cit.* See also NLRB files, "Present Status of National Labor Relations Act," memorandum, undated and unsigned, pp. 3–4 and "Status of Litigation of the National Labor Relations Board," memorandum by T. I. Emerson, September 10, 1936, pp. 3–4.

169. *Virginian Railway Company* v. *System Federation*, 300 U.S. 515 (1937).

had long been received generously by the Supreme Court, as in the *Texas and New Orleans* case,"[170] and because of the basic similarity in the provisions of the Railway Labor Act and the Wagner Act.[171]

170. *Texas & New Orleans Railway Co.* v. *Brotherhood 281* U.S. 548 (1930).
171. Cortner, *op. cit.*, pp. 156 and 186.

6 The New Labor Policy Is Constitutional

The nine justices of the Supreme Court, in what the editor of *United States Law Week* described as "the role of silent listeners," heard oral arguments in the five Wagner Act test cases on February 9, 10, and 11, 1937.[1] More than a dozen attorneys argued for more than a dozen hours in the large court room where each day "every seat was filled and there were long lines of persons standing outside hoping to obtain admission when others left."[2]

Chairman Madden and the solicitor general of the United States, Stanley Reed, had been discussing the overall strategy of the board's arguments in the Supreme Court and who should participate in those arguments as early as November 11, 1936.[3] It was finally decided that Stanley Reed, J. Warren Madden, NLRB General Counsel Charles Fahy, and Charles Wyzanski, special assistant to the attorney general (and former solicitor for the Department of Labor in the days of the old NLRB) would argue

1. Dean Dinwoodey, "Commerce Is Key To Wagner Act Test," *The New York Times*, February 14, 1937, sec. 4, p. 7E, col. 3.
2. NLRB files, "Supreme Court Arguments," memorandum from Robert Watts to all attorneys, February 16, 1937.
3. NLRB files, "Memorandum of a Conversation with Solicitor General Reed," memorandum from J. W. Madden to the files, November 11, 1936. "He asked whether there were people here who had had a part in the drafting of the statute and would therefore know a good deal about what was intended by it. He was told that Mr. Levy, Mr. Witt and Mr. Emerson were hereabout, and that Professor Calvert Magruder, of the Harvard Law School had been General Counsel at the time and had had a great deal to do with the drafting of the statute. Mr. Reed thought that we should have a conference which would include Mr. Magruder." *Ibid.*

the test cases on behalf of the United States and the NLRB. Chairman Madden recalls that

> One day I said to Stanley Reed, "I would like to argue the *Jones and Laughlin* case." And he looked sort of surprised and said, "Well, I'll think about it." And then a couple of days later he told me that it would be all right. I think that what happened in the meantime was that he consulted the chief justice because it really was quite irregular. Here, *I* had decided, along with my colleagues, Jones and Laughlin's case against Jones and Laughlin. Then it had gone through an intermediate court and now it was in the Supreme Court and it was a good deal like the situation where a trial court decides a case and then it goes through a court of appeals and then it goes to the Supreme Court and here the trial judge turns up in the Supreme Court saying, in effect, "I was right. And I'd like to try to persuade you, eminent gentlemen, that I was right the first time." And so at any rate the Court made no objection to it and I think that the chief justice told Reed that as long as I was a lawyer he wouldn't have any objection to it. So it gave me, really, quite an extraordinary opportunity to get into perhaps the most important case of the century in its economic and social effects.[4]

The employers were represented, among others, by Earl F. Reed, chief draftsman of the American Liberty League's 1935 report on the unconstitutionality of the Wagner Act,[5] and by John W. Davis, Democratic candidate for president in 1924, a signer of the Liberty League report, and one of the nation's leading corporation lawyers.

There were two fundamental questions of constitutional law involved in the Wagner Act test cases: whether Congress and, therefore, the NLRB had authority under the commerce clause to apply the provisions of the Wagner Act to employer-employee relations and whether those provisions were valid under the due process requirements of the Constitution. The company attorneys maintained that the Wagner Act arbitrarily deprived employers of their liberty and property without due process of law by de-

4. Oral history interview with J. W. Madden, *op. cit.*, p. 60.
5. See Chapter V, pp. 172–173.

stroying "the freedom of individual employers and employees to bargain with each other equally and individually in regard to their own private relations and private occupations," by making collective bargaining compulsory in all industries, by compelling the restoration of an employer-employee relationship which the employer chose to terminate, and by denying to employers their constitutional right to a jury trial in directing the reinstatement of employees with back pay.[6]

Although these same due process arguments ran through all the test cases, the arguments of counsel centered principally on the commerce clause question. The board developed the *Jones and Laughlin* case almost entirely around the commerce question, the crucial issue of the Wagner's Act's application to manufacturing.[7] The Division of Economic Research, therefore, made its major effort in that case and supplied the kind of economic and industrial relations evidence essential to the success of the legal strategy. Many industrial relations experts, including William Leiserson, Sumner Slichter, John A. Fitch, Hugh Kerwin, and David Saposs, had testified at the hearing in the *Jones and Laughlin* case in Washington in April 1936. Their experience and opinions ranged over general industrial relations "facts": that employers' refusals to recognize unions had caused widespread industrial strife in the nation's basic industries, that outstanding strikes (the Southwest Railway strike in 1886, the anthracite coal strike in 1902, the steel strike in 1919, and so forth) had seriously obstructed commerce, that unfair labor practices had been a major cause of industrial conflict, that collective bargaining had been working most satisfactorily in many industries, and that "governmental intervention of some kind [had] been the rule in major labor disputes for more than half a century."[8] As required

6. See Senate Document Number 52, *Arguments in the Cases Arising Under the Railway Labor Act and the National Labor Relations Act Before the Supreme Court of the United States*, 75th Cong., 1st Sess. (Washington: GPO 1937). See also Dinwoody, *op. cit.*, and *The New York Times*, September 15, 1936, p. 13, col. 1.
7. NLRB files, "Supreme Court Arguments," memorandum from C. Fahy to J. W. Madden, November 23, 1936, p. 2.
8. NLRB Division of Economic Research, *Government Protection of Labor's Right to Organize* (Washington: GPO, 1936) Bulletin Number 1. These hearings before the NLRB were held in Washington

by the legal strategy, the economic testimony became more specific and shifted to the economic structure and labor relations history of the steel industry: the industry's place in the American economic system, its concentration of ownership and integration of production, its national and international market—and the Homestead strike of 1892, the U.S. Steel Corporation strikes of 1901 and 1910, the steel strike of 1919, the threatened steel strike of 1934, the company union movement, and the industry's use of espionage and the coal and iron police to prevent union organization for collective bargaining.[9] The NLRB's Supreme Court brief summarized this expert testimony and supported it with references to government reports, scholarly journals, and labor relations textbooks and histories.[10] The Economic Division also supplied the last and most critical economic evidence needed to complete the NLRB lawyers' plan of attack—the interstate nature of the operations of the Jones and Laughlin Steel Corporation, particularly its Aliquippa plant where the alleged unfair labor practices occurred.[11]

Jones and Laughlin told the Supreme Court that, whereas the board had "made some effort to adhere to the ordinary standards of relevancy" at the opening hearings in Pittsburgh, "the bars to irrelevant and prejudicial material were entirely dropped"[12] in Washington. The company characterized the economic data as "a miscellany of economic and political opinions," "hypothetical evidence," and pure speculation based upon magazine articles, newspaper clippings, doctoral theses on labor relations, and "a best seller, 'Steel Dictator.'"[13] The corporation's most serious complaint was that the "evils in other branches of the industry and in other industries were used to blacken the reputation of the respondent."[14] The employer maintained, finally, that since its

from April 2 to April 8, 1936. The verbatim testimony of the expert witnesses appears in the record, pp. 398–970, *NLRB* v. *Jones & Laughlin Steel Corporation*, 83 F. 2d 998 (5th Cir. 1936).

9. NLRB Division of Economic Research, *op. cit.*, pp. 33–34.
10. Brief for petitioner, pp. 21–31, *NLRB* v. *Jones & Laughlin Steel Corp.*, 301 U.S. 1 (1937)
11. *Ibid.*, pp. 52–72.
12. Brief for respondent, p. 19, *NLRB* v. *Jones & Laughlin Steel Corp.*, 301 U.S. 1 (1937).
13. *Ibid.*
14. *Ibid.*, p. 20.

operation had not been interrupted by the strike or impaired in the slightest way by the discharge of the complaining employees, "it [was] a defiance of reason and good judgment to argue that guesswork evidence . . . can bridge the distance between the discharge of thirteen employees and the movement of interstate commerce."[15]

In the NLRB-Department of Justice strategy sessions, Stanley Reed and Charles Wyzanski took the position that the board "would probably win the transportation case [and] the *Associated Press* case which was in the area of communications" because of the decision of the Supreme Court in the *Texas and New Orleans* case.[16] (The opinion in that case had been written by Chief Justice Hughes for a unanimous court.) They had little hope, however, that the board could win any of the manufacturing cases.[17] The board and Fahy, on the other hand, insisted that "the government

15. *Ibid.*, p. 21.
16. Oral history interview with P. Levy, *op. cit.* See also oral history interview with C. Fahy, *op. cit.* In the *Texas & New Orleans* case, Chief Justice Hughes found that the Railway Labor Act of 1926 was designed to protect interstate commerce from interruption by providing "a machinery to prevent strikes." A unanimous Court had "no doubt of the constitutional authority of Congress to enact the prohibition" against employer interference with the employees freedom of choice in the selection of representatives:

"Exercising this authority, Congress may facilitate the amicable settlement of disputes which threaten the service of necessary agencies of interstate transportation. In shaping legislation to this end, Congress was entitled to take cognizance of actual conditions and to address itself to practicable measures. The legality of collective action on the part of employees in order to safeguard their proper interests is not to be disputed. . . . The Railway Labor Act of 1926 does not interfere with the normal exercise of the right of the carrier to select its employees or to discharge them. The statute is not aimed at this right of the employers but at the interference with the right of employees to have representatives of their own choosing. As the carriers subject to the Act have no constitutional right to interfere with the freedom of the employees in making their selections, they cannot complain of the statute on constitutional grounds." 281 U.S. 548 (1930).
17. Oral history interview with P. Levy, *op. cit.* Levy believed that the "harsh treatment" which Solitor General Reed had received from the judges of the Sixth Circuit Court of Appeals when he argued the

should try for the whole shooting match" since the NLRB's total operation was most dependent upon victory in the "typical" manufacturing case.[18] Fahy believed that it might be possible to "break down" the Supreme Court's feeling about manufacturing and the commerce clause by "availing ourselves of the opportunity afforded by the three manufacturing cases to keep hammering away—so that when the tournament is over there is little likelihood of failure to have presented all that is possible."[19] Yet, because the board's prospects were grim, it was decided to present the test cases to the Supreme Court in a manner which "gave the Court the opportunity to draw the line of constitutionality in various places; against all the cases; against the manufacturing cases but not against the interstate communications and transportation cases; against the small clothing manufacturing case but not against the large steel and automotive cases."[20]

Ironically, the enormity of what the government and the NLRB were asking of the Supreme Court was most aptly described by Jones and Laughlin attorney, Earl F. Reed:

What the petitioner is asking is that the traditions and precedents of a century be cast aside and that we change the meaning of the Constitution by a judicial decree and say that things that for a century have not been the business of the

---

Fruehauf Trailer Co. case before them and the Court's adverse decision in that case "had an influence on the [Justice Department's] formulation of the issues. *Ibid.*, p. 44.

18. *Ibid.*
19. NLRB files, "Supreme Court Arguments," memorandum from C. Fahy to J. W. Madden, November 23, 1936. Levy recalled that "the upshot was that Fahy requested Reed to hear his side of the question before making a final decision on the makeup of the briefs. Everybody was in good humor and Reed was very amenable. I was present when Fahy argued what amounts to the argument about the argument in Reed's office. The other gentlemen who were also from the Department of Justice were also present. Reed said, as I recall, right then that he saw no reason why every argument that any of us who felt strongly about it should not be included." Oral history interview with P. Levy, *op. cit.*
20. Madden, *op. cit.*, p. 246. See also Robert L. Stern, "The Commerce Clause and the National Economy, 1933–1946," *Harvard Law Review*, vol. 59, no. 5 (May 1946), p. 677.

Federal Government are now to be subject to regulation, because of the remote possibility that these discharges and things of this kind may obstruct commerce.[21]

The Supreme Court and the *Carter Coal* Case

At the outset of the New Deal, however, many scholars of constitutional law believed that over the years the Supreme Court had established sufficient conflicting precedent on such questions as the extent of federal power over interstate commerce to enable the justices "to produce within broad limits nearly any constitutional result they pleased."[22] The nine Supreme Court justices in 1937 were, in the words of labor historian Irving Bernstein,

> . . . divisible by three. The largest bloc consisted of the conservative four—George Sutherland, Pierce Butler, Willis VanDevanter, James C. McReynolds, opposed by the liberal three—Louis D. Brandeis, Benjamin N. Cardozo, [Harlan Fiske] Stone, and, last, but most important, because they held the balance of power, the uncertain two—[Chief Justice Charles Evans] Hughes and Owen J. Roberts."[23]

It became clear in 1935 and 1936 that the constitutional result chosen by a majority of these men could have led only to the nullification of the Wagner Act.

21. Document Number 52, *op. cit.*, p. 142.
22. Schlesinger, *The Politics of Upheaval, op. cit.*, pp. 451–452. For a comprehensive analysis of the Supreme Court in this period, see Robert H. Jackson, *The Struggle for Judicial Supremacy*, (New York: Knopf, 1942); Merlo J. Pusey, *Charles Evans Hughes* (New York: The Macmillan Company 1951); Cortner, *op. cit.*; and E. S. Corwin, *Twilight of the Supreme Court* (New Haven: Yale University Press, 1934).
23. Bernstein, *Turbulent Years, op. cit.*, pp. 635–636. All nine were old men, the youngest being Justice Roberts who was sixty-two in 1937. *Ibid.*, p. 636.

The battle was joined in 1935. On January 7, the court in the "Hot" oil cases struck down the provision of the National Industrial Recovery Act regulating the petroleum industry as an unconstitutional delegation of power to the President. On February 18, in one of the Gold Clause cases, the court held that Congress had no authority to modify the redemption terms of government gold bonds. On May 6, in a 5 to 4 decision the court set aside the Railroad Retirement Act. May 27 was "Black Monday." The Supreme Court struck three times. It nullified the Frazier-Lemke Act, which provided relief to farm mortgages. In seeming defiance of its own precedent, the court held that the President was without power to remove a Federal Trade Commissioner, a decision that infuriated Roosevelt. Most important, in the Schechter case the court set aside the National Industrial Recovery Act. At a press conference later in the week the President said that the Supreme Court had turned back the Constitution to "the horse-and-buggy" conception of interstate commerce. Where, he asked, would the federal government find the powers to deal with national economic problems? . . . .

In 1936 the court again took up the bludgeon, now from its sparkling, new, marble Roman palace. "It is a magnificient structure," Howard Brubaker noted in the *New Yorker*, "with fine big windows to throw the New Deal out of." On January 6, by a vote of 6 to 3, the court struck down the Agricultural Adjustment Act . . . . On February 17 . . . the court sustained the Tennessee Valley Authority's right to use government property to generate power, a narrow victory. On April 6 the court hobbled the investigatory powers of the Securities and Exchange Commission, and Sutherland gratuitiously attacked the SEC with what Cardozo called "denunciatory fervor." Early in May the court nullified the Bituminous Coal Conservation Act in the Carter case, in part by a 5 to 4 vote . . . . On the last day of the term, still again 5 to 4, the court struck down the New York minimum wage law for women in the laundry case, Morehead v. Tipaldo . . . . "We finished the term of the Court yesterday," Stone wrote his sister, "I think in many ways one of the most disastrous in its history."[24]

24. *Ibid.*, pp. 638–640.

Of all these reversals for the New Deal, the Supreme Court's decision in the *Carter Coal* case[25] was the most devastating to the cause of the NLRB. The Bituminous Coal Conservation Act (the Guffery Coal Act) contained essentially the same labor provisions as those in the Wagner Act and the attorneys for the government used the same "commerce arguments" in the *Carter* case that the board was using in the Wagner Act test cases— proving "beyond doubt that labor disputes in the coal industry had interferred not only with interstate commerce in coal itself but with interstate rail transportation and a great proportion of all industry as well."[26] The government also introduced the same kind of economic evidence that the board was preparing in the test cases "for the purpose of showing that the respondent is engaged in interstate commerce."[27]

The Supreme Court's decision made it seem certain, however, that the NLRB's attempts to apply the Wagner Act to manufacturing were hopeless. Despite the fact that 97 percent of the Carter Company's coal was shipped outside its home state of West Virginia and that "seven coal-producing states filed briefs supporting the government's contention that the act did not endanger state's rights and that federal regulation was the only solution for the coal industry,"[28] a majority of the Supreme Court ruled that production was not commerce but merely a "step in preparation for commerce,"[29] that the "local character of mining, of manufacturing, and of crop growing is a fact, and remains a fact, whatever may be done with the products,"[30] and that "the relation of employer and employee is a local relation . . . . over which the federal government has no legislative control."[31] The majority characterized the government's reliance on previous Supreme Court decisions in the antitrust cases and the *Swift*,

25. *Carter v. Carter Coal Co.*, 298 U.S. 238 (1936).
26. Stern, *op. cit.*, p. 676.
27. NLRB files, "Procedure in Showing Interstate Commerce," legal memorandum (496) from C. Fahy, pp. 1–4. See also NLRB files, "Supplement No. 1 to Memorandum on Procedure in Showing Interstate Commerce," legal memorandum (497) from C. Fahy, pp. 1–2.
28. Bernstein, *Turbulent Years, op. cit.*, pp. 476–477.
29. *Carter v. Carter Coal Co.*, 298 U.S. 238 (1936), at 303.
30. *Ibid.*, at 304.
31. *Ibid.*, at 308.

Stafford, and *Olsen* flow of commerce cases as "superficially considered"[32] in that the government, in the opinion of the Court, failed to make the "final and decisive inquiry, whether here [the] effect [on interstate commerce] is direct . . . or indirect."[33]

Although allowing "that the production of every commodity intended for interstate sale and transportation has some effect upon interstate commerce,"[34] the Court found that the Bituminous Coal Act sought to regulate "local controversies and evils affecting local work" and that "such effect as they may have upon commerce, however extensive it may be, is secondary and indirect."[35] The majority agreed that the only "perceptible difference" between the *Carter* case and the *Schechter* case was that "in the Schechter Case the federal power was asserted with respect to commodities which had come to rest after their interstate transportation; while here [*Carter Coal Co.*] the case deals with commodities at rest before interstate commerce has begun."[36] The Supreme Court found that "the difference is without significance."[37]

The Outlook for Constitutionality

The NLRB took the public position that "officially and authoritatively the [*Carter Coal Co.*] decision [had] no effect whatever on the Wagner Act."[38] But the chairman's explanations were unconvincing and betrayed some of the frustration and dejection prevalent at the board. Speaking in Pittsburg five days after the

32. *Ibid.,* at 304. See Cortner, *op. cit.,* pp. 99–102 and appendix: *Swift & Company* v. *United States,* 196 U.S. 375 (1905); *Stafford* v. *Wallace,* 258 U.S. 495 (1922); and *Chicago Board of Trade* v. *Olsen,* 262 U.S. 1 (1923).

33. *Carter* v. *Carter Coal Co.,* 298 U.S. 238 (1936) at 307.

34. *Ibid.*

35. *Ibid.,* at 308–309.

36. *Ibid.,* at 309.

37. *Ibid.*

38. NLRB files, "Address of J. Warren Madden Before the Labor Institute," Pittsburgh, Pennsylvania, May 23, 1936, p. 1.

Supreme Court's *Carter Coal* decision, Chairman Madden told his audience that "decisions which relate to work on a commodity before the commodity has begun to move on an interstate journey [*Carter Coal Co.*], or after it has reached the end of an interstate journey [*Schechter Poultry Co.*], [did] not justify a prediction that the court will apply the same rule to work on a commodity which is at mid-point in a long interstate journey."[39] (The chairman referred to stockyards, meat packing plants, "a great steel mill," and truck factories.)

He reminded his listeners that the Wagner Act was not before the Supreme Court in the *Carter* case and that what the Court had said about manufacturing in that case was obviously dicta "recognized by all courts and lawyers as not having the weight or importance of decisions."[40] The chairman pointed out that the Supreme Court had not yet adopted the doctrine "that there is something about labor relations, as distinguished from all other sorts of relations, which prevent labor relations from having a bearing upon interstate commerce . . ." and that such a doctrine "would ignore . . . what every man in the street knows, namely, that strikes in industries which stand in a current of interstate commerce not only affect that current but frequently stop it completely. . . ."[41] If such a doctrine were applied, the chairman said, "it would seem that the discussion had passed into a realm of legal mysticism, which it would be useless to pursue farther. . . ."[42] He concluded by stating the predicament of powerlessness caused by the *Carter Coal* decision—a decision which one historian has called "a staggering blow against the whole idea of national power":[43]

In the litigation involving the Guffey Act, the national government asserted the power, and most of the interested states through their officers expressed a desire that the national government should have the power, yet the Constitution, as interpreted, had lodged the power in the states, which didn't want it and thought they couldn't usefully

39. *Ibid.*, p. 3.
40. *Ibid.*, pp. 1 and 6.
41. *Ibid.*, p. 4.
42. *Ibid.*
43. Bernstein, *Turbulent Years, op. cit.*, p. 478.

exercise it. Such a phenomenon clearly calls for thoughtful consideration by those interested in public affairs.[44]

On May 21, 1936, just three days after the *Carter Coal* decision, the board sent a "highly confidential" memorandum to all regional directors instructing them that, because of the Supreme Court's ruling, "certain types of cases will have to be completely eliminated for the present and others must be discouraged as much as possible."[45] Most significantly, the regional directors were told that manufacturing cases were now "in general less desirable."[46] The board's regional directors, in turn, reported the harsh realities of the post-*Carter* case reactions in the field: "The prevailing belief among employers that the Supreme Court is going to hold the Act unconstitutional, and that consequently they can violate the law with impunity,"[47] the "hesitancy on the part of unions to file charges because of the prevailing belief that the Act is unconstitutional,"[48] and the "increasing feeling of unrest and more danger of strikes"[49] because of the "disgust and impatience [of labor] coupled with the belief that the only way to effect reforms in industrial relations is by extending economic organization and the use of economic power resulting from such organization."[50] (Elinore Herrick, director of the New York

44. NLRB files, "Address of J. Warren Madden Before the Labor Institute," *op. cit.*, p. 7.
45. *Smith Committee Hearings*, *op. cit.*, p. 5542. This memorandum gave several other reasons for the curtailment of hearings, including lack of funds and staff, but Chairman Madden made it quite clear at a subsequent meeting of the regional directors in June 1936 that the May 21, 1936 memorandum "came out as a result of the Carter Coal Company decision. . . ." See minutes of a conference of regional directors, June 19, 1936, Box 157.
46. *Smith Committee Hearings*, *op. cit.*, vol. 24, part II, p. 5542, memorandum from Wolf to regional directors, May 21, 1936.
47. NA, RG233, "Discussion of Problems at Conference," memorandum from Bertram Edises, attorney, Twentieth Region, San Francisco, to B. Wolf, June 11, 1936, Box 157.
48. NA, RG233, memorandum from Robert H. Cowdrill, director, Eleventh Region, Indianapolis, to B. Wolf, June 8, 1936, Box 157.
49. NLRB files, "Regional Offices' Comments on Current Labor Situation for May 1936," Thirteenth Region, Chicago, p. 7.
50. NLRB files, "Regional Offices' Comments on Current Labor Situation for May 1936," Sixth Region, Pittsburgh, p. 4.

regional office, in her usual frank way told the board "that if we are in for a summer of suspended animation . . . . The Directors must be given strong support and backing by the Board," since "you [the board] only see a union delegate when he appeals. We have to see them every day."[51])

One day after the board's confidential memorandum to its regional directors, the AFL's general counsel, Charlton Ogburn, wrote a letter to Chairman Madden urging that "the Board should at least carry these arguments [on constitutionality] to their logical conclusion in the court of last resort before modifying its views about its own jurisdiction," particularly since, in Ogburn's opinion, "the Guffey decision [left] the law about where the Schechter decision left it with regard to the subject matter of commerce. . . ."[52] Ogburn saw the Supreme Court in its *Carter Coal* opinion going "back to ancient days . . . . where commerce is treated almost as if it were confined to transportation"—"a limitation upon the power of the national government over interstate commerce, which was within a few years repudiated by the Supreme Court itself, and the Court has never gone back to this old narrow doctrine of interstate commerce until it passed upon the N.R.A. in the Schechter case, and upon the Guffey Act this week."[53] Ogburn, agreeing with those who maintained that the Supreme Court had "under its own decisions" the "complete discretion to uphold or not uphold the New Deal laws," found, as others were finding, that the board's constitutional difficulties were being caused not so much by Supreme Court case precedent as by the men of the Supreme Court:

We must . . . consider how five Justices out of nine of the Supreme Court will look at a given question. We must consider their political philosophy and their economic views. We have seen that the Justices divide five against four or six against three on these vital questions according to their own personal and political philosophy. We know that five Justices of the present court are dominated by a doctrine of

51. NA, RG233, memorandum from E. Herrick to B. Wolf, June 12, 1936, Box 157.
52. NA, RG233, letter from Charlton Ogburn to J. W. Madden with attached memorandum, "Effect of Guffey Act Decision on the National Labor Relations Act," May 22, 1936, Box 143.
53. *Ibid.*, p. 2.

laissez faire. We know that five of these Justices believe in the so-called principles of rugged individualism . . . . we are dealing not with the full power of Congress under the Constitution to regulate commerce among the States and with foreign countries, we are dealing rather with the way in which five or six men out of nine would limit the power of Congress by their own ideas of what is meant by commerce. . . .[54]

The board called its regional directors and field staff to Washington for a meeting on June 18, 1936. The gathering came at a time when the board had just received word that the Fifth Circuit Court of Appeals had ruled in the *Jones & Laughlin* case that "the Constitution does not vest in the Federal Government the power to regulate the relation as such of employer and employee in production or manufacture."[55] There was no doubt that the Fifth Circuit had based its opinion on the Supreme Court's *Carter Coal Co.* decision. Fahy told the group that "in view of the Supreme Court under the Guffey Act [the Bituminous Coal Act] . . . other Circuit Courts will make similar decisions this summer."[56]

In this pessimistic setting, Chairman Madden remarked that apparently "our judges have ceased to pay that respect to the other branches of government" which traditionally required the courts to adopt a "strong presumption that these other branches of government have not exceeded the constitutional power . . ." and that "Perhaps the reverse [was] true that they approach the problem almost with a presumption that the legislative and executive branches of the government have violated the Constitution."[57] The serious reversals of recent months, the dismal prospects for the Wagner Act, and the frustration of knowing that "what shall be done about it is not within [the board's] hands" must have weighed heavily upon the usually idealistic chairman when he confided to the directors and the field staff that

54. *Ibid.*, pp. 3, 5.
55. *The New York Times*, June 16, 1936, p. 1, col. 3.
56. NA, RG233, minutes of a meeting of the departmental and field staff of the National Labor Relations Board, June 18, 1936, Box 157.
57. *Ibid.*

I shall be obliged to have a feeling closely resembling nausea when I continue to hear, perhaps more frequently in the future than in the past, the statement that what we have is a government of laws and not of men. That statement is nonsense when analyzed. It seems to me that it is particularly demonstrable nonsense at this time, when by these narrow divisions of the men who sit in the seat of decision, we get these important consequences.[58]

In the same vein, board member Edwin Smith, in a written but never published paper, stated that the *Carter Coal* decision had "left a pretty thin ray of hope that the Supreme Court will find the National Labor Relations Act constitutional as applied to manufacturing."[59] He felt that the majority of the Supreme Court had revealed themselves "as temperamentally and by their intellectual processes opposed to constructions of the language of the Constitution which would countenance federal intervention in this field."[60] He wrote further that "the changes which have made modern industry . . . something quite different than the members of the Constitutional Convention could have conceived" made it "utter folly . . . to attempt to read now the intentions of these minds 150 years ago toward things then non-existent."[61] Smith believed that if the Wagner Act was found unconstitutional, "the powerful, predatory forces which are opposed to unionization of labor will resume full sway."[62] He recommended that labor should seek a "constitutional amendment which will confirm once and for all Congress' power in the field of regulation of labor relations."[63] In a handwritten notation at the top of a draft of Smith's manuscript, Charles Fahy indicated that he had "no objection except that Mr. Smith is a member of the Board. In some other hands it would be fine."[64]

58. *Ibid.*
59. NLRB files, three-page typewritten statement by E. S. Smith, undated and untitled, p. 1.
60. *Ibid.*
61. *Ibid.*, p. 2.
62. *Ibid.*, p. 1.
63. *Ibid.*, p. 3.
64. *Ibid.*, p. 4.

One of the most revealing indicators of the board's assessment of its chances in the courts came in the form of an announcement during the June conference of regional directors of a "modified policy" concerning the regional directors' use of mediation in the adjustment of cases. The same board which had instructed its regional directors that the NLRB was to be a "rigorous law enforcement operation rather than a mediation or conciliation operation" now had board member Edwin Smith tell the directors that, since the NLRB planned to "take relatively few manufacturing cases . . . to a hearing and decision," mediation was "the most important job before the regional director" and that they should be "perfectly frank" in telling workers that "the most we can do for them is likely to be through mediation."[65] The board's secretary, Benedict Wolf, added that even where "full compliance with the law cannot be secured it is well to get all you can. . . ."[66] (Wolf wanted "to see the Act amended to provide that the Board shall be constituted, in addition to its present functions, a Board of Mediation." He believed that "such an amendment would make this Board the chief mediating agency in the country and give its prestige a tremendous boost. . . .")[67]

Injunctions and the District Courts

The NLRB in 1936 had to contend not only with the judges of the Supreme Court and the U.S. circuit courts of appeals but also with

65. NA, RG233, minutes of a conference of regional directors, June 19, 1936, Box 157.
66. *Ibid.*
67. NLRB files, memorandum by B. Wolf, n.d., pp. 7–8. See also NLRB files, "Suggested amendment of the National Labor Relations Act to provide for mediation in the maritime industry, and in the interstate trucking and bus industries," memorandum from B. Wolf to the National Labor Relations Board, n.d., and NLRB files, "Suggested amendment of the National Labor Relations Act to provide for mediation in the maritime industry," memorandum from E. S. Smith to B. Wolf, December 3, 1936. See also *Smith Committee Hearings, op. cit.*, vol. 16, pp. 3332–3333 and 3385–3391.

the judges of the federal district courts, many of whom were ready "to seize an opportunity to declare invalid legislation which displease[d] their conception of policy."[68] This "predisposition on the bench" in 1935 and 1936 resulted in an unprecedented 1,600 injunctions issued by "well over a third of the entire corps" of federal court judges restraining various acts of Congress.[69]

Although the board was free of injunction suits during its first two months of operation, by November of 1935 "the United States Marshall honored the Board with almost daily visits, to serve papers upon the members charging them with being trespassers and intermeddlers and seeking to enjoin them from doing what they were appointed to do."[70] Most of the employers moved to halt NLRB proceedings before a word of testimony had been heard on the merits of their cases, charging that the Wagner Act was unconstitutional and that the holding of hearings by the board would cause an employer irreparable injury for which there would be no adequate remedy "in that [hearings] would involve expense, impair existing employer-employee relationships, affect adversely the good will of the company, subject the company to the possible necessity of producing records under subpena, and might involve criminal prosecution."[71] According to the NLRB's *First Annual Report,*

> Immediately following the institution of [the] first suit, a Nationwide and apparently concerted endeavor was made to utilize the same injunctive method to prevent the Board from proceeding with many other hearings scheduled before it. Not only did the attorneys filing the injunction suits become most ingenious in devising all possible allegations of injury, but, strikingly enough, the growth and fantastic character of these allegations showed a gradually increasing uniformity. In the first bills of complaint the allegations of

68. Seymour S. Mintz, "Suits to Enjoin the National Labor Relations Board," *The George Washington Law Review*, vol. 4, no. 3 (March 1936), p. 999.
69. Schlesinger, *The Politics of Upheaval, op. cit.,* pp. 447–448.
70. NLRB files, address of J. W. Madden during the National Radio Forum sponsored by the *Washington Star*, September 6, 1937, p. 2 (mimeographed).
71. NLRB, *First Annual Report, op. cit.,* p. 47.

damage were not very detailed, then some other counsel would think of other possible injuries and add them to those previously alleged in suits already filed. Subsequent suits would incorporate all damages alleged in previous suits, plus whatever additional ones the particular attorney could think of; and this total would be contained in the next suit, with further additions.

The process was like a rolling snowball. The allegations in a pleading filed by an employer in Georgia, for example, would show up in precisely the same wording in a pleading filed in Seattle. There came a very rapid and widespread exchange of pleadings all over the country until all had exhausted their ingenuity in conjuring up the many and gross injuries which it was alleged a hearing before the Board would entail.[72]

Of the total of 103 injunction suits that were filed against the board in district courts, 83 were instituted before June 30, 1936. Chairman Madden, annoyed at the time by circuit court delays in deciding the test cases, told a Senate appropriations committee that "the Board was in the anomalous situation of having district judges who are directed by the statute not to disturb our cases, reach out with anxiety to get them" [while] "the Circuit Courts of Appeals which are directed by the statute to handle our cases expeditiously, have great hesitation in doing anything with them."[73] (The chairman, pleading for additional funds, also told

72. *Ibid.*, pp. 47–48. Charles Fahy recalled that "In the injunction litigation we were faced with quite a formidable national movement . . . in support of the injunction litigation. There was a brief published by a very distinguished group of lawyers, some of the best-known lawyers in the United States, which had been printed and given very widespread circulation throughout the country. It was used by lawyers pretty widely scattered throughout the country in the arguments and briefs which they filed in support of their efforts to enjoin the board. And sometimes, too, in one of these suits, the plaintiff would be some poor, moderately single employee who was seeking, because of his or her opposition to a union, to enjoin the operations of the act, but would be represented by one of the great New York law firms." Oral history interview with C. Fahy, *op. cit.*, p. 16.

73. *The New York Times*, February 2, 1936, p. 9, col. 1.

the committee that when the board "finds that [its] adversary in the injunction suit is John W. Davis or Mr. Wood of *Cravath and Wood* we do not feel that it is fair to the government to have this $2,800 boy, [the salary of NLRB attorneys] to determine a great constitutional question.")[74]

Even in the "hostile judicial atmosphere of that day,"[75] however, the board's inexperienced lawyers won almost all of the injunction cases by convincing most of the district court judges before whom they appeared that the Wagner Act provision for circuit court review of any final order by the board was "an entirely adequate remedy" and that, since employers could not demonstrate that a board hearing would cause the type of damage that would justify an injunction under equity principles, "it was unnecessary for the district courts to consider the constitutionality of the act."[76]

Board attorneys who argued the injunction cases throughout the country found that the legal thinking of many district court judges reflected not only their conservative philosophy of political economy but also their "deep ignorance of labor relations."[77] Associate General Counsel Robert Watts,[78] who was in charge of

74. *Ibid.*
75. Oral history interview with P. Levy, *op. cit.* It is also fair to point out, however, that much of the NLRB's injunction work was handled by experienced attorneys such as Charles Fahy, Robert Watts, Thomas Emerson, Malcom Halliday, Lawrence Knapp, and Philip Levy.
76. NLRB, *First Annual Report, op. cit.*, p. 48. For a detailed statement of the NLRB's position in litigating the injunction suits, see NLRB files, "Judicial Interference With Proceedings of the N.L.R.B. Or Its Regional Agencies," memorandum by Robert S. Erdahl (mimeographed); "Effect of Courts Doubt as to Constitutionality of the National Labor Relations Act on an Application for a Preliminary Injunction," memorandum from A. N. Somers to C. Fahy, January 28, 1936; "Brief In Opposition to Application for Preliminary Injunction," memorandum circulated by C. Fahy to all attorneys, February 3, 1936.
77. NLRB files, "Supplement to Chester Wright's Labor Letter," April 4, 1936, p. 2.
78. Watts graduated from Bates College and the Yale Law School. He was appointed as an assistant United States attorney for the southern district of New York and became chief assistant United

the board's injunction litigation and who argued many of the injunction cases in the district courts, found it "appalling to go before the District Courts in various parts of the country and get the most amazing revelations as to what the Court thought this Act was before it was explained."[79] Some of the lower court judges thought that the Wagner Act provided for compulsory arbitration, while others believed the act was merely a conciliation statute.[80] Judge John P. Barnes of the Northern District of Illinois, for example, found that a "combination of majority rule and compulsory unilateral arbitration [was] the heart of the act"[81] and Judge Merrill E. Otis of the Western District of Missouri, whose injunction order brought the work of the Kansas City Regional Board "to a complete and utter halt,"[82] wrote in his opinion that

> the individual employee still can confer, still can petition, but he cannot bargain. If his employer bargains with him as an individual, as a man, as an American citizen, that is unfair; it is prohibited. The individual employee is dealt with by the act as an incompetent. The Government must protect him even from himself. He is the ward of the United States, to be cared for by his guardian even as if he were a member

States attorney for that district. After two years in that post, Watts resigned to become a member of a private law firm in New York City where he practiced until 1934 when he joined the old NLRB and was placed in charge of litigation. He became associate general counsel for the NLRB shortly after the board began its work in September 1935.

79. NA, RG233, minutes of a meeting of the departmental and field staff of the National Labor Relations Board, June 18, 1936, Box 157. Robert Watts told his attorneys in the field that "We should keep in mind that the courts are in fact not familiar with the Act and may have many entirely erroneous ideas about it." He instructed the attorneys to explain to the court such things as the creation of the board, the unfair labor practice provisions of the act, and the fact that the board had no power of enforcement and that "the full right of review [was] given to the Circuit Court of Appeals. . . ." *Ibid.*

80. *Smith Committee Hearings, op. cit.*, vol. 13, p. 2583. See also NLRB files, *First Annual Report op. cit.*, p. 49.

81. *The New York Times*, March 25, 1936, p. 1, col. 5.

82. Oral history interview with George Pratt, *op. cit.*, p. 91.

of an uncivilized tribe of Indians or a recently emancipated slave.[83]

George Pratt, the regional director in Kansas City, recalled that

one of our staff members in Washington . . . at the time was Malcolm Ross, otherwise known as Mike Ross. He was in the Publicity Department, . . . the public relations fellow . . . and he was always writing songs. And one of the songs that he wrote was "Judge Otis Regrets." . . . there was a popular song, "Mrs. Otis Regrets She Cannot Have Lunch Today" . . . . and he wrote this song, "Judge Otis Regrets That Commerce Is Not Involved, For Manufacturing Is Purely a Local Thing . . . ." And he put that to some music or the guitar or something of the sort and . . . for quite a long time at our get-togethers . . . this [was] one of our songs that we would sing. . . .[84]

The NLRB was forced to commit "a large portion" of its undermanned legal staff "to the task of protecting the Board from these attacks."[85] In many of these cases, the "litigation was long and wearisome" so that "by the time the Board had extricated itself from these legal entanglements and went back to pick up the merits of the case, nothing recognizable remained of the situation."[86] This was, perhaps, the most severe consequence of the injunction suits since many unions became convinced that the Wagner Act was not useful to them and, therefore, they ignored the law. According to Robert Watts,

. . . unions and complainants who have come, in good faith, to the Board, relying upon the act of Congress for relief, have suddenly, in a manner totally inexplicable to them, found themselves stopped and unable to present their cases to the Board. They have been in effect prevented from continuing their organizing and collective bargaining and, in

83. *Smith Committee Hearings, op. cit.,* vol. 13, p. 2581. See also *The New York Times,* December 22, 1935, p. 1, col. 1.
84. Oral history interview with G. Pratt, *op. cit.,* pp. 90–91.
85. *Smith Committee Hearings, op. cit.,* vol. 13, p. 2583.
86. NLRB files, address of J. W. Madden during the National Radio Forum sponsored by the *Washington Star, op. cit.,* p. 2.

many instances, as I have been informed by representatives of labor organizations that while these collateral attacks were going on, they did not feel they could bring their disputes before the Board, but they, of necessity were relying upon the guerilla warfare of industrial disputes to protect their rights to organize and bargain.[87]

Although the board's position was eventually sustained in all of the injunction cases, by June of 1936, eleven district court judges had issued twenty decisions granting injunctive relief to employers in ten judicial districts.[88] The Eighth Circuit Court of Appeals, moreover, by affirming Judge Otis' ruling on August 5, 1936, "for all practical purposes" blocked the board from functioning in that court's jurisdiction. The Second, Fifth, and Sixth Circuit Courts of Appeals affirmed the denial of injunctions by district court judges in their jurisdictions, but the refusal of those courts to enforce board orders in the *Friedman-Harry Marks* case on July 13, 1936, in the *Jones and Laughlin* case on June 15, 1936, and in the *Fruehauf Trailer Co.* case on June 30, 1936 "in effect confined the Board's activities in those jurisdictions to cases involving interstate transportation and communication."[89] Finally, after the Supreme Court's decision in the *Carter Coal* case, the Court of Appeals for the District of Columbia made it possible for the board to be "blocked by any employer who care[d] to take his case to Washington" by granting temporary injunctions to employers pending a hearing on their appeals from the adverse decisions of lower courts.[90] As one board attorney

87. *Smith Committee Hearings, op. cit.,* vol. 13, pp. 2583–2584.
88. These figures were compiled by the author from the NLRB's *Second Annual Report, op. cit.,* pp. 37–38.
89. NLRB files, "Present Status of National Labor Relations Act," unsigned legal memorandum, n.d., pp. 10–15. For an almost identical version of this memorandum, see NLRB files, "Status of the National Labor Relations Board," memorandum by T. I. Emerson, September 10, 1936. The cases mentioned are *NLRB* v. *Friedman-Harry Marks Clothing Co.,* 85 F. 2d 1 (CCA 2d July 13, 1936); *NLRB* v. *Jones & Laughlin Steel Corp.,* 83 F. 2d 998 (CCA 5th June 15, 1936); and *NLRB* v. *Fruehauf Trailer Co.,* 85 F. 2d 391 (CCA 6th, June 30, 1936).
90. NLRB files, "Present Status of National Labor Relations Act," unsigned legal memorandum, n.d., p. 11. When the board issued a complaint against the Goodyear Tire & Rubber Co., for example,

put it, "in short, pending final determination of the constitutional questions, the Board's activities in all fields except transportation and communication seem virtually at an end."[91]

An Alternative Route to Constitutionality

The NLRB's predicament was particularly grave since the board in 1936 had little public or political support. Those at the NLRB realized that the Wagner Act was not passed because the New Deal administration or the general public deeply desired it. The lack of any public contempt toward those who defied the act, moreover, emphasized the NLRB's lack of public support and made the board certain that the Wagner Act would never be accepted as the law of the land until the Supreme Court declared it to be the law of the land. The board also believed that "public intelligence" about the NLRB was "under a great hardship" in that "practically all of the important newspapers of the country" were either suppressing or misinterpreting facts about the work of the board.[92] Chairman Madden complained, for example, that whereas New York City papers "gave large front-page spreads to adverse decisions by obscure District Court Judges in remote

---

"on charges growing out of the . . . beatings of union organizers at Gadsden, Alabama, the Company applied for an injunction in the Supreme Court of the District [of Columbia]. The injunction was denied and the Board's motion to dismiss granted, but the Court at the same time granted a 'temporary injunction' pending appeal." *Ibid.*, pp. 11–12. See also NLRB files, "Status of the National Labor Relations Board," memorandum by T. I. Emerson, September 10, 1936, pp. 7–8.

91. NLRB files, "Present Status of National Labor Relations Act," unsigned legal memorandum, n.d., p. 17. See also NLRB files, "Status of the National Labor Relations Board," memorandum by T. I. Emerson, September 10, 1936, p. 8. NA, RG25, informal files, letter from Robert B. Watts to Clifford O'Brien, February 3, 1936, *Carlisle Lumber Company* case.
92. NLRB files, letter from J. W. Madden to Harwood L. Childs, managing editor, *The Public Opinion Quarterly*, July 21, 1936.

parts of the country," they "gave very small treatment well tucked away inside of the paper" to the decision of the Circuit Court of Appeals in New York upholding the constitutionality of the Wagner Act in the *Associated Press* case.[93]

The NLRB's position was especially weak and vulnerable to attack since it had isolated itself during its first year of operation. The board had not developed any power base in Congress and had not sought to influence the president or any other important people in the administration. The board, consequently, was still haunted by President Roosevelt's reluctant support of the public policy of collective bargaining and by the president's readiness to restrict the jurisdiction of the old NLRB in the San Francisco *Call-Bulletin* episode.[94] When, during the shipping strikes of 1936, many newspapers, particularly the Scripps-Howard chain, urged the government to transfer the board's jurisdiction over maritime labor relations to the Railway Labor Act's National Mediation Board, Chairman Madden wrote to his regional director in New Orleans that "if jurisdiction over shipping were removed from us, and if the Supreme Court should deny us jurisdiction over manufacturing and over production enterprises, we really would have very little left, and an office such as yours would have practically nothing left."[95] Benedict Wolf was certain "that, after maritime, would go trucking and buses would follow, and then to communications, etc., leaving the Board only a field of doubtful jurisdiction."[96]

It was only because of the persistent efforts of the NLRB's "special investigator," Heber Blankenhorn,[97] that the board was willing to counter the opposition of the courts by exerting direct pressure on public opinion and the Congress. Blankenhorn was considered as a "mystery man" at the board, a "professional detective" who "always gave the appearance that something

93. *Ibid.*
94. See Chapter IV, pp. 109–122.
95. NLRB files, letter from J. W. Madden to Charles H. Logan, November 14, 1936.
96. NLRB files, memorandum by B. Wolf, n.d., p. 6. This memorandum was an excellent source for the analysis of the board's situation in 1936.
97. For other references to Blankenhorn, including his background and job description with the NLRB, see Chapter IV, pp. 115–116, fn. 26.

sinister was going on."[98] One historian has written that

[Blankenhorn] became a familiar figure in Washington liberal and labor circles. Wiry, balding, and bespectacled, he prowled through government buildings in a worn army trenchcoat, apparently always engaged in clandestine activities. Boris Shiskin, an economic researcher for the American Federation of Labor, remembered him as "a man of considerable parts . . . . By his choice and his gifts, he was really very much an operator on a grandiose scale. He had big visions of things to be done . . . ." Blankenhorn's goal—a strong labor movement—never receded; his technique—publicity—never changed.[99]

"Just as soon as the Wagner Act was passed," Blankenhorn concluded that "when you lay prohibitions on employers, there is a tendency to have recourse to a third party to do the things that are forbidden."[100] His experience in supervising the Interchurch World Movement's field investigations of the great steel strike of 1919 convinced him that employers would not "have your labor law [but would] have labor detectives, gas, and guns in the mills, gunmen as deputy sheriffs, vigilante committees if need be, legalistic obstructiveness and propaganda to 'unconstitutionalize' any enactments that interfere with these things."[101] On September 30, 1935, at the urging of Blankenhorn, the board authorized him to conduct what he referred to as "a preliminary investigation, greatly restricted in scope and personnel," into these "long rooted"—employer practices.[102]

98. Oral history interview with Louis G. Silverberg, *op. cit.*, p. 40.
99. Jerold S. Auerbach, *Labor And Liberty: The LaFollette Committee and the New Deal* (New York: The Bobbs-Merrill Company, 1966), p. 60.
100. NA, RG233, minutes of a conference of regional directors, June 19, 1936, Box 157.
101. U.S. Congress, Senate, Subcommittee of the Senate Committee on Education and Labor, *Hearings on Senate Resolution 266*, 74th Cong., 2d Sess. (Washington: GPO, 1936), p. 265. (hereinafter referred to as *Hearings on Senate Resolution 266*).
102. NA, RG25, "Cooperation of the National Labor Relations Board with the Civil Liberties Sub-Committee of the Committee on Education and Labor, U.S. Senate, 1935–39," memorandum for the board

What Blankenhorn really wanted, however, was a congressional investigation.[103] Chairman Madden remarked at the June 1936 conference of regional directors that "a good deal of the time . . . we scarcely knew where Blankenhorn was, but when he turned up again, it developed that he had either been at the Hill or had been out in the regions finding out about this [investigation]. . . ."[104] Blankenhorn was, in fact, on a "campaign to salvage the Wagner Act," writing letters to Senators LaFollette and Wagner and "buttonhol[ing] senators on the Committee on Education and Labor. . . ."[105] He told them that "the Wagner Act put the cart before the horse in establishing a law without full investigation of capital-labor relations throughout the country" and he advocated reviving a "little United States Commission on Industrial Relations" (of 1912–1915) to make that investigation.[106] "Practically single handed," Blankenhorn mobilized the drive for a civil liberties investigation by Congress.[107]

He travelled throughout the country spurring union leaders on to communicate with members of Congress, personally obtaining passage of resolutions at the American Federation of Labor Convention of 1935 encouraging the investigation of undercover agencies (and getting AFL President William Green to send a questionnaire to all AFL unions "for the express purpose of collecting information"), planning investigations "with officers of textiles, hosiery, miners, ladies garments, men's clothing,

---

by Heber Blankenhorn, n.d., p. 7. Records of NLRB II relating to the Smith Committee investigation, File L-3, LaFollette Committee.

103. NLRB files, "Position of Undercover Agencies Investigation," memorandum from H. Blankenhorn to J.W. Madden, J. M. Carmody, and E. S. Smith, December 17, 1935.

104. NA, RG233, minutes of a conference of regional directors, June 19, 1936, Box 157.

105. Auerbach, *op. cit.*, p. 62.

106. NA, RG233, minutes of a conference of regional directors, June 19, 1936, Box 157. See the United States Commission on Industrial Relations, 1912–1915, *Final Report and Testimony* (Washington: GPO, 1916) 11 vols. and the United States Commission on Industrial Relations, 1912–1915, *Final Report of the Commission on Industrial Relations* (Washington: GPO 1915).

107. NA, RG233, minutes of a conference of regional directors, June 19, 1936, Box 157.

machinists and other metal trades, railway clerks, printing trades, steel, auto and rubber unions," assembling documents from past investigations of industrial espionage as well as "documentary evidence of espionage since July 5, 1935," and using the resources and hearings of the NLRB's regional boards "for uncovering espionage."[108]

Blankenhorn took the results of his preliminary investigation to Senator Robert LaFollette of the Committee on Education and Welfare "by letter [on] December 3, 1935" and to Senator Robert Wagner "in conferences [on] December 28, 1935." He reported later that "their advice immediately confirmed the judgment of the Board that an adequate investigation could be carried out only by the Congress" and that the "senators were supported in this view by unions of the A.F.L. whose cooperation in collecting data and witnesses had been obtained during the Board investigations; also independently of the Board investigation, by civic and religious organizations, some of which held public meetings . . . ."[109]

Blankenhorn emphasized to Senators LaFollette and Wagner that a congressional investigation would expose "that connection between plant munitioning, professional espionage, and legal obstruction"[110] by "hold[ing] up to public scrutiny the conduct of leading industrialists (. . . Ernest T. Weir, Tom Girdler, Eugene Grace, Alfred P. Sloan and Henry Ford)" and exposing their links to "Liberty League lawyers (. . . Earl Reed, John W. Davis, and Raoul Desvernine)."[111] This evidence of antilabor practices

108. NLRB files, three memorandums from H. Blankenhorn to J. W. Madden, J.M. Carmody, and E. S. Smith: "Work at AF of L Convention," October 7, 1935; "Position of undercover agencies investigation," December 17, 1935; "Undercover agency in Brown Shoe Case, St. Louis," November 6, 1935. See also *Smith Committee Hearings, op. cit.,* vol. 20, pp. 4260 and 4265 and vol. 21, p. 4422.

109. NA, RG25, "Cooperation of the National Labor Relations Board with the Civil Liberties Sub-Committee of the Committee on Education and Labor, U.S. Senate, 1935–1939," memorandum for the National Labor Relations board by H. Blankenhorn, n.d., p. 8. Records of NLRB II relating to the Smith Committee Investigation, File L-3, LaFollette Committee.

110. *Hearings on Senate Resolution 266, op. cit.,* p. 57.

111. Auerbach, *op. cit.,* p. 61.

would, if released throughout the spring and summer of 1936, "become a mighty weapon in the approaching presidential campaign" and "would convince the rank and file of labor that Congress had not passed the Wagner Act merely as a sop to forestall legitimate labor demands."[112]

On February 21, 1936, Senator LaFollette promised to introduce a resolution calling for a Senate inquiry into civil liberties violations and "Blankenhorn led a small group in drafting a suitable resolution; by mid-March they had finished the draft."[113] Although there was great pressure to extend the hearings to the entire field of civil liberties, LaFollette's Senate Resolution 266 which he submitted on March 23, 1936 confined the Committee on Education and Labor to "an investigation of violations of the rights of free speech and assembly and *undue interference with the right of labor to organize and bargain collectively.*"[114]

Blankenhorn had pointed out a "new road to salvation."[115] Rather than "establishing the law" by "fixing our eyes on the courts, particularly the Supreme Court, and that little handful of precedents imbedded in *Texas and New Orleans, . . .* etc." (a process which Blankenhorn said looked "like standing the pyramid on its head, trying to erect a very broad structure on the narrowest imaginable base"), Blankenhorn advocated that the board "[take its] eyes from the courts . . . and [undertake] to turn the facts of labor relations into broad new precedents for the consideration of courts":[116]

> The other process or way of looking at law establishing, begins with the base, to make it as broad as possible, and to build on that . . . . In other words building with the facts as they are, which means investigation and the hearing or publicizing of those facts is one most essential phase of the process of law establishing. Therefore this investigation by the Senate committee simply returns to a major phase of

112. *Ibid.*, pp. 61–62.
113. *Ibid.*, pp. 47 and 62.
114. *Ibid.*, pp. 62–63 (emphasis added).
115. NA, RG233, minutes of a conference of regional directors, June 19, 1936, Box 157. (E. S. Smith used this phrase in introducing Blankenhorn to the conference.)
116. *Ibid.*

establishing our Act by bringing most broadly and definitely to the consciousness of the country the essential facts of actual capital-labor relations.[117]

In March 1936, Nathan Witt, who was assistant general counsel in charge of the Review Division, strongly supported the Blankenhorn approach of "going around the corner a bit"[118] to "establish" the Wagner Act:

A further advantage of presenting material of this kind [evidence of labor espionage and "union smashing"] is that, as far as American public policy is concerned, it is actually non-controversial in that, apart from the small group which profits when workers are spied upon and terrorized, the reaction of the public (including judges and Senators) is certain to be that these practices violate the best in the American tradition, and that their indulgence is incompatible with our free institutions. When Judge Otis learns more about the Bergoffs and the Pinkertons, even he may no longer believe that the Act reduces American workers to the status of slaves or wards. So with other judges. Those judges who vote the way the New York Times thinks, do so because they believe the New York Times is right, and arguments will not change their minds. They may believe differently, however, when they learn that protection of the right to organize includes protection of workers from practices which Americans traditionally despise.[119]

Blankenhorn explained to the board that a Senate investigation would give the board the opportunity to "restate on a national platform what it has done, including certain cases heard in outlying areas and not so well known nationally [and to] state the position it is in vis-a-vis the courts and organized legal opposition."[120] (He felt, for example, that "it would be a public

117. *Ibid.*
118. NA, RG233, "Hearings on the LaFollette Resolution," memorandum from N. Witt to the National Labor Relations Board, March 30, 1936, p. 1–2, Box 124.
119. *Ibid.*
120. NLRB files, memorandum from H. Blankerhorn to J. W. Madden, J. M. Carmody, and E. S. Smith, March 26, 1936.

service to correct what critics say 'these dozen Board cases in the Courts are all that the Board found in a year's work!'").[121] Blankenhorn also saw the investigation as a powerful weapon against the injunction in that the enjoined hearings could be presented in full before a Senate committee investigating interferences with labor's rights. He doubted "that anybody [was] going to attempt to stop a Senate supoena to a hearing"[122] and he was confident that "it ought not to take more than one or two such hearings to make companies hesitant about rushing to courts for injunctions. . . ."[123]

As far as the board and Blankenhorn were concerned, therefore, the Senate investigation was to be used "to eliminate obstacles to enforcement of the Wagner Act, in order to stand the NLRB on its feet, and to realize the promise of labor organization and collective bargaining."[124] Senator LaFollette, moreover, needed the board as much as the board needed the Senate investigation. LaFollette wanted his subcommittee to report favorably on his Senate Resolution 266 with "comparatively few witnesses presenting as strong material as possible"[125] and the NLRB was ready and waiting with expert witnesses, documented case records, and the results of Blankenhorn's investigation of espionage. Senator LaFollette realized that "the NLRB had a great deal more to offer than other governmental agencies" and he "look[ed] upon the Board's assistance as the backbone of the investigation."[126]

Chairman Madden was the first witness called when the hearings on the LaFollette resolution began on April 10, 1936 and his testimony was followed immediately by that of Heber

---

121. NLRB files, letter from H. Blankerhorn to J. W. Madden, October 16, 1936.
122. NA, RG233, minutes of a conference of regional directors, June 19, 1936, Box 157.
123. *Smith Committee Hearings*, "Adjunctive 'Enforcement' of our Law," memorandum from H. Blankenhorn to J. W. Madden, May 22, 1936, vol. 20, p. 4317.
124. Auerbach, *op. cit.*, p. 64.
125. *Ibid.*, p. 65.
126. NA, RG233, "LaFollette Investigation," memorandum from H. Blankenhorn to J. W. Madden and E. S. Smith, October 1, 1936, p. 1, Box 124.

Blankenhorn. Madden used the *Freuhauf* case to demonstrate that the "very dirty business" of espionage was "rapidly becoming . . . the chief obstacle to the realization of the policy of our statute."[127] Blankenhorn "became the star witness of the preliminary hearings," submitting his report on espionage "charging industry with supporting 'an extensive and lucrative business of labor espionage and strikebreaking' . . . . angrily . . . declar[ing] several prominent Liberty League lawyers guilty of association with companies engaged in antilabor practices"[128] and concluding that "only Congress can get at it adequately."[129] Board members John Carmody and Edwin Smith and Associate General Counsel Robert Watts also appeared before the subcommittee to add their supportive testimony.[130] As stated in the Board's *First Annual Report*, "Testimony for the Board and given by agents of the Board comprised more than half the record (344 pages) of these hearings, which resulted in the passage of Senate Resolution 266. . . ."[131]

After Senate Resolution 266 was approved by the Senate on June 6, 1936, the board, "recognizing the importance of the investigation and its bearing on the law the Board administers," decided to assist the LaFollette Committee "to the fullest extent possible."[132] The board designated Heber Blankenhorn to act as full-time liaison with the committee, stated that all "Regional Directors may be given assignments directly by the Committee . . . or by Mr. Blankenhorn," and instructed the regional directors "to cooperate fully with any assignments so made."[133] Although

127. *Hearings on Senate Resolution 266, op. cit.*, pp. 2–3.
128. Auerbach, *op. cit.*, p. 66.
129. *Hearings on Senate Resolution 266, op. cit.*, p. 277.
130. *Ibid.*, pp. 26–32; 278–290; and 291–294.
131. National Labor Relations Board, *First Annual Report, op. cit.*, p. 32.
132. NLRB files, "Memorandum for Senator LaFollette," memorandum from H. Blankenhorn, August 6, 1936. See also NA, RG25, "Minutes of Executive Committee of the Board," July 27, 1936. Records of NLRB II relating to the Smith Committee investigation, Legal Division, office of the general counsel, minutes of executive meetings of the board.
133. NLRB files, "Memorandum for Senator LaFollette," memorandum from H. Blankenhorn August 6, 1936. See also NA, RG25, "Minutes of Executive Committee of the Board," July 27, 1936. Records of

other government agencies loaned personnel to the committee,[134] Blankenhorn considered the investigation the "Board's baby" and so the burden of the committee's field work was carried by the board's regional staffs.[135]

Subcommittee secretary, Robert Wohlforth, who supervised the LaFollette investigation, told a NLRB regional director that "without the help of you fellows on the Board, the Committee never would have been able to collect its data nor prepare its cases with any degree of effectiveness."[136] Approximately thirty-six NLRB employees were "detailed" to the Senate Civil Liberties Committee in 1936 for periods ranging from several days to one

NLRB II relating to the Smith Committee investigation, Legal Division office of the general counsel, minutes of executive meetings of the board, and memorandum from B. Stern to all regional directors, July 29, 1936. Records of NLRB II relating to the Smith Committee investigation, Legal Division, office of the general counsel, File I-4, instructions to staff which may be questioned by the committee.

134. The committee had the cooperation "in the shape of loans of personnel or other facilities" of the following government agencies: the department of Labor (especially the Bureau of Labor Statistics and Wages and Hours Division), the Department of Agriculture (especially the Bureau of Agricultural Economics, Farm Security, Farm Credit Administration, and Rural Electrification Administration), Bureau of Internal Revenue, Securities and Exchange Commission, Public Works Administration, Federal Communications Commission, Railroad Retirement Board, Government Printing Office, United States Housing Authority, National Bituminous Coal Board, and the Treasury Department. (Senate Resolution 266 authorized the investigating Committee "to employ and to call upon the executive departments for clerical and other assistants. . . .") See: NA, RG25, "Cooperation of the National Labor Relations Board with the Civil Liberties Sub-Committee of the Committee on Education and Labor, U.S. Senate, 1935–1939," memorandum for the National Labor Relations Board by H. Blankenhorn, n.d., p. 2. Records of NLRB II relating to the Smith Committee investigation, File L-3, LaFollette Committee.

135. NA, RG233, minutes of a conference of regional directors, June 19, 1936, Box 157. See also NA, RG233, "January Hearings," memorandum from Robert Wohlforth to all staff members, December 22, 1936, p. 1. Exhibit Number 1635, Box 35.

136. NA, RG233, letter from Robert Wohlforth to E. J. Eagen, April 2, 1937. Exhibit Number 1635, Box 35.

year.[137] The committee's only complaint about the board's personnel was that they were too thorough for a congressional committee that needed to "dwell on the sensational and often on the
extreme" in order to command wide attention and to influence
public opinion.[138] Blankenhorn felt that what was needed was the
selection of the more serious and sensational of the abuses from
the "mass of petty detail," that is, "selection . . . on the basis of
what will make the best Senate hearing":[139]

> Surprise and gratification have been expressed by La-
> Follette over "the Board's staff, which was thrown into this
> thing suddenly but seemed to know the subject already and
> who certainly know how to investigate." At the same time the
> difference between our people's methods and a Senate com-
> mittee's exigencies has caused some waste of effort, as well as
> headaches for me. Our people have gone at it with the detailed
> thoroughness characteristic of Board cases, and with an
> expectation of the same amount of time for hearings usual in
> Board cases. But the senators are the boss, and time for
> hearing is extremely limited; the hearings have to score
> major points and must not be lost in supporting details, and
> finally their decisions on what they wanted presented, may be
> very suddenly made and unmade and for reasons which
> cannot always be foreseen by their advisors. The Senators

137. NA, RG25, "Tabulations Summarizing Details of National Labor
     Relations Board's Employees To Senate Civil Liberties Committee
     By Years, 1936–1939" and "List Of Personnel Detailed By The
     National Labor Relations Board To Senate Civil Liberties Com-
     mittee, 1936–1939." Records of NLRB II relating to the Smith
     Committee investigation, File L-3, LaFollette Committee. See also
     Smith Committee Hearings, op. cit., vol. 24, part II, pp. 5788–5791.
     Jerold Auerbach found that "the committee acquired most of its
     staff by the simple expedient of borrowing from the National Labor
     Relations Board." Auerbach, *op. cit.*, p. 85.
138. For the reference to a congressional investigating committee's
     desire for publicity, see Auerbach, *op. cit.*, p. 83.
139. NLRB files, "LaFollette investigation: Informal report," memoran-
     dum from H. Blankenhorn to J. W. Madden, August 7, 1936. See also
     NA, RG233, "Hearings on the LaFollette Resolution," memorandum
     from N. Witt to the National Labor Relations Board, March 30, 1936,
     p. 1, Box 124.

have, of course, relied heavily on their advisors but in some cases briefs, including scores of pages of elaborately worked out questions, have been suddenly thrown into the discard by them. . . .[140]

The NLRB investigators did whatever was necessary to make the investigation a success. For example, when Associate General Counsel Robert Watts anticipated that LaFollette Committee subpoenas "might frighten the detective agencies into destroying their records . . . . he devised a scheme whereby NLRB field agents would approach janitors in buildings where the recalcitrant companies maintained offices and get permission to obtain the contents of their wastebaskets."[141] A board employee who participated in the Washington end of this operation remembered that

Somebody got the bright idea that some of these people might start destroying their records and that's exactly what happened. We had people in the field [who] got trash out of the offices of these people . . . . Trash was all brought into Washington, it was the most amazing sight. People were coming in from out of town with suitcases full of trash . . . . I heard somebody say that he had to bribe the superintendent of an office building in some city to let him have the trash out of a certain room. Probably millions of pieces of torn-up paper. And everybody that could be found in the National Labor Relations Board went to work in this hot summer of 1936 trying to put together torn-up records and gluing them together with little pieces of gummed tape. And probably the most interesting thing that stands out in my memory was that because we were dealing with little scraps of paper we couldn't have any electric fans. And we'd spread this stuff out on tables and desks and try to find little things that matched and the jigsaw puzzle was gradually put together and we reconstructed I don't know how many hundreds and thousands of records . . . . And it was hot because we couldn't open a window for fear of having a draft or a breeze blow

140. NA, RG233, "LaFollette Investigation," memorandum from H. Blankenhorn to J. W. Madden and E. S. Smith, October 1, 1936, p. 2, Box 124.
141. Auerbach, *op. cit.*, p. 93.

everything apart after we were getting it set up. Well, we did that. I remember the summer of 1936 very well.[142]

Malcolm Ross, the director of information for the NLRB in 1936, believed that the LaFollette Civil Liberties Committee was an important factor in the survival of the board:

> The disclosures of the LaFollette Committee being sensational, also made good copy. The newspaper coverage given the colorful testimony of finks and criminals on company payrolls shamed much of the opposition into silence. It worked on the public conscience where appeals to reason had failed. While this is discouraging to the scholarly approach, it demonstrates the wisdom of giving a full airing to both sides of a public question.[143]

The Supreme Court's Decision

Only those who were privy to the Supreme Court's deliberations, however, know why the Court sustained the Wagner Act. The NLRB had relied almost exclusively on the "scholarly approach" to the Supreme Court, appealing to reason with precise legal analyses of the five carefully chosen test cases. Yet, however reluctantly, the NLRB did admit the importance of "the other side of the public question" of the constitutionality of the Wagner Act. The board had created an Economic Division to supplement legal principles with economic and industrial relations facts and had given Heber Blankenhorn virtual autonomy in his artful endeavors "to turn the facts of labor relations into broad new precedents for the consideration of the courts."[144]

No one could have ignored "the facts of industrial relations" in 1936 and 1937 since major and often violent strikes erupted around

142. Oral history interview with Herbert Glaser, *op. cit.*, pp. 12–13.
143. Malcolm Ross, "The G—— D—— Labor Board," in Louis G. Silverberg, ed., *The Wagner Act: After Ten Years* (Washington: BNA, 1945), p. 68.
144. See Chapter VI, pp. 211–223.

the country in almost every important industry—maritime, electrical, automobiles, trucking, steel, lumber, glass, ship-building, textiles, shoes, publishing, retail trade, and rubber.[145] In addition, the AFL which had been torn by "discord, dissension, division and disunion" formalized organized labor's war with itself in August 1936 by expelling the ten rebellious unions that advocated industrial unionism.[146] These new and militant CIO (Committee for Industrial Organization) unions launched organizing drives in the mass production industries in 1936, most often unleashing a dramatic and "marvellously effective"[147] weapon— the sit-down strike. The number of sit-down strikes increased from 8 during the first 9 months of 1936 to 282 during the eight-month period from August 1936 through March 1937—with an all-time high of 170 of those occuring in March, just one month before the Supreme Court announced its Wagner Act decisions.[148]

President Roosevelt, moreover, spurred on by his "immense victory" in the November 1936 presidential election, announced his "court packing" plan on February 5, 1937, four days before the Supreme Court heard oral argument in the Wagner Act cases:

> The proposal was to give a justice who reached seventy the opportunity to retire on full salary for life. If he retired the President would name a successor. If he continued to serve, the President would be allowed to name another justice, up to a maximum of six new members of the court.[149]

145. For an excellent description of industrial unrest in 1936 and 1937, see Bernstein, *Turbulent Years, op. cit.*, pp. 432–634. See also Louis Stark, "Wave of Strikes Marks Recovery in Industry," *The New York Times* December 20, 1936, p. 7E, sec. 4, col. 1.
146. The AFL's expulsion order named the United Mine Workers, Amalgamated Clothing Workers, Oil Workers, Mine, Mill, Ladies' Garment Workers, Textile Workers, Flat Glass Workers, Iron, Steel and Tin Workers, Auto Workers and Rubber Workers. See Bernstein, *Turbulent Years, op. cit.*, p. 423.
147. *Ibid.*, p. 499.
148. These statistics were compiled from a chart which appeared in the May 1939 issue of the *Monthly Labor Review* and which is reproduced in *Smith Committee Hearings, op. cit.*, vol. 13, p. 2740.
149. Bernstein, *Turbulent Years, op. cit.*, p. 641. The plan also permitted the president to appoint an additional judge (up to a total of 50) for

The president soon abandoned his attempts to justify his Court plan with expressions of concern for the advanced age and heavy workload of the justices of the Supreme Court. It became clear by early March that he was attacking the Supreme Court because it "was disregarding the national will and thwarting the national interest."[150]

Many observers believed that the Supreme Court simply yielded to these "forces of political and social unrest [that] beat upon the Court in the spring of 1937."[151] In January 1937, one month before the board made its oral arguments before the Supreme Court, Heber Blankenborn suggested to Chairman Madden "that auto, steel, and coal may possibly 'render constitutional' the Wagner Act."[152] He told the chairman that "strikes there may reinforce your words to the Justices, who besides 'reading the election returns' may possibly scan the news of tie-ups" and he reminded Madden that "it would not be the first time that Labor Board history had something to do with strike talk. June 16, 1934 was the date set for a steel strike, at the same time that the first Wagner Act was failing and the first Board passing out. That strike threat was a principal cause of Congress passing Public Resolution 44, creating the second Labor Board . . . ."[153] "The concept may dawn even on the Court," Blankenhorn wrote, "that a Government Labor Board is in some measure a necessary alternative to a general labor war."[154]

After the Supreme Court decisions, Blankenhorn, in a memorandum that would become an issue four years later before a House investigating committee, felt that his "basic concept had been borne out by events."[155] He believed, however, that the publicity surrounding the President's Court plan and the hidden

---

each lower federal court judge who failed to retire "within six months after reaching retirement age." See Cortner, *op. cit.*, p. 151.

150. Pusey, *op. cit.*, vol. 2, p. 749.
151. Cortner, *op. cit.*, p. 177.
152. NLRB files, letter from H. Blankenhorn to J. W. Madden, January 4, 1937.
153. *Ibid.*
154. *Ibid.*
155. *Smith Committee Hearings, op. cit.*, vol. 20, pp. 4282–4283, memorandum by H. Blankenhorn, April 19, 1937.

effects of the capitulation of General Motors to John L. Lewis and the United Automobile Workers on February 11, 1937 and of the United States Steel Corporation to the Steel Workers' Organizing Committee on March 2, 1937 were the decisive factors influencing Justice Roberts to switch his vote from the "conservatives" to the "liberals":

> Of the various impingements, one, Roberts' financial connections, could hardly be disregarded; in fact it would have to be first thought of . . . . the word of Philadelphia and New York to Roberts, whether spoken or to be inferred from the newspapers, was "We have surrendered the nut of the Wagner Act, we are in no position to fight on that line now, your decision might as well favor the Act and at least save yourself" . . . . financiers had no promising expectations of accomplishing the undoing in steel and autos; they had instead a lively fear that John Lewis' union could reach out from the economic to the political pressure—in fact they knew that Lewis was already reaching into the political field on the Court issue.[156]

Other people vigorously denied that the Supreme Court (particularly Chief Justice Hughes and Associate Justice Roberts) changed its judicial views for political reasons.[157] The NLRB's general counsel, Charles Fahy, for example, preferred a "more professional approach" to the Supreme Court's "transition in the application of principles" and maintained that "Justice Roberts' position was a thoroughly sincere legal one."[158] Fahy has written:

> Speculation has arisen as to how and why this [the "transition"] came about at that time . . . . From their

156. *Ibid.*
157. Pusey, *op. cit.*, vol. 2, pp. 766–772 and Felix Frankfurter, "Mr. Justice Roberts," *University of Pennsylvania Law Review*, vol. 104, no. 3 (December 1955), pp. 311–317.
158. Charles Fahy, "Review of Some Early Developments and Later Influences of Wagner Act Litigation," *Labor Law Developments*, proceedings of the Fifteenth Annual Institute on Labor Law, The Southwestern Legal Foundation, 1969, p. 286. In a letter to the author on July 21, 1972, Judge Fahy expressed his conviction that Blankenhorn's remarks were "unfair to a great man and jurist."

previous positions, not infrequently in dissent, it was reasonable to predict that Justices Brandeis, Stone and Cardozo would not repudiate Congress' enactment of the Wagner Act. I think the same should be said of Chief Justice Hughes, one of the foremost exponents after Marshall of the federal commerce power. The position of Justice Roberts, who joined these four to make a fifth, was more uncertain. In speculating about a matter of this sort I believe one must take some account of the relation of the Wagner Act to human relations. When a judge believes that the conditions under which men, women, and children work need not . . . be left to individual arrangements, but may be subject to legislative regulation, such a judge is likely to look favorably upon the source resorted to by the legislature to engage in the regulation. Justice Roberts concluded in March 1937, in the case of *West Coast Hotel v. Parrish* to join with Chief Justice Hughes, and Justices Brandeis, Stone, and Cardozo, to uphold the law of the State of Washington, . . . prescribing minimum wages for women, overruling *Adkins v. Children's Hospital* . . . . It then became predictable that Justice Roberts probably would join the same members of his Court, as he did two weeks later, in upholding the Wagner Act under the commerce clause . . . . The thinking of a judge entrusted with constitutional decision-making is affected in one matter by his view in another.[159]

As Heber Blankenhorn put it in April 1937, "a proved answer . . . is unlikely." When it is recognized, however, that "the connection between interstate commerce and labor relations in the coal mines shown in the *Carter* record far exceeded in quantity and effect anything appearing in the Labor Board cases, [and] that there had been no change in the membership of the Court,"[160] it is reasonable to discount the effect of the board's strategy and arguments and to give major credit to environmental conditions— that is, to the "facts of industrial relations."

For whatever reason, the Supreme Court was ready to have its mind changed and the board had provided the justices with all of the legal reasoning and economic material the Court needed to

159. *Ibid.*, pp. 286–287.
160. Stern, *op. cit.*, p. 681.

justify its rejection of precedent. In all of the test cases the Supreme Court accepted the board's arguments that the act did not invade the constitutional rights of employers under the due process clause. In the crucial case involving interstate commerce, the *Jones and Laughlin* case, the Court followed the board's economic outline step by step from general propositions to particular case applications:

> We are asked to shut our eyes to the plainest facts of our national life and to deal with the question of direct and indirect effects [on commerce] in an intellectual vacuum . . . .
>
> Experience has abundantly demonstrated that the recognition of the right of employees to self-organization and to have representatives of their own choosing for the purpose of collective bargaining is often an essential condition of industrial peace. Refusal to confer and negotiate has been one of the most prolific causes of strife. . . .
>
> These questions have frequently engaged the attention of Congress and have been the subject of many inquiries. The steel industry is one of the great basic industries of the United States, with ramifying activities affecting interstate commerce at every point. The Government aptly refers to the steel strike of 1919–1920 with its far-reaching consequences. The fact that there appears to have been no major disturbance in that industry in the more recent period did not dispose of the possibilities of future and like dangers to interstate commerce which Congress was entitled to foresee and to exercise its protective power to forestall. It is not necessary again to detail the facts as to respondent's enterprise. Instead of being beyond the pale, we think that it presents in a most striking way the close and intimate relation which a manufacturing industry may have to interstate commerce. . . .[161]

In support of this portion of its opinion, the Supreme Court made footnote references to documents supplied by the board's Division of Economic Research: the *Final Report of the Industrial Commission* (1902); the *Final Report of the Commission on Industrial Relations* (1916); the National War Labor Board, *Principles*

161. 301 U.S. 1, 41–43.

and Rules of Procedure (1919); and Senate Report No. 289, *Investigating Strikes In Steel Industry.*[162]

On April 12, 1937, the Supreme Court rejected "metaphysical concepts" and spoke "in terms which anyone, be he layman, economist or even lawyer, could understand": The Wagner Act and the NLRB were constitutional.[163]

A proud Senator Wagner "took to the radio" on April 12, 1937 at the end of what *The New York Times* called "one of the happiest days of his public career."[164] He reminded his listeners that he had started the struggle for a national labor relations law and a national labor board and that he had been "confronted by the most difficult fight" in his political life. But the Senator wanted the fighting ended now that the Supreme Court had approved the Wagner Act and the NLRB in what he called "an act of industrial statesmanship." The Supreme Court decisions earlier that day had changed a controverted measure into a "bulwark of industrial peace and justice" and Senator Wagner appealed to employers and unions to submit their differences to the NLRB:

> Now that the Supreme Court has sanctioned the National Labor Relations Act and approved the board administering it, let employers and workers come freely before the board with their difficulties.
>
> . . . Let no one any longer take the law into his own hands through self-appointed interpreters of what the Constitution means, through hired police or spies, or through any precipitate and unreasonable resort to force of any kind.
>
> Let everyone read the decisions of the Supreme Court itself, and after having read the decisions, let everyone accept the underlying principles of democracy and fair dealing.
>
> Now the court has acted so wisely and so well, a new prospect is opened to peace and decent relations throughout our nation-wide industries. A pathway to industrial accord and economic progress has been cleared. Let industry and

162. See 301 U.S. 1, 43, fnn. 8 & 9.
163. Stern, *op. cit.*, p. 680.
164. *The New York Times*, April 13, 1937, p. 20, col. 1. See also "Four 5–4; One 9–0," *Time*, April 19, 1937, pp. 14–15.

labor march along that path together toward a clearer atmosphere of mutual understanding and good-will.[165]

The NLRB had won its constitutional battle but, despite Senator Wagner's idealistic appeals, the Supreme Court decision simply shifted the war to other battlegrounds.

165. *The New York Times*, April 13, 1937, p. 20, col. 1.

7 Labor Policy Made and About to Be Remade

On April 12, 1937 at the NLRB "it was just wild." A "great joy" and a "whole feeling of victory . . . ran through the office—[it was] like a carnival almost for that day and days afterward."[1] There was, of course, good cause for celebration. Almost four years after Senator Wagner first assembled the members of his National Labor Board in August 1933, the Wagner Act had become the law of the land and the NLRB a permanent governmental authority with powers of adjudication.

Much of historical importance had happened in those four years. The initial approach of the NLRB was one of partisan representation, agreement through mediation, hearings conducted as nonlegalistic and informal friendly discussions, emphasis on communication and voluntary cooperation, and reliance on public sentiment and the prestige of its members as defenses both against employers, who would not permit the board to tamper with the balance of power between themselves and their employees, and against the NRA, which readily compromised the labor provisions of the NIRA in order to retain the cooperation of business in the recovery program. This approach had been tried, found wanting, and rejected.

At first, gradually and without authorization from the White House, the NLB and the old NLRB transformed themselves into quasijudicial bodies of full-time, paid neutrals, deciding cases rather than suggesting compromises, obtaining competency in handling questions of law, adopting more legalistic, judicial methods, shifting from friendly persuasion to formal hearings (including evidence, uniformity in procedures, and rules and

1. Oral history interview with C. Fahy, *op. cit.*, p. 32 and with H. Glaser, *op. cit.*, p. 28.

regulations), and asserting the independence and impartiality of the boards.

Even before the Wagner Act, employer defiance had forced the NLB and the old NLRB to develop a common law of labor relations by defining, on a case-by-case basis, the rights of employers under Section 7(a) and to seek the translation of this common law into an enforceable statute. As a result, the old NLRB's legal staff worked closely with Leon Keyserling in revising Senator Wagner's labor disputes bill so that the new Wagner bill reflected the agony of the NLB and the old NLRB. Almost all of its provisions could be traced to the experiences of these two boards. Events finally imposed the culmination of the work of the NLB and the old NLRB on the president and the Wagner Act became law on July 5, 1935.

The work of the NLB and the old NLRB had been brought to fruition by the Wagner Act NLRB: the Supreme Court had confirmed the Wagner Act as the law of the land and the NLRB as an administrative agency of the federal government. But the Supreme Court's decisions brought no reprieve to the new board from the pressure of economic and political power which constantly surrounded the formulation and administration of the national labor policy. The opponents of the new national labor policy simply shifted their attacks from the act to the board itself. Victory celebrations were brief at the board in April 1937.

Battles Yet to Be Fought

Despite the fact that the Supreme Court's decision had confirmed the Wagner Act as the law of the land and the NLRB as a permanent governmental authority and despite the appeals for labor peace and the submission of disputes to the NLRB, the opponents of the board and the act simply sought other ways to destroy the Wagner Act and the NLRB. Their attacks were shifted from the act to the board itself and included a powerful new dimension— "the clamor of legislators against the board."[2]

2. Luther A. Huston, "NLRB Under Fire In Congress," *The New York Times*, August 1, 1937, p. 6E, sec. 4, col. 3.

Not all of the NLRB's difficulties were caused by hostile forces outside the board, however. Now that the constitutional battle had been won, the board's internal problems became more pressing and more important. As J. Warren Madden put it, "prior to our Supreme Court decisions . . . we were all so busy fighting the common enemy that we didn't have very many disagreements."[3] Harry Brickman, the recently retired chief of the NLRB's Operations Analysis Section and a messenger with the board in 1937, remembered the good fellowship of those early years:

> We had an institution, a Saturday afternoon baseball game. We used to work half a day on Saturday, in the morning, and we'd developed a practice of, when work was done, of going out to the Potomac Park . . . where there were a number of softball diamonds . . . and we'd go out there and play games, the clericals against the professionals. Well, the chairman and the general counsel played with the professionals every Saturday. They wouldn't miss it and we had some other eminent people on the professional staff playing against us and they almost invariably beat us, too. [The] chairman played second base. Well, this gives you an idea of what kind of people they were. They weren't stuffed shirts. . . . They were very fine people and virtually universally respected and loved.[4]

Yet, internal divisions and conflicts surfaced almost immediately after the Supreme Court decisions. There was serious disagreement within the NLRB, for example, over just how much influence the work of the Division of Economic Research had on the Supreme Court.

Many experts were convinced that the need for economic analysis in labor cases was an accepted fact, making the NLRB's Division of Economic Research an indispensable element in the administration of the National Labor Relations Act:

> These services, especially that of economic research, are a powerful complement to the Board's legal work. No small amount of the success that the NLRB has had before the courts may be attributed to facts that it has been able to present on the respective industries. . . . Public policy cannot

3. Oral history interview with J. W. Madden, *op. cit.*, p. 97.
4. Oral history interview with Harry Brickman, *op. cit.*, pp. 30–31.

be determined or enforced in a vacuum, or by legal precedents alone. Adjudication as well as legislation must be based on the facts of economic and social conditions. Only in this way can the law be vital. For the purpose of finding these facts a bureau of economic research is invaluable.[5]

The New Republic stated it less academically but more dramatically:

In the labor cases before the federal courts, economic data were yanked out of cloistered classrooms and dusty bookcovers, and boldly injected into hearings and briefs of the National Labor Relations Board. Instead of pleading on purely legalistic ground as decided by case so-and-so, in court Whosis, the Board through its Economics Division, brought in evidence in terms of human values, in language so real, and so respectably substantiated by recognized economists, that decision after decision was rendered in the Board's favor. The courts treated the economic evidence with utmost seriousness and frequently quoted from it.[6]

On the other hand, Charles Fahy, the board's general counsel during these critical years, agreed that it was "prudent, wise, and helpful" to present economic data to the Supreme Court, but felt that the economists "thought their contribution was more important than it was." Fahy "thought more in terms of a lawyer using economic data, rather than in terms of an economist" and recognized that "there was some pride of profession" involved.[7]

The Economic Division's response to the Supreme Court's decisions were made in the assertive language of an insecure department seeking to solidify its position and to attain first-class citizenship in the organization. The division's strongest declarations went beyond picayune squabbles over professional prestige to question the appropriateness and the value of the essentially legalistic approach the board had adopted. The division was

5. James E. Pate, "The National Labor Relations Board," *Southern Economic Journal*, vol. 6, 1939–1940, pp. 57–58.
6. Rose M. Stein, "Congress Gets Its Pound of Flesh," *The New Republic*, vol. 103, November 4, 1940, p. 621.
7. Oral history interview with C. Fahy, *op. cit.*, pp. 28 and 30–31. In Fahy's opinion "there was [not] anything serious that interferred in any way with the relationship between the lawyer and the Economic Division." *Ibid.*, p. 31.

questioning the meaning of the Wagner Act itself—whether Congress intended the NLRB to be a judicial agency or an "industrial relations" agency. The Division of Economic Research's section of the NLRB's *Second Annual Report*, for example, asserted the economic and sociological basis of the NLRA and told of a "trend toward enlightenment" wherein "the public consciousness is being focused on the economic factors inherent in the problems confronting the Board."[8] The enthusiasm with which the report was written led to a disconcerting (at least to the board's lawyers) exaggeration:

The decisions of the Supreme Court with their full use of the economic evidence presented in each case, *coupled with the complete disregard for finely spun legal distinctions* reaffirmed the appropriateness of the "economic approach" for which the famous Brandeis brief was the precedent.[9]

One week after the Wagner Act decisions, David Saposs came forward with specific proposals intended to get the Division of Economic Research involved more substantially in the NLRB's case work. The chief economist wanted to have the NLRB's jurisdiction in future cases decided in the field "by a member of the staff trained in economics, working in cooperation with the regional attorney."[10] He requested that "in important cases" an economist proficient in labor relations "assist, not only in the preparation of evidence prior to the hearing, but also at the hearing" and that after the hearing, there be close cooperation between the division and the review attorney handling the case.[11] Saposs also recommended that data for all major industries be prepared, that educational material on appropriate labor relations issues be published "for the public, employers, workers, and legislators," and that the NLRB establish "for *all* our staff" a reading course, supplemented by lectures, "in the history and practices of labor relations. . . ."[12]

8. National Labor Relations Board, *Second Annual Report, op. cit.*, p. 46.
9. *Ibid.*, p. 47 (emphasis added).
10. NLRB files, "Suggested Plan of Activities for the Division of Economic Research," memorandum from D. J. Saposs to J. W. Madden, E. S. Smith, D. W. Smith, C. Fahy, R. Watts, N. Witt, B. Wolf, P. Levy, April 19, 1937, pp. 1–2.
11. *Ibid.*, p. 2.
12. *Ibid.*, p. 3. See also NLRB files, "Suggested Subjects for General

The board's general counsel replied to this apparent empire building by telling Saposs that "any advice to the Regional Attorneys on [the] interpretation of Supreme Court decisions" should go out from the office of the general counsel.[13] In a memorandum to Saposs, dated May 13, 1937, he said,

Should we obtain soon several Circuit Court decisions to the effect that the jurisdiction of the Board applied to ordinary manufacturing enterprises engaged in interstate commerce, which I am convinced we should, we could then eliminate, in ordinary manufacturing cases, all economic material except that which is necessary to prove the operations of the particular respondent.[14]

Charles Fahy was opposed to the establishment of any general rules governing the use of economic data and suggested, instead, that the use of such materials in "borderline cases" and in circuit court briefs should be treated "as a separate problem in each case as it arises." He also maintained that it was "no longer necessary to prove the history of labor relations in ordinary manufacturing cases," that it was not feasible for the Economic Division to review drafts of board decisions, and that no "general preparation of material for Circuit Court Briefs should be undertaken by the Economic Division" except to review any economic material which a particular brief might contain.[15] The board sustained the recommendations of General Counsel Fahy.[16]

Research by the Division of Economic Research," memorandum from D. J. Saposs to J. W. Madden, E. S. Smith, and D. W. Smith, May 25, 1937, pp. 1–3. Educational literature would include studies of collective bargaining, union responsibility, the bargaining unit, bargaining in good faith, antiunion attitudes of employer associations, independent unions, and sit-down strikes.

13. NLRB files, memorandum from C. Fahy to D. J. Saposs, June 12, 1937.

14. NLRB files, "Economic Material as Evidence in Hearings," memorandum from C. Fahy to D. J. Saposs, May 13, 1937, p. 1.

15. *Ibid.*, pp. 1–2. See also NLRB files, "Reconsideration of Economic Data Required in Cases Before the Board," memorandum from C. Fahy to J. W. Madden, E. S. Smith, D. W. Smith, R. Watts, B. Wolf, N. Witt, P. Levy, D. J. Saposs, September 2, 1937, pp. 1–3.

16. See NLRB files, "Jurisdictional Proof and Cooperation Between Legal Staff and Economic Division," memorandum from C. Fahy to regional attorneys and attorneys in regional offices, September 22,

The internal disagreement over the proper role of the Division of Economic Research continued but it was obscured for a while as the tremendous post-April 1937 expansion of the NLRB's workload increased the amount if not the scope of the division's activities. The whole issue, however, became a *cause célébre* in 1940 in public hearings conducted by a hostile House investigating committee which had little interest in clarifying the place of economic analysis in the work of the NLRB. Instead, this committee took advantage of the deepening divisions within the board over this and other issues, to conduct a personal attack on David Saposs, linking him with alleged communists at the board and charging him and his division with bias and with the improper administration of justice.[17]

The deluge of cases that hit the NLRB after the April 12, 1937 Wagner Act decisions (when the board "could no longer ask labor to withhold cases so that the Board's litigation strategy would not be upset")[18] also created many problems that would be exploited by the board's opposition in later years. Compared to the number of cases which swamped the board in the months immediately after the Supreme Court's decision, the NLRB had hardly functioned at all from September 1935 to April 1937. During the approximately 18-month "preconstitutional" period, the average number of cases coming to the NLRB and its 21 regional offices each month was 150 and in only three of those months were more than 200 cases handled. In May 1937, the first full month after the Court's decision, 1,064 cases were filed with the NLRB, followed by 1,283 in June and another 1,325 cases in July. Almost 10,000 cases were filed in 1937—more than seven times the number of cases handled by the NLRB in 1936.[19] (The increase in the number

---

1937. The Economics Division expanded from four to twelve members between June 30, 1937 and June 30, 1938, but this was due to an increased NLRB caseload rather than to an expansion of the Division's jurisdiction. See *Smith Committee Hearings, op. cit.*, vol. XIII, p. 2728.

17. See, for example, *Smith Committee Hearings, op. cit.*, vol. 17, pp. 3413–3486 and vol. 26, pp. 6895–6910.
18. Madden, *op. cit.*, p. 246.
19. These statistics are taken from *Smith Committee Hearings, op. cit.*, vol. 13, pp. 2587, 2729. See also Luther A. Huston, "National Labor Board Is Deluged With Cases," *The New York Times*, July 27, 1937, p. 6E, sec. 4, col. 1 and *The New York Times*, May 3, 1937, p. 9, col. 11.

of NLRB representation elections was particularly impressive. Whereas the board conducted a total of only 66 elections in the 18-month "preconstitutional" period, an average of 4 elections a month, it conducted 31 NLRB elections in April, 70 in May, 111 in June, and 185 in July 1937.)[20]

Regional boards pleaded for increased staff, reporting that "we cannot even in a 14 hour day work fast enough to keep up with the new cases that flood us. The legal staff is overworked. We cannot try the cases that must be prosecuted quickly enough,"[21] that "the office staff is beginning to show the strain of long hours and the constant pressure under which everyone is working,"[22] that "matters are piling up so fast that I think it is important to tell you that unless something is done I feel the situation will get out of hand,"[23] and that "there is at no time in the reception room less than half a dozen people and oftentimes it is crowded into the hall. . . ."[24]

The work of the NLRB which had been delayed by injunctions and other forms of noncompliance was now delayed by an overwhelming volume of work. Elinore Herrick, the regional director in New York City, felt that this was a "vital defect" and that unless the board succeeded in reducing the time consumed in adjudicating cases, the NLRB would be "thoroughly discredited in the eyes of the public—then watch the employers introduce legislation to sabotage the law. . . . Labor looks to us now and, if disappointed, will wash their hands of the whole affair, relying upon their economic strength in the first instance."[25]

20. Emily Marks and Mary Bartlett, "Employee Elections Conducted By National Labor Relations Board," *Monthly Labor Review*, vol. 47, July 1938, pp. 32–33.

21. NLRB files, "Regional Offices' Comments On Current Labor Situation For May, 1937," p. 1.

22. NA, RG25, "Regional Directors' Conference," memorandum from Stanley Root, regional director, 4th Region, to B. Wolf, June 8, Region IV, Philadelphia, 1934–1937.

23. NA, RG25, memorandum from Philip G. Phillips, Region IX, to B. Wolf, May 25, 1937, p. 1. Records of NLRB II, office of the secretary, Region IX, Cincinnati, 1934–1937.

24. NLRB files, "Regional Offices' Comments On Current Labor Situation For April, 1937," p. 4.

25. NLRB files, memorandum from E. Herrick to J. W. Madden, E. S. Smith, D. W. Smith, and B. Wolf, April 26, 1937, p. 2.

The board's *Second Annual Report* noted that " the number of cases pending at the end of each month was increasing at an alarming rate"[26] and J. Warren Madden told a House investigating committee in 1940 that the board had still not recovered from the tremendous increase in its workload:

> ... the flood of work coming along at the time that it did, when we had no staff, no adequate staff, no money to increase our staff—we didn't get the money until several months later—that then the problem of acquiring the staff and training them and attacking this backlog of work is a problem which has been with us ever since that time, and which has put us behind in our work and kept us there down to this very day.[27]

The board responded to the crisis of delayed decisions by almost tripling its staff in fourteen months. (The bulk of this expansion actually took place in about ten months, since the board had "to call a halt to expansion" until Congress increased the NLRB's appropriation in August 1937.)[28] The NLRB, which had a staff of 119 in Washington and in the regional offices on September 1, 1935, reported a total staff of 182 in June 1936, 262 in June 1937, and 692 in June 1938.[29] Given what Chairman Madden called the "greeness and newness of a lot of our help"[30] and the fact that

26. NLRB, *Second Annual Report, op. cit.*, pp. 2–3.
27. *Smith Committee Hearings, op. cit.*, vol. 13, p. 2587.
28. NA, RG25, memorandum from C. Fahy to all attorneys and attorneys in regional offices, August 2, 1937. Records of NLRB II relating to the Smith Committee investigation, Legal Division, office of the general counsel, File I-4, "Instructions to Staff Which May be Questioned by the Committee," p. 1. See also NLRB, *Second Annual Report, op. cit.*, p. 2.
29. *Smith Committee Hearings, op. cit.*, vol. 13, pp. 2586–2728. From June 30, 1937 to June 30, 1938, the administrative staff in Washington increased from seventy-three to 175, the litigation staff from thirty-eight to fourty-five, the Review Division from eleven to sixty-four, trial examiners from eleven to twenty-four, and the Economics Division from four to twelve. Attorneys in the field increased from twenty-four to ninety-five and examiners from twenty-eight to ninety-seven.
30. NA, RG233, minutes of regional directors conference—trial examiners meeting, October 29, 1937, p. 47, Box 38, Exh. Number 1836.

they had been recruited "as rapidly as possible,"[31] it was inevitable, however, that the personnel "explosion" would cause a new set of problems for the board.

General Counsel Charles Fahy felt it necessary to caution the board's attorneys in Washington and in the field "not to try to prevent material evidence from being introduced by [employers]," not to be "excessive in the use of [their] authority," not to "engage in loose threats of what they are going to do to this and that employer," and to remind them that " the personal inclinations of the individual attorney in connection with the split in the labor movement should never enter into his official conduct in the administration of the Act."[32] Although Fahy, in August 1937, doubted that agents of the board ever threatened employers and attributed such "rumors" to "distortions of innocent remarks,"[33] his December 1937 memorandum to the NLRB's attorneys clearly demonstrated that he had come to accept the reality of the rumors:

> There has been called to our attention the fact that some attorneys seem to have been very careless in their handling and expressions about the subpoenas which they have available for use in the preparation and trial of cases. For example, some attorneys, it is reported, make loose remarks about what they might do to so and so by subpoenaing him, *in a manner which may be construed as bragging or "strutting" about the power they have* through the availability and use of subpoenas . . . . I want to warn all attorneys now about the above. All of our attorneys should have enough common sense and sense of responsibility to realize that subpoenas entrusted to them by the Board should be used discriminately, not used as threats or occasions for boasting as to what you might or might not do. . . .[34]

George Bokat, who later became the board's chief trial examiner, knew nothing about an examiner's work when he joined the board in October 1937 except that trial examiners were "indi-

31. NA, RG25, memorandum from C. Fahy to all attorneys and attorneys in regional offices, *op. cit.*, p. 1.
32. *Ibid.*, pp. 1–2.
33. *Ibid.*, p. 2.
34. NLRB files, "Use of Subpoenas," memorandum from C. Fahy to all attorneys in the field, December 15, 1937 (emphasis added).

viduals . . . who act[ed] like judges."[35] A few days after he was hired, Bokat heard his first case armed only with "a copy of the rules and regulations, a copy of the Act, and some travel vouchers —that was my [Bokat's] orientation and knowledge.[36] He recalled that particularly because of the per diem system, "The board pick[ed] up some individuals who did not do the kind of job that you would expect people who were sitting as judges to do. . . ."[37] It was clear that some trial examiners did treat employers' counsel harshly.

Several instances of injudicious conduct were discussed at the NLRB's conference of regional directors in October 1937. For example,

> The individual [a trial examiner] thought by a few introductory remarks he might bring about a settlement of the case. He talked on for about thirty minutes, in which time he spoke on his family history and of the fact that in the South his family had a large number of slaves, how the Union army had come down to free the slaves, and went on from where it might be necessary for any army to come up North to free the working man. It was a pretty poor way to start off the hearing, and the respondent's attorney was fit to be tied, and more fit to be tied when he found out that the court reporter hadn't taken the speech down. He demanded the Trial Examiner repeat the speech, but he couldn't do it, of course.[38]

As early as July 1937, Senator Nye, Republican of North Dakota, publicly charged that the board was "a partisan body rather than a judicial institution"[39] and Representative Rankin, Democrat from Mississippi, coauthor of the Tennessee Valley Authority Act and a leading supporter of the Roosevelt administration, claimed to "have affidavits from responsible people in Tupelo to the effect that these representatives of the so-called Labor Relations Board boasted that they were going to close every

---

35. Oral history interview with George Bokat, March 17, 1969, p. 6, on file in the Labor Management Documentation Center, ILR, Cornell.
36. *Ibid.*, p. 7.
37. *Ibid.*, p. 9.
38. NA, RG233, minutes of a regional conference, October 28, 1937, p. 3, Box 38, Exh. No. 1836.
39. *The New York Times*, July 23, 1937, p. 1, col. 4.

factory in the city before they quit, and that when they got through with it there would be no Tupelo left."[40]

Chairman Madden was "enormously" disturbed by these charges (particularly since *The New York Times* reported that Representative Rankin was "expected to ask the administration to remove the present members of the board or curtail their activities").[41] Despite the denials of the regional director who allegedly threatened the cotton mill owners in Tupelo, the chairman informed him that the board had "more than a suspicion . . . that you may have said something of the kind."[42] Chairman Madden reprimanded the director and tried to impress upon him the consequences for the board of such irresponsible statements:

> In one way or another we have gotten those people dreadfully stirred up, and it is not possible to get for workers the benefits of our law if we have this kind of resistance. It may be too late in Tupelo, but it seems to me that your diplomatic powers ought to be sufficient, when backed up by the very considerable legal power which we now have, so that people ought not to feel so savage about the Board and its work. . . . The community seems to think that you gave the strikers in the cotton mill case the impression that if they would hold out strongly, they would get what they demanded. . . . [that] was never any of our affair. The holding of the election to determine representatives and the arrangement of conferences was our affair . . . and that is all that we should have done. . . .
>
> If the judges from whom we must get enforcement of our orders get the impression that we are a lot of rough and ready dictators, they will cut the effectiveness out of our decisions to the point where we cannot accomplish anything.
>
> The reason I am writing you like this is that we are greatly bedeviled by being put on the defensive by matters of this kind which could not possibly under any circumstances do us any good and which in fact consume our time and energy and undermine the reputation which we are trying to make by

40. *The New York Times*, July 27, 1937, p. 1, col. 4.
41. *Ibid.*
42. NLRB files, letter from J. W. Madden to Charles H. Logan, director, 15th Region, August 7, 1937, pp. 1–2.

doing an orderly and dignified job. We have had instances from other regions where staff people have apparently not known how to apply the powers, which we have recently succeeded in obtaining, with dignity and consideration for the feelings and rights of others. We are necessarily exposed to a large amount of criticism by reason of the fact that employers dislike our law and that the split in the labor movement creates a critical attitude even on the part of labor. Much of that criticism could be obviated if we would take thought before we speak and act.[43]

Certainly, the board's field staff had no easy time in bringing the Wagner Act to Tupelo, Mississippi. As described by an NLRB attorney on the scene who felt that the chairman's criticisms were "not based upon full knowledge of the situation":

Tupelo has been and is a feudal stronghold; it happens that the ideals of our legislation have clashed with a philosophy no longer nationally accepted. Since its organization, our Board received criticism from the same type of men who have ruled Tupelo. In this case they happen to be a peculiarly uneducated and arrogant group with which to deal. It seems to me that the Board cannot expect its employees to do their job without receiving the bitter opposition of that type of men and *that occasionally their feeling will find a voice in Congress.* One of the newspapers in Tupelo went so far as to advise the use of bloodshed if it were necessary to keep organizers for the C.I.O. out of town. Under such circumstances we have two alternatives: to submit to the bigoted and outworn ideals of the town's masters or to attempt to enforce the law and run the risk of criticism . . .; it seems to me inevitable that in some instances employers will . . . attempt to embarrass the Board in its functions by using Congress as a sounding board.[44]

The first instance of congressional protest foreshadowed not only an anti-NLRB alliance of certain legislators and business but also a potentially devastating attempt to discredit the board

43. *Ibid.*
44. NLRB files, letter from G. Van Arkel to J. W. Madden, August 9, 1937, pp. 3–4 (emphasis added).

in the eyes of the public by linking the NLRB with communism. The efforts that Senator Nye and Representative Rankin made in July 1937 to stigmatize the board as a "kangaroo court" which "conspir[ed] with communist influences" and which was no more than an "adjunct" of the radical CIO[45] were developed over the years and culminated in the 1940 final report of the Special House Committee to investigate the NLRB which purported

> . . . to show how members and employees of the Board were profoundly influenced by the doctrines and teachings of a leftist philosophy which the committee believes incompatible with a truly democratic system of government. Fraternizing with Communist sympathizers attending meetings of societies behind whose innocuous names lurks the Communist incubus, accepting suggestions and instructions from Communists and near-Communists—all these and many other instances of improper associations and activities have convinced the committee that many of the employees of the Board are unfit for the task of fair and impartial administration of the Act. Amid such a luxuriant growth of alien philosophies, no democratic process would long have a chance of survival.[46]

Chairman Madden realized that with industry hostile, with "a very bad press," and with "congressional sharpshooters" opening fire, "we [the board] needed friends, and it was a misfortune to lose any of those we had."[47] The bitter division within the ranks of organized labor made it inevitable, however, that the board would alienate either or both the AFL and the CIO and, therefore, lose at least one of its best and most powerful friends. Lloyd Garrison, the former chairman of the old NLRB, advised Chairman Madden in January 1936 that

46. *The New York Times*, July 23, 1937, p. 1, col. 4 and July 27, 1937, p. 1, col. 4.
46. U.S. Congress, *Report of the Special House Committee to Investigate the National Labor Relations Board*, 76th Cong., 3d Sess. (Washington: GPO, 1941), p. 4.
47. Madden, *op. cit.*, p. 248. See also Luther A. Huston, "NLRB Under Fire In Congress," *The New York Times*, August 1, 1937, p. 6, sec. 4, col. 3.

... it would seem to me better for the board not to be forced to take sides in such a struggle; and however impartial you are, and however much your decision in a particular case turns upon the peculiar facts, you will inevitably be charged by one group or the other with taking sides. And I wonder also if it might not be better for labor to fight out the struggle itself without governmental intervention.[48]

Garrison proposed that the Wagner Act be amended to keep the board out of craft-industrial union disputes over the appropriate unit for collective bargaining.[49] The chairman told Garrison that the board "had not been greatly embarrassed yet by the craft-industrial dispute" and that (although labor's civil war had not been "foreseen when the Wagner Act became law") the board's "general tendency has been to refrain from having our statute tinkered with at this session of Congress because of the conflict and confusion in the labor movement itself, as well as the fact that there are many enemies of the statute on the other side, who would like to take a kick at it."[50]

The board had not been embarrassed before the split in the labor movement simply because it had decided to "keep hands off [jurisdictional disputes within the AFL] and leave to the governing body of the Federation the responsibility for deciding these jurisdictional disputes."[51] After the expulsion of the CIO, however, the NLRB could no longer dodge the issue. As Chairman Madden stated it,

... it seemed to us that there was no use talking any longer about asking these labor organizations to have their affairs settled in their own parent body, when as a matter of fact there was a divorce inside the family and there were two

48. NLRB files, letter from L. K. Garrison to J. W. Madden, January 18, 1936.
49. *Ibid.*
50. NLRB files, letter from J. W. Madden to L. K. Garrison, February 1, 1936. See also *The New York Times*, September 7, 1937, p. 3, col. 4.
51. *Smith Committee Hearings, op. cit.*, vol. 13, p. 2584. See, for example, *In the Matter of the Axton-Fisher Tobacco Company and International Association of Machinists, Local No. 681, and Tobacco Workers' International Union*, 1 NLRB 1036.

parent bodies, and they simply didn't recognize the authority of the one parent any longer.[52]

In the chairman's opinion, "the Board had no possible right under the law to refuse to give to these people [the CIO] the status which the law gave them, and that to have refused to have done so would have been a completely arbitrary act on the part of the Board."[53] At the same time, however, Chairman Madden understood that the AFL believed that it had a "proprietary interest" in the Wagner Act since the act could not have been enacted without AFL support and that " the CIO was a rebel movement which had no right to call upon the Act or the Board for protection."[54] When, for example, the board first decided to order an election to resolve a representation dispute between a CIO and an AFL union in the *Interlake Iron Corporation*[55] case, AFL President William Green telephoned Chairman Madden to protest:

Mr. Green: Mr. Madden, I am calling up this morning to protest in the name of the American Federation of Labor very vigorously against the decision of your Board to hold an election in the Interlake Iron Company. I think it is a complete distortion of the Wagner Labor Relations Act. It means simply that you have decided in behalf of one union against the other, not for the purpose of making it possible for nonunion workers to organize and engage in collective bargaining as the Act provides, but you have gone definitely on the side of the CIO, and I protest as the President of the American Federation of Labor and in behalf of the Federation that we shall not accept the decision, that we shall fight it with all the power and vigor we possess.

52. *Smith Committee Hearings, op. cit.*, vol. 13, p. 2586. See *In the Matter of Interlake Iron Corporation and Toledo Council Committee for Industrial Organization*, 2 NLRB 1036.

53. *Ibid.*, p. 2585.

54. J. W. Madden, *op. cit.*, p. 248.

55. 2 NLRB 1036.

Mr. Madden: As you know, I am very sorry that you feel that way about it. . . . The conflict that is going on within the labor movement, of course, puts the Board in a very difficult position.

Mr. Green: There is an impression gaining every day among the officers and members of the Federation that your Board is definitely CIO, and that your agents are definitely CIO. . . . This decision will confirm that impression.

Mr. Madden: I shall be very sorry if people feel that way.

Mr. Green: In the Axton Fisher and in the Teamsters-Brewery workers you took the right position, one that we could approve, that of refraining from interfering in inter-union fights. . . .

Mr. Madden: I know there are perils in it, and it is extremely hard for us. I am sorry that you feel the way you do.

Mr. Green: I wanted you to know that we won't let it run—we will not acquiesce in that.[56]

Not all of the board's problems with organized labor involved appropriate bargaining unit determinations, however. In Chairman Madden's words "some of the hottest controversies" were fought over the board's application of Section 8 (1) of the Wagner Act: "It shall be an unfair labor practice for an employer—to interfere with, restrain or coerce employees in the exercise of the rights guaranteed in Section 7."[57] (Section 7 reads: "Employees shall have the right to self-organization, to form, join, or assist labor organizations, to bargain collectively through representatives of their own choosing. . . .")

In the spring and summer of 1937, for example, many regional boards reported that "employers seem[ed] to consider that the AFL [was] the lesser of the two evils, and in a number of instances

56. RG, 233, verbatim transcript of telephone conversation between William Green and J. W. Madden, June 29, 1937, Box 140.

57. NLRB files, address of J. W. Madden at the 57th annual convention of the American Federation of Labor at Denver, Colorado, October 5, 1937, p. 7. See also *Report of Proceedings of the 57th Annual Convention of the American Federation of Labor,* Denver, Colorado (Washington: Judd and Detweiler, 1937), pp. 231–236.

evidence [had] been secured that the employer [was] aiding the AFL group,"[58] that "management has either rushed into a closed shop contract with an AFL union before the preferences of the employees was clear or it [was] putting pressure on the employees to join an AFL union,"[59] that the AFL had taken over company unions,[60] that employers were "subversively encouraging their employees to join AFL unions,"[61] that "AFL affiliates [were] preferred wherever Chambers of Commerce and Boards of Trade members gather,[62] and that the AFL was "attempting to take advantage of an antipathy among employers directed toward the CIO as being communist and radical."[63]

On August 30, 1937, the board, in the *National Electric Products Company* case, declared void a closed shop contract between the company and an AFL union on the grounds that the AFL's International Brotherhood of Electrical Workers was given its status in the plant by interference and coercion by the management.[64] Philip Levy, the board attorney who prepared and drafted the board's decision in that case, believed that it was "impossible to overstate the impact of that decision" and that "it became a rallying point" for the AFL "in its growing criticism of the Board as favoring the CIO."[65]

The decision was headlined on the front page of *The New York Times*,[66] the Executive Council of the AFL "unsparingly criticized" the board and condemned its action in the case[67] and the

58. NLRB files, "Regional Offices' Comments On Current Labor Situation For June, 1937," C-52, p. 8.
59. *Ibid.*, p. 3.
60. *Ibid.*, p. 8.
61. NA, RG25, memorandum from Alice M. Rosseter, regional director, San Francisco to B. Wolf, April 27, 1937. Records of NLRB II, office of the secretary, Region XX, correspondence and reports relating to regional offices 1934–1937.
62. NLRB files, "Regional Offices' Comments On Current Labor Situation for May, 1937," C-51, p. 2.
63. *Ibid.*, p. 11.
64. *In the Matter of National Electric Products Corporation and United Electrical and Radio Workers of America, Local No. 609*, 3 NLRB 475.
65. Oral history interview with P. Levy, *op. cit.*
66. *The New York Times*, September 1, 1937, p. 1, col. 2.
67. *The New York Times*, September 2, 1937, p. 8. col. 3.

president of the IBEW delivered a "scathing attack" on the board pledging that his union would "resist the decision with all the power it command[ed] and with the support and backing of the AFL."[68] Chairman Madden wrote later:

The AFL unions which had nearly always in the past had to do their organizing the hard way, over the employer's resistance, were at a loss to understand why, when at last the employer was willing to smooth the path for them, they should be frustrated by the law which they had done so much to obtain.[69]

The AFL had privately warned the board that unless the NLRB stopped "bastardizing" the act, the Federation had no choice but to make whatever alliances were necessary to obtain amendments to the Wagner Act that would curb the board and protect AFL craft unions. Charlton Ogburn, general counsel of the AFL, wrote to Chairman Madden on May 24, 1937 "that it [was] going to be difficult to prevent the Executive Council of the American Federation of Labor from themselves taking notice and adopting some steps which, to say the least, would be unfortunate."[70] On June 1, 1937, the board's regional director in Cincinnati reported to Chairman Madden that Mr. Ogburn had "[come] in for a long conversation":

Ogburn told me (in confidence, which I assume means that he wants to be sure I write you) that if the Act is used against the Federation, the Federation will have no other alternative than to see that the Act is properly amended. He then mentioned that Senator Steiwer had been trying to approach him for some time as to the possibility of the Federation utilizing the services of the Republican block. He mentioned that people ought to realize that appropriations are very essential and that with the present split in Congress that it was possible that appropriations could be blocked. He did not wish to cooperate with Senator Steiwer but he said if things got bad enough, and the Federation was double-crossed, there would

68. *The New York Times*, September 2, 1937, p. 1, col. 6.
69. Madden, *op. cit.*, p. 249.
70. NA, RG233, letter from Charlton Ogburn to J. W. Madden, May 24, 1937, p. 2, Box 143.

be nothing left for them to do but to play ball with persons who would play ball with them.[71]

The AFL's bitterness toward the board "broke out dramatically" at the federation's October 1937 convention in Denver where "it was open season on the Board." After an apparent "change of heart," the Executive Council of the AFL had invited Chairman Madden to address the convention. Madden remarked that the division in the labor movement had added "enormously to the difficulty" of the board's work. He told the delegates that "situations in which the meaning and purpose of the law are plain and the application of it would, in a calm atmosphere, be easy, become in the minds of the contestants confused with hot emotions, and victory over the adversy is demanded, regardless of the law and regardless of the facts." He also emphasized, courageously under the circumstances, that the meaning of Section 7 and 8 (1) of the act were "plain beyond question": "They did not say and they do not mean that it shall be an unfair labor practice for an employer to coerce his employees to join a union unless he coerces them to join an American Federation of Labor Union."[72]

Chairman Madden faced a "cool and partly hostile audience of labor leaders" who "applauded Mr. Madden politely, but without enthusiasm before and after he spoke" but who gave him no applause during his speech.[73] After the chairman's speech, the board and its employees "were raked fore and aft in language seldom heard at an AFL convention."[74]

71. NA, RG233, memorandum from Philip G. Phillips to J. W. Madden, June 1, 1937, p. 1, Box 141.
72. NLRB files, address of J. W. Madden at the 57th annual convention of the American Federation of Labor, Denver, Colorado, October 5, 1937, R-357, p. 7. See also *Report of Proceedings of the 57th Annual Convention of the American Federation of Labor, op. cit.*, p. 235. Louis Stark, "Secretary Perkins 'Rebuked' By A.F.L.," *The New York Times*, September 23, 1937, p. 8, col. 3; Irving Bernstein, *Turbulent Years, op. cit.*, p. 664.
73. Louis Stark, "Labor Board Chief Denies It Favors C.I.O. Over A.F.L.," *The New York Times*, October 6, 1937, p. 1, col. 1.
74. Louis Stark, "Speakers Score Labor Board," *The New York Times*, October 14, 1937, p. 1, col. 1.

Joseph Padway, an AFL attorney, declared that it was unwise "for organized labor to surrender jurisdiction over its internal affairs and over all its relations with employers, particularly contractual relations, to boards and bureaus." He cautioned that "unless the law [was] speedily amended there [was] but one thing left to do, and that [was] to remove the tyrannical hand of bureaucracy from the shoulders of organized labor" by repealing the Wagner Act.[75]

The principal anti-NLRB speech was delivered by John Frey, the president of the AFL Metal Trades Department and a member of the convention's Resolutions Committee, who charged that the administration of the Wagner Act had been placed "very largely" in the hands of men and women who were "unqualified by training and experience or judicial balance." Although his criticisms exempted Chairman Madden, he accused board member Donald Wakefield Smith of being an "amiable incompetent" and Edwin S. Smith of fraternizing with John L. Lewis and "representatives of the Russian Embassy." Frey told the delegates that the board had "done more during recent months to destroy the practice of collective bargaining and to interfere with its progress, than all of the efforts of all of the anti-union forces in the country combined" and he concluded by calling for a "housecleaning."[76]

The AFL convention unanimously adopted the report of the Resolutions Committee which instructed the Executive Council to "assemble" the evidence in proof of the maladministration of the act, recommended that William Green and the Executive Council be authorized to petition the president of the United States "for prompt and adequate relief," and also recommended that the Wagner Act be amended.[77]

Although there certainly were individuals on the board, on the board's staff, and in the regional offices who were less than neutral on the issue of conservative and radical unions, it became increasingly clear that both the AFL and the CIO were simply using

75. *Report of Proceedings of the 57th Annual Convention of the American Federation of Labor, op. cit.*, p. 253.
76. *Ibid.*, pp. 487 and 489–490. See also Bernstein, *Turbulent Years, op. cit.*, p. 664.
77. *Report of Proceedings of the 57th Annual Convention of the American Federation of Labor, op. cit.*, pp. 486, 500.

the board as a tool in their efforts to defeat each other. At the same time that the AFL was meeting in Denver, a CIO conference of "several hundred organizers, field workers and union executives" in Atlantic City, New Jersey unanimously adopted a resolution condemning the labor board for its decisions "favoring craft organizations."[78] (The CIO was particularly upset over the NLRB's "Globe Doctrine" in which the board, in cases where either a craft or an industrial unit was equally appropriate, agreed to be bound by an election held separately among the employees of the craft unit to determine whether they preferred to be a separate unit or to be part of a larger industrial unit.)[79] Heber Blankenhorn, who attended this conference, reported to Chairman Madden that, although it would be a "mistake to underestimate the feelings against certain Board decisions":

> To the C.I.O. leaders, their move in criticising the Board was part of their fight with the A.F.L. They saw themselves throwing brick-bats through the Board's plate glass window straight at Bill Green. Leaders like Hillman were skeptical when told that cumulative criticism might damage the Board's authority and be an excuse for "Amending" the law. When ... I showed Hillman editorials in the Washington Post and in the Philadelphia papers, referring to a Board threatened with discredit and calling for Wagner Act amendments, he showed only irritation and silence. He and others were emphatic ... that they would not tolerate "Amendments" to the Law. ... I suggested their indication was mighty feeble. ...
>
> Tactical, and temporary, considerations that moved them were a bit mixed: If the A.F.L. could push the Board around, they'd show the A.F.L. the C.I.O. could too; incidentally, it

---

78. Louis Stark, "Secretary Perkins 'Rebuked' By A.F.L.," *op. cit.*, and Louis Stark, "Speakers Score Labor Board," *op. cit.*

79. *In the Matter of the Glove Machine and Stamping Company and Metal Polishers Union Local No. 3; International Association of Machinists, District No. 54; Federal Labor Union 18788 and United Automobile Workers of America*, 3 NLRB 294. See also Joseph Rosenfarb, *The National Labor Policy and How It Works* (New York: Harper & Brothers, 1940), pp. 356–357 and 363–375.

would dispose of the talk of Board bias in favor of C.I.O.; it might change the Board's mind about whittling away industrial unionism; .... In short, the usual pressure tactics ....

The main part of this C.I.O. feeling was based on the belief that Board decisions were threatening industrial unionism by interfering to find a place for craft unionism. Right or wrong there was no questioning the vehemence of such fears in the minds of men like Murray, Bittner, Hillman, Golden and auto leaders .... [Murray said] Our people have fought hard for the kind of union they are now in and they will turn against anything or anybody that fails to let them have what they want.[80]

As Historian Irving Bernstein has written, "the Chief Justice had hardly concluded the reading of his Jones & Laughlin decision" when the Chamber of Commerce, the National Association of Manufacturers, and their "friendly members of Congress" proposed amendments to "equalize" the Wagner Act and to limit the power of the NLRB.[81]

The NLRB decided to oppose even friendly amendments since the board was "anxious not to have the Act opened up for good amendments out of fear that by so doing a flood of bad ones will come in which will be hard to defeat."[82] The board adopted this attitude in the belief that unfriendly amendments would be "contained politically" by democratic majorities in both houses and by key friends such as the Democratic chairman of the Senate Committee on Education and Labor, Elbert Thomas of Utah, who could be counted on to bottle up amendments. (Senator Thomas had told Heber Blankenhorn that he had "told everybody my position which is that no amendments to the Wagner Act are desirable, that the Act and the Board constitute an experiment

80. NA, RG25, memorandum from H. Blankenhorn to the National Labor Relations Board, October 18, 1937, pp. 1–3. Records of NLRB II relating to the Smith Committee investigation, Legal Division, office of the general counsel, LaFollette Committee cooperation file.
81. Bernstein, *Turbulent Years*, *op. cit.*, p. 663.
82. NA, RG233, letter from E. S. Smith to A. L. Wirin, April 24, 1937, Box 149.

which is proceeding satisfactorily and should be allowed to proceed without change for a considerable period.")[83]

According to Heber Blankenhorn, Senator LaFollette disagreed with this strategy:

> Senator LaFollette said that he was not as optimistic as some about staving off amendments. He said that privately he disagreed with the attitude of Senator Thomas, and as he understood it, of the Board. "Or rather, while I am against any amendments, of course, I think we had better be prepared to offer amendments from friends of the Bill, rather than leave the field to hostile amendments in case the opposition puts a pistol to our heads. You may have to concede something, rather than run the risk of having the whole dam go out."[84]

Senator LaFollette had prepared "several . . . amendments to the Wagner Act embodying the results of his committee's investigation intending these to be 'thrown into the hopper as make weights' in case . . . other amendments came up for discussion."[85] Although this tactic proved unnecessary, there was no doubt on all sides that "the firing this far [had been] somewhat sporadic" and that "the rumble of heavy guns in the rear" promised a major attack to come.[86] The situation would become increasingly grave as the AFL moved closer to what *Fortune* called "the essential paradox"[87]—an alliance with the enemies of the board.

The Supreme Court decisions, therefore, had granted the NLRB no reprieve from the pressure of economic and political power which constantly surrounded the formulation and administration of the national labor policy. On April 15, 1937, the board, in the midst of its victory celebrations, had already begun to travel the bitter road from Wagner to Traft-Hartley.

---

83. NLRB files, memorandum from H. Blankenhorn to J. W. Madden, E. S. Smith, and D. W. Smith, December 4, 1937. See also Bernstein, *Turbulent Years, op. cit.*, p. 663.
84. NA, RG233, "Wagner Act Amendments," memorandum from H. Blankenhorn to J. W. Madden, December 8, 1937, Box 143.
85. NLRB files, memorandum from H. Blankenhorn to J. W. Madden, E. S. Smith, and D. W. Smith, December 4, 1937.
86. Luther A. Huston, "NLRB Under Fire In Congress," *op. cit.*
87. "The G— D— Labor Board," *Fortune*, vol. 18, October 1938, p. 52.

Index